LEADING
PERFORMANCE
MANAGEMENT

IN LOCAL GOVERNMENT

Edited by David N. Ammons

ICMA PRESS

ICMA *Leaders at the Core of Better Communities*

ICMA advances professional local government worldwide. Its mission is to create excellence in local governance by developing and advancing professional management of local government. ICMA, the International City/County Management Association, provides member support; publications, data, and information; peer and results-oriented assistance; and training and professional development to more than 9,000 city, town, and county experts and other individuals and organizations throughout the world. The management decisions made by ICMA's members affect 185 million individuals living in thousands of communities, from small villages and towns to large metropolitan areas.

www.icma.org/press

Library of Congress Cataloging-in-Publication Data

Leading performance management in local government / David N. Ammons, editor.
  p. cm.
 Includes bibliographical references.
 ISBN 978-0-87326-178-4
 1. Local government--Labor productivity--United States. 2. Performance standards--United States. 3. Municipal services--United States. 4. Municipal government--United States. 5. Performance--Management. I. Ammons, David N. II. International City/County Management Association.
 JS363.L43 2008
 352.6'6--dc22
                              2008032861

Design: Charles Mountain, Robert Mench

Printed in the United States of America

2015 2014 2013 2012 2011 2010 2009 2008

5 4 3 2 1

Contents

Foreword

Performance management encompasses all that managers do to use objective information to design, direct, and improve government services as well as facilitate results-based policy decisions of elected officials. Local governments are the ideal laboratories for experiments in performance improvement and outcome-based governance.

Evidence of strengths—or weaknesses—of public services is most readily observed in those governments closest to the day-to-day lives of the general public—the tens of thousands of villages, boroughs, towns, cities, and counties throughout the United States and around the world. Performance matters. So identifying services and practices in need of improvement and focusing organizational resources, talents, and policies to achieve improved results—as well as celebrating successes—should be the lodestar of all city and county managers, department heads, and other public officials. This professional bearing and steadfast attitude is what transforms good local government organizations into truly great ones.

ICMA's newest book on performance management, *Leading Performance Management in Local Government,* brings together in one place many of the very best articles on how to seize that opportunity and make the most of it.

Performance measurement was the subject of David Ammons's first collection of articles for ICMA, entitled *Accountability for Performance: Measurement and Monitoring in Local Government,* published in 1995. Since then, management based on a clear vision of desired outcomes and objective measures of progress toward that vision has become well established as a measure itself of management and leadership excellence.

But the transition from measurement and monitoring to enhanced management capacity is not an easy one. In this collection of new articles on converting measures of performance to true management tools, Professor Ammons follows the efforts of ICMA and other organizations to tie measures to vision and goals and to standardize measurement in order to track internal progress in service delivery as well as make comparisons with other organizations *for the express purpose of learning "effective practices" from others.* The promise and the pitfalls of performance measurement are apparent in the success and sometimes the failings of local governments engaged in working toward evidence-based management.

What is most important in every instance of success is the local government's commitment to agreeing on a vision for the future, defining what needs to be done to reach that future, deciding who needs to do it, and then measuring progress and adjusting strategies and tactics as the local government team works toward that future.

We are grateful to David Ammons for compiling this book and to the individuals and organizations that granted ICMA Press permission to use their material. We also wish to thank Mary Marik for her editorial expertise. ICMA staff members who helped create this volume are Ann I. Mahoney, director of publishing; Michael Lawson, director of the ICMA Center for Performance Measurement™; Christine Ulrich, editorial director; and Nedra M. James, publications assistant.

Robert J. O'Neill, Jr.
Executive Director
ICMA

About the Editor and Authors

Following are the affiliations of the editor and authors at the time of writing.

Editor

David N. Ammons is Albert Coates Professor of Public Administration and Government at the University of North Carolina at Chapel Hill. He specializes in productivity improvement, performance measurement, and benchmarking in local government. His research has appeared in such journals as *Public Administration Review, Public Performance and Management Review, American Review of Public Administration,* and *State and Local Government Review.* Among his books on public sector management are *Municipal Benchmarks: Assessing Local Performance and Establishing Community Standards,* 2nd ed. (Sage Publications, 2001) and *Tools for Decision Making: A Practical Guide for Local Government,* 2nd ed. (CQ Press, 2008). Early in his career, Ammons worked in municipal government, serving in various administrative capacities in the cities of Fort Worth, Texas; Hurst, Texas; Phoenix, Arizona; and Oak Ridge, Tennessee. Ammons earned his Ph.D. from the University of Oklahoma. He was elected a fellow in the National Academy of Public Administration in 2006. e-mail: Ammons@sog.unc.edu.

Article authors

Robert D. Behn, Lecturer, John F. Kennedy School of Government, Harvard University.

Barbara J. Cohn Berman, Vice President, Fund for the City of New York and National Center for Civic Innovation; Director, Center on Governance Performance, New York.

William J. Bratton, Chief, Los Angeles Police Department; formerly Police Commissioner, New York City.

Paul M. Coates, Associate, Epstein & Fass Associates, New York.

David Edwards, Leads the design and implementation group of Atlanta Mayor Shirley Franklin's program for reforming municipal government.

Paul D. Epstein, Principal, Epstein & Fass Associates, New York.

Harry P. Hatry, Principal Research Associate and Director of the Public Management Program at the Urban Institute, Washington, D.C.

Theodore H. Poister, Professor of Public Administration, Department of Public Administration and Urban Studies, Andrew Young School of Policy Studies, Georgia State University.

William C. Rivenbark, Albert and Gladys Hall Coates Associate Professor for Outstanding Faculty Achievement, University of North Carolina at Chapel Hill.

Dennis C. Smith, Associate Professor of Public Policy, Wagner School, New York University.

Stephen K. Straus, Assistant Professor, Public Administration Program, North Carolina State University; Director, North Carolina Legislative Internship Program.

David Swain, Associate, Epstein & Fass Associates, New York.

James E. Swiss, Associate Professor, Public Administration Program, North Carolina State University.

John Clayton Thomas, Professor, Department of Public Administration and Urban Studies, Andrew Young School of Policy Studies, Georgia State University.

Jonathan Walters, Writer, *Governing* Magazine.

Lyle D. Wray, Associate, Epstein & Fass Associates, New York.

Introduction

David N. Ammons

Many local governments adopt mission statements declaring impressive aspirations and vowing to provide high-quality services to their citizens. A relatively small subset of this high-aspiration group consists of governments that adopt *performance management* tactics to energize their declarations. These local governments establish management systems and apply a variety of techniques designed to convert aspirations and promises into reality. Not trusting eloquent mission statements alone to somehow inspire favorable results, these governments use performance management tactics to influence results directly. In short, they take the proverbial bull by the horns, often struggling with the beast but ultimately leading it where they want it to go.

Performance management is the intentional application of strategies and techniques to achieve desired results. It is not passive; instead, it is action oriented. It includes a host of practices designed to influence performance. It is more than merely declaring goals and trusting that program officials and employees will somehow achieve them. It is more than simply measuring performance and hoping that the act of measurement will provide all the impetus needed. Performance management incorporates a wide array of tactics, used in a variety of combinations, to achieve some or all of the following along the path to producing real results:

- Heighten awareness among supervisors and employees of the importance of good performance and favorable results (addressing the need for an organizational culture conducive to focusing on results).

- Establish performance expectations (via mission, goals, objectives, performance targets).

- Sharpen the accuracy of performance perceptions and increase awareness of performance gaps (via performance measurement, benchmarking).

- Identify the causes of performance deficiencies—or, in the case of solid performers, factors that prevent a good program from achieving great results—and prescribe corrective action (via program evaluation, performance auditing, operations analysis, benchmarking, continuous improvement, others).

- Motivate program officials and employees to improve performance (via performance reviews, including "stat" systems and effective performance appraisals; pay-for-performance systems; managed competition; programs allowing greater managerial discretion in exchange for favorable program results; gainsharing; others).
- More effectively incorporate meaningful performance data into management and policy decision processes (for example, budgeting, planning, performance appraisal, employee development plans, work plan development, others).

Local government officials sometimes claim to be engaged in performance management simply because their community has adopted a strategic plan or because their departments report performance measures in the annual budget document. Although both are signs that a given local government *might* engage in performance management, neither sign is sufficient to guarantee that it does so. Strategic plans almost always address an organization's overarching mission and goals, but some fall short of operationalizing the goals into meaningful objectives that focus departmental efforts on specific, measurable targets. Many strategic plans fail to prompt performance management practices that would more aggressively influence results and give the plan its greatest chance of success.

Similarly, the fact that a local government possesses a set of performance measures—even a good set—does not guarantee the *meaningful use* of those measures to improve performance. Performance management relies on good performance measurement, but effective performance management is much more than merely compiling and reporting measures. Persons engaged in performance management use the measures to influence performance results. Many more officials can validly claim to measure performance than can honestly report using their measures to improve results.

Performance measurement

At the urging of ICMA and other prominent professional associations,[1] many local governments have adopted the practice of measuring performance. In a large portion of these governments, measurement practices are limited, with the government tabulating only the most basic service outputs in a handful of departments—for example, outputs such as applications processed, fire emergency responses, meters read, or swimming pool attendance. In others measurement practices are extensive and thorough, covering all or most major departments and extending beyond the mere tabulation of service outputs to address service quality, effectiveness, and efficiency as well. Altogether, the number of city and county governments engaged in measurement—at the rudimentary, intermediate, and advanced levels—is quite large.

Government observers reported a measurement groundswell during the last decade of the twentieth century—an "enthusiasm for measuring service performance that approached fervor," in the view of Janet Kelly and David Swindell (2002, 611)—coinciding with the publication of David Osborne and Ted Gaebler's *Reinventing Government* (1992) and the National Performance Review's push for greater accountability at the federal level. Surveys of local government officials during that period and even earlier seem to bear out this assessment, with high percentages of local governments—60, 70, or even 80 percent—reporting that they collected performance measures (Poister and McGowan 1984; Poister and Streib 1989, 1994; Cope 1987; O'Toole and Stipak 1988). Do these numbers overstate the actual practice of *serious performance measurement,* especially considering the minimal measurement done by some governments? Perhaps they do. Other surveys, along with studies involving the actual examination of performance reporting documents, suggest that the proportion of cities and counties with at least moderately well-developed sets of measures for most departments is considerably lower (GASB and NAPA 1997; Poister and Streib 1999; Streib and Poister 1999; Ammons 1995b). Whichever filter is used—broad gauge or narrow—it remains clear, however, that a substantial number of local governments are engaged today in efforts to measure and report performance.

Benefits of performance measurement

Surveyed officials in cities and counties that collect performance measures tend to be enthusiastic about doing so, believing that their governments are "better off" because they engage in this practice (Melkers and Willoughby 2005). Measures are purportedly helpful in strategic management, strategic planning, budgeting, management-by-objectives processes, program evaluation, and incentive systems, among other uses (Poister and Streib 1999, 2005). Many of these survey responses, however, are more general than specific, prompting researchers to declare that "favorable ratings of the effectiveness of [performance measurement] systems" tend "to outstrip reported impacts" (Poister and Streib 1999, 334; Streib and Poister 1999). To a large degree, it seems, many local government proponents of performance measures have responded to surveys on faith that their measures can, will, or probably already have been helpful in improving performance, even if they are unable to cite specific examples. The vagueness of their responses suggests that many of these officials represent governments that measure performance but have not actually stepped up to performance management. Until more governments move from performance measurement to performance management, the full potential of measurement's value remains largely untested.

Recent developments in performance measurement

ICMA last published a collection of writings on performance measurement in 1995 in a book entitled *Accountability for Performance* (Ammons 1995a). The ensuing decade witnessed significant initiatives in the field of local government performance measurement. During this period, for instance, large-scale comparative performance measurement projects—in particular a national project sponsored by ICMA and a single-state project based at the University of North Carolina—demonstrated how to overcome the difficulties of interjurisdictional comparison and provide information that participating local governments could use to gauge their performance relative to that of other cities and counties.[2] Unlike previous attempts by others, the ICMA and North Carolina projects have operated for more than a decade, in testimony to their value to participating governments.

ICMA's Center for Performance Measurement.

The ICMA Center for Performance Measurement (CPM) enables participating local governments to share program data, benchmark their performance to comparable jurisdictions, and improve service delivery by implementing best management practices and efficient use of resources.

CPM now includes more than 200 jurisdictions, ranging in size from under 5,000 to over 3,000,000 million residents. Coordinated, consistent data collection makes possible interagency benchmarking as well as internal performance measurement comparisons. Participating jurisdictions can compare their own data to the full sample or use the electronic database to customize comparisons based on population, climate, urban density, method of service provision, community demographics, and other characteristics.

Service areas evaluated include:

· Police services

· Fire services

· Neighborhood services (code enforcement, housing, libraries, parks and recreation, refuse collection, road maintenance)

· Support services (facilities management, fleet management, human resources, information technology, purchasing, risk management)

· Youth services.

Second, a series of projects in New York, Iowa, and elsewhere—often under the sponsorship of the Alfred P. Sloan Foundation—experimented with the involvement of citizens in performance measurement (Holzer and Kloby 2008). For years, cities and counties had surveyed citizens to gauge satisfaction with public services, but this was different. Citizens in these communities were engaged in the identification of relevant service dimensions for measurement and, in some cases, in the design of measures or as field observers in the measurement activity itself. Proponents praised these projects for emphasizing collaboration among public officials and citizens, for adding a citizens' perspective—a service receiver's perspective—to the measures, and for heightening the profile and credibility of performance measures in these communities (Holzer and Yang 2004; Callahan 2004).[3]

Third, the balanced scorecard approach to performance measurement, adapted from the version developed for private corporations by Robert Kaplan and David Norton, began to appear in local governments. The originators' scorecard was intended to reduce the tendency of corporations to overemphasize short-term financial gains at the expense of their long-term health by providing balance between "short- and long-term objectives, between financial and non-financial measures, between lagging and leading indicators, and between external and internal perspectives" (Kaplan and Norton 1996, viii). In the adapted version used by the city of Charlotte, North Carolina, often highlighted as the foremost example of the balanced scorecard in a local government, the four prescribed perspectives of the original balanced scorecard—financial, customer, internal business processes, and learning and growth—were renamed and reordered as *serve the customer, run the business, manage the resources,* and *develop employees.* Charlotte's scorecard ensures that attention is directed to all four. Several other cities and counties have followed Charlotte's lead.

Finally, the decade was highlighted by an initiative that, more than any other, addressed the lingering concerns that performance measurement all too often failed to lead to improved performance and better results. Time after time in one local government after another, performance measures had been adopted but performance management tactics were never deployed. The introduction in New York City of a police management system called Compstat was an important breakthrough in this regard, for it demonstrated the power of combining performance measurement with strong leadership for effective performance management. Operating with computer statistics—hence the name, Compstat— police management pinpointed problem areas for crime and in regularly scheduled, recurring meetings with precinct officials insisted on solutions. New strategies, constant reassessment of progress, and a relentless focus on results led to dramatic reductions in crime. The success of Compstat spawned a variety of spin-offs. In some cases Compstat's progeny, like the parent, focused on police services. In others—such as Baltimore's CitiStat—the tactics of Compstat were applied more broadly to other local government services (Smith and Grinker 2005).

Performance management

Performance measurement is an important ingredient in performance management, but it is only one ingredient among many. Public officials engaged in performance management are not content to set goals and objectives, track performance, and hope for good results. Instead, they take steps to improve the odds of success—sometimes by creating conditions especially conducive to success and sometimes by taking even more aggressive steps to achieve desired results.

Performance management is not passive; it is active. It is not just putting a system in place and going through the motions; it is exercising the leadership necessary to make the system work (Behn 2002). Local governments that best epitomize performance management are tied both by rhetoric and by action to the achievement of measurable results. Attention to performance data in these governments is not restricted to one office, one management level, or one time of the year; instead, it permeates the organization and is constant rather than cyclical (Plant 2006). Managers talk with supervisors about objectives and measures, and supervisors talk with workers. Interactive inquiry addressing problems and seeking solutions occurs throughout the organization (Metzenbaum 2006). Furthermore, the local governments most intent on performance management have multiple programs in place to advance their efforts, not just one (Holzer and Yang 2004).

Robert Behn observes that many public managers mistakenly claim to engage in performance management simply because their organization has adopted a system of performance measurement, performance budgeting, or performance pay—whether the systems are functioning effectively or not. Without active leadership, these systems are merely passive systems of rules, deadlines, and reports. Too many managers think that simply adopting the system will be enough to improve performance.

> The procedures created by the system are themselves [assumed to be] adequate. Once such a performance-management system is established, goes the never-stated assumption, everything will function on automatic pilot . . . .

> Real performance management requires an active strategy. It requires energetic leadership. It requires a leader, or a team of leaders, to make a conscious effort to change the behavior of the individuals who work for the organization and its collaborators (Behn 2002, 19).

The systems and tactics of performance management set the stage for achieving desired results. But setting the stage does not make it happen. *Leadership makes it happen.*

Contents of this book

The articles in this book will lead the reader from a brief overview of performance measurement and related topics to a more extensive examination of the practices of performance management. The focus on measurement is brief, for many other publications devoted to this topic are readily available.

Section I: Measuring and Reporting Performance

The four articles that make up the book's first section, "Measuring and Reporting Performance," address the basics of performance measurement, citizen perceptions of local government services, methods of data collection, and one city's approach to performance reporting. The article, "The Basics of Performance Measurement," introduces the reader to the fundamentals of performance measurement, clarifying essential concepts that can make the difference between measures that are suitable for use in performance management and those that are not.

Local government officials sometimes doubt that performance issues will be understood by people outside of government or that citizens actually want more information from government. In "Ten Significant Observations about How People View Local Government," Barbara J. Cohn Berman sets the doubters straight on these misconceptions and shares other observations gleaned from citizen focus groups.

How does one go about gathering data for useful and reliable performance measures? Harry P. Hatry, in "Methods of Gathering Data," offers five principal options: administrative data from agency records, customer surveys, trained-observer ratings, role playing (the public sector equivalent of "secret shoppers" to assess the consumer's experience in seeking and receiving services), and special technical equipment (for instance, profilometers to gauge street roughness).

David Edwards and John Clayton Thomas round out Section I with "Developing a Municipal Performance-Measurement System: Reflections on the Atlanta Dashboard," about how one city measures and reports its performance.

Section II: From Performance Measurement to Performance Management

The five articles in Section II, "From Performance Measurement to Performance Management," describe various approaches taken by local governments across the United States to achieve greater levels of efficiency and effectiveness. Not content to merely declare their performance aspirations in eloquent mission statements or to rest their hopes on the act of measuring performance, these governments have taken additional steps to create favorable conditions and in some cases to more aggressively push their organizations toward improved performance.

"Organizations Managing for Results" by Paul D. Epstein, Paul M. Coates, and Lyle D. Wray, with David Swain, describes the impressive results of performance management efforts by the local governments of Baltimore, Charlotte, New York City, Phoenix, Prince William County, San Jose, and Savannah. The authors show how these organizations learned from performance feedback, incorporated the lessons into management practice, and improved results.

James E. Swiss and Stephen K. Straus provide a step-by-step guide for establishing a system designed to get results: "Implementing Results-Based Management in Local Government." The authors acknowledge that implementing such a system requires a considerable commitment of energy and resources, but they demonstrate through examples from a training and employment services program and a fleet maintenance department the substantial benefits possible from such an effort.

"Factors Influencing the Use of Performance Data to Improve Municipal Services" examines patterns of data use by a group of North Carolina cities engaged in a cooperative benchmarking project. David N. Ammons and William C. Rivenbark conclude that the types of measures on which officials rely, the willingness of the officials to embrace comparison, and the act of incorporating measures into key management systems are three characteristics that tend to separate heavy users of performance measures for service improvement from light users.

In "Monitoring Quality and Productivity," Theodore H. Poister shows the importance of tying performance measures to the "nuts and bolts of service delivery systems" when the intent is to manage service quality and productivity. There the need is for frequent and detailed indicators of performance, contrasting sharply with performance measurement needs for other purposes such as strategic management or budgeting, where annual data might suffice. The experience of the city bus system of Williamsport, Pennsylvania, illustrates his points.

Researchers have found that "the most innovative and productive agencies institutionalize productivity and performance improvements by identifying, implementing, measuring and rewarding major cost savings and performance enhancements in their agencies" (Holzer and Yang 2004, 20). Should rewards extend beyond providing greater support to successful programs? Should employees be rewarded for better performance and improved results? Should the rewards be financial? Some say yes, while others have their doubts (Metzenbaum 2006). In the next article, David N. Ammons and William C. Rivenbark address the topic of "Gainsharing in Local Government," one approach to rewarding employees monetarily for achieving results. Although hardly widespread, adoptions of gainsharing plans by local governments are sufficiently numerous—7 percent of respondents in one recent survey (Melkers and Willoughby 2005)—to be regarded as more than a mere blip on the performance management screen.

Section III: The "Stat" Approach: Compstat, CitiStat, and Others
Public sector managers who practice performance management are not content to develop goals and hope for the best—or even to develop goals, measure performance, and become cheerleaders for excellent performance. Managers who practice performance management will do all of these things plus they take intentional steps to more directly influence performance improvement. Performance management is active, not passive, and one of its most active embodiments in recent years is the stat approach to performance management, appearing first as Compstat in New York City, later as CitiStat in Baltimore, and in various other forms across the nation. This approach to performance management is the focus of the three articles of Section III, "The 'Stat' Approach."

Dennis C. Smith and William J. Bratton describe the original "stat" system in "Performance Management in New York City: Compstat and the Revolution in Police Management." They note not only the most obvious characteristics of Compstat—the meetings, the questioning, the pursuit of strategies to get better results—but also the changes it brought in structure and philosophy. Robert D. Behn, who has studied Compstat and other stat systems, agrees that the elements of the system could be adopted in other cities, but he suggests that leadership in New York City has given Compstat its energy and success:

> Yes, it is a system. Yes, a mayor could require a police chief to establish a Compstat system. Yes, the police chief could jump through all of the required hoops. But Compstat—as conceived and implemented by William Bratton, Louis Anemone, and Jack Maple—is not merely a system. It is how the top executives of the New York Police Department exercise leadership. It is a vehicle for getting the key managers throughout the organization to focus weekly on first their performance deficiencies and then on possible strategies for producing better results. But without the active leadership by the department's top executives, Compstat is just another passive procedure."

Behn is the author of the final two articles, "The Core Drivers of CitiStat" and "The Varieties of CitiStat." In these articles he identifies success factors in CitiStat and outlines key options for local governments wishing to adopt this promising approach to performance management.

Endnotes
1. Other organizations encouraging local governments to measure and report performance include the American Society for Public Administration, Government Finance Officers Association, Governmental Accounting Standards Board, and National Academy of Public Administration.

2. For more information on the ICMA project, see www.icma.org. For information on the North Carolina project, see www.sog.unc.edu.

3. Despite the enthusiasm for citizen involvement in performance measurement among its proponents, scholars note that public officials have not

embraced the idea in large numbers (Streib and Poister 1999), that there are relatively few cases of sustained implementation (Holzer and Kloby 2008), and that some of the hoped-for effects of

citizen involvement—namely the longer-lasting effectiveness associated with greater employee inclusiveness—have not been confirmed in subsequent research (Melkers and Willoughby 2005).

References

Ammons, David N., ed. 1995a. *Accountability for Performance: Measurement and Monitoring in Local Government.* Washington, D.C.: ICMA.

———. 1995b. "Overcoming the Inadequacies of Performance Measurement in Local Government: The Case of Libraries and Leisure Services." *Public Administration Review* 55, no. 1:37–47.

Behn, Robert D. 2002. "The Psychological Barriers to Performance Management," *Public Performance & Management Review* 26, no. 1:5–25.

Callahan, Kathe. 2004. "Performance Measurement and Citizen Participation." In *Public Productivity Handbook,* 2nd ed., ed. Marc Holzer and Seok-Hwan Lee, 31–42. New York: Marcel Dekker.

Cope, Glen Hahn. 1987. "Local Government Budgeting and Productivity: Friends or Foes?" *Public Productivity Review* 41:45–57.

GASB (Governmental Accounting Standards Board) and NAPA (National Academy of Public Administration). 1997. *Report on Survey of State and Local Government Use and Reporting of Performance Measures.* Washington, D.C.: GASB.

Holzer, Marc, and Kathryn Kloby. 2008. "Helping Government Measure Up: Models of Citizen-Driven Government Performance Measurement Initiatives." In *International Handbook of Practice-Based Performance Management,* ed. Patria de Lancer Julnes et al., 257–281. Los Angeles: Sage Publications.

Holzer, Marc, and Kaifeng Yang. 2004. "Performance Measurement and Improvement: An Assessment of the State of the Art." *International Review of Administrative Sciences* 70, no. 1:15–31.

Kaplan, Robert S., and David P. Norton. 1996. *The Balanced Scorecard.* Boston: Harvard Business School Press.

Kelly, Janet M., and David Swindell. 2002. "A Multiple-Indicator Approach to Municipal Service Evaluation: Correlating Performance Measurement and Citizen Satisfaction across Jurisdictions." *Public Administration Review* 62, no. 5:610–621.

Melkers, Julia, and Katherine Willoughby. 2005. "Models of Performance-Measurement Use in Local Governments: Understanding Budgeting, Commu-nication, and Lasting Effects." *Public Administration Review* 65, no. 2:180–190.

Metzenbaum, Shelley H. 2006. *Performance Accountability: The Five Building Blocks and Six Essential Practices.* Washington, D.C.: IBM Center for the Business of Government.

Osborne, David, and Ted Gaebler. 1992. *Reinventing Government: How the Entrepreneurial Spirit is Transforming the Public Sector.* Reading, Mass.: Addison-Wesley.

O'Toole, Daniel E., and Brian Stipak. 1988. "Budgeting and Productivity Revisited: The Local Government Picture." *Public Productivity Review* 12, no. 1:1–12.

Plant, Thomas. 2006. "The Performance Measurement Paradox in Local Government Management." *Public Management* 88, no. 4:16–20.

Poister, Theodore H., and Robert P. McGowan. 1984. "The Use of Management Tools in Municipal Government: A National Survey." *Public Administration Review* 44, no. 3:215–223.

Poister, Theodore H., and Gregory Streib. 1989. "Management Tools in Municipal Government: Trends over the Past Decade." *Public Administration Review* 49, no. 3:240–248.

———. 1994. "Municipal Management Tools from 1976 to 1993: An Overview and Update." *Public Productivity & Management Review* 18, no. 2:115–125.

———. 1999. "Performance Measurement in Municipal Government: Assessing the State of the Practice." *Public Administration Review* 59, no. 4:325–335.

———. 2005. "Elements of Strategic Planning and Management in Municipal Governments: Status after Two Decades." *Public Administration Review* 65, no. 1:45–56.

Smith, Dennis C., and William J. Grinker. 2005. *The Transformation of Social Services Management in New York City: "Compstating" Welfare.* New York: Structured Employment Economic Development Corporation [Seedco].

Streib, Gregory D., and Theodore H. Poister. 1999. "Assessing the Validity, Legitimacy, and Functionality of Performance Measurement Systems in Municipal Governments." *American Review of Public Administration* 29, no. 2:107–123.

Section I:

Measuring and Reporting Performance

The Basics of Performance Measurement

David N. Ammons

Performance measures are all around us. The car we are thinking about purchasing recorded 21 city miles and 36 highway miles per gallon of gasoline in federal tests. Students in the local school district earned an average score of 1120 on the SAT exam for college admission, well above the statewide average. The label on your box of breakfast cereal proudly declares that a single serving of the contents will provide 24 percent of your daily dietary fiber needs. Your favorite team, at eleven wins and only one loss, has a winning percentage of .917, good for first place. These measures help us assess the performance of auto manufacturers, school districts, food processors, and sports teams. We see performance measures such as these every day.

Does a single measure tell us the whole story? No, a single measure provides only a glimpse. But a comprehensive set of measures—called *metrics* in the private sector—offers more than a glimpse. A good set of measures provides a more complete picture of an organization's performance.

Performance measures in local government gauge the quantity, quality, efficiency, and impact of the work of a city or county government. These measures usually focus on the work of crews, programs, or entire departments rather than the work of individual employees.

A good set of performance measures can reveal a great deal about an operation. If it is a really good set, it will tell us much more than simply *how much* work has been performed by the group being measured. The measures of "how much" are sure to be present in the set—we will see, for example, that the fire department responded to 14,706 fire alarms and 11,376 emergency medical calls, completed 9,754 inspections, and presented fire prevention education programs to 656 classes and other audiences—but the set will also include measures of "how well" and "how efficiently." There will be measures showing us that firefighters responded to emergency calls in 5 minutes and 17 seconds on average from the time of initial call (even quicker from the time of dispatch); that the community experienced 1.7 structural fires per 1,000 population; that 89 percent of all

3

structural fires were confined to the room of origin; that fire losses were less than 0.3 percent of the value of all property protected; that 91 percent of local residents are satisfied with the fire department's performance; and that the city's public protection classification has climbed from a 4 to an even more favorable 3. Yes, a good set of performance measures reveals a lot about an operation.

The logic and uses of performance measurement

The logic of performance measurement is simple and compelling:

- *Performance measurement provides vital information for management and oversight.* Those who manage a program and those who have oversight responsibility for it should know what is being done and how well it is being done.

- *Performance measurement focuses attention on priorities and results.* The identification of key objectives for a department or program and the measurement of progress toward these objectives focuses the attention of program officials and employees, and, where needed, prompts the development of new strategies to achieve the program's objectives.

- *Performance measurement identifies successful strategies.* Evidence of performance progress will reveal strategies that are working. In contrast, evidence of performance decline or performance gaps will challenge the status quo, leading managers to revise their strategies or test new approaches and, perhaps in especially severe cases, prompt decision makers to consider service delivery alternatives or even program discontinuation.

- *Performance measurement enhances accountability.* Those who pay for public programs deserve an accounting that reassures them that funds are being spent properly, that programs are being managed efficiently, and that expectations for service quantity, quality, and results are being met.

Robert Behn (2003) offers generalized categories of uses for performance measurement—to evaluate, control, budget, motivate, promote, celebrate, learn, and improve. More specific applications include:

- *Performance reporting,* both internal and external to the local government, as a method of accountability for performance

- *Directing operations,* making adjustments where measures indicate areas or patterns of deficiency

- *Testing new procedures or equipment,* comparing new measures with prior results or comparing pilot project results to measures elsewhere

- *Contract monitoring* to ensure that promises regarding service quantity and quality are being kept

- *Supporting planning and budgeting systems* by providing objective information on the condition of programs and services

- *Program evaluation,* which often begins with routinely collected performance measures and proceeds with the compiling of new measures specific to the needs of more detailed analysis
- *Benchmarking,* usually by comparing the performance measures of one's own organization to professional standards or to the results achieved by respected counterparts, often as a catalyst for improving local operations.

Most local governments that are among the leaders in performance measurement use their measures for more than one purpose. For virtually all of them, some form of accountability—the first of the uses listed above—is one of those purposes. Rarely, however, do the leaders stop with simply reporting their performance. Most apply measures in other ways that more directly influence improvements in services and programs, ways such as those that make up the balance of the list.

The principal types of performance measures

To usefully serve the various purposes of performance measurement, a set of measures must be multidimensional. It must focus not just on the quantity of services provided by a department or program but also on the quality of services, the efficiency with which services are provided, and the extent to which objectives are being achieved. An especially good set of measures may even assess the overall productivity of a program—often by means of an index that taps both efficiency and effectiveness—and the impact that the program or service is having on service recipients or the community as a whole.

Local governments can develop sets of performance measures that will gauge quantity, efficiency, quality, effectiveness, impact, and productivity by concentrating their attention on four categories of performance measures: output (also known as workload), efficiency, outcome (also known as effectiveness), and productivity.[1] Concentrating only on output measures, as so many local governments do, will yield information of limited value. It will not produce the multidimensional measures needed to manage performance.

Output (workload) measures

Output or workload measures are the simplest of all measures. They report raw counts of activities or services—for example, calls received, work orders completed, city council minutes prepared, zoning applications processed, or tons of asphalt laid. They tell us nothing about quality or efficiency—only about the workload of the department or program. If persons engaged in performance measurement are sometimes called "bean counters," this is the type of measure that best earns them the label, for it consists merely of raw counts of output.

Calling output measurement bean counting might be a little harsh—but only a little—for raw output measures alone have very little of the managerial or policy value associated with higher-order measures. This is not to suggest that local governments should discontinue output measurement. Output measures remain important for at least three reasons.

First, tracking outputs over time will show whether demand for a given service is going up, going down, or holding steady. Second, output measures reveal the scale of an operation and, when viewed alongside measures of efficiency and outcome, show whether an efficient and effective program is also a high-volume operation. Third, and most important, workload measures often are necessary for calculating the higher-order measures of efficiency and effectiveness. So even bean counting can have value.

Unfortunately, many city and county governments begin and end their performance measurement with output measures—raw counts of workload. It is impossible to tell from output measures alone whether a given program performs well or poorly, gets results or does not. Workload measures alone rarely prompt program officials to reconsider service delivery strategies. They are easy and safe. They rarely challenge the status quo, as shifts in efficiency and outcome measures do from time to time. In most instances, raw output measures have relatively little managerial or policy value.

Table 1 displays a set of performance measures for the Water Operations Division of the city of Bend, Oregon. Within this set are output measures reporting figures on "how much" or "how many" for water production, water main installations, and other tasks. These workload measures would have limited managerial value if they stood alone; but they are accompanied by effectiveness and efficiency measures that are more likely to draw management attention and spur new strategies to reduce water consumption, reduce line losses, minimize main breaks, and increase employee efficiency. The workload figures provided the ingredients for calculating these effectiveness and efficiency measures, and, by revealing the scale of the water operations, they provide a useful context for considering these effectiveness and efficiency measures.

Efficiency measures

Managerial and policy value ramps up considerably with measures of efficiency—for good efficiency measures relate outputs to the resources consumed to produce them. Local government officials can consider whether the current level of efficiency in a given program meets expectations, whether steps should be taken to improve efficiency, or, more fundamentally, whether a given allocation of resources produces a sufficient return in services or other benefits to warrant continued funding.

Sometimes the relationship between outputs and inputs is expressed as a unit cost—for example, the cost per accounts payable transaction or the cost per swimmer at the public pool. Or the ratio can be reversed and expressed as units of service per $1,000 of expenditure. Other efficiency measures express the relationship between outputs and resources in other ways. Some remove dollars from the ratio and substitute in their place another major form of resource input, such as staff-hours or labor-hours, thereby producing measures such as transactions processed per staff-hour or curb miles swept per operator-hour. When cost accounting systems are inadequate to support unit cost calculations and staff-hour calculations are impractical, some governments choose less precise measures that nevertheless address efficiency, even if only roughly—for example, average daily backlog or average turnaround time are measures that emphasize the importance of promptness and encourage diligence.

Table 1. Performance measures: Water operations in the City of Bend, Oregon.

	FY 03–04 Actual	FY 04–05 Actual	FY 05–06 Target	FY 06–07 Target
Output Measures				
Surface/groundwater produced	4,302 mg	3,765 mg	4,196 mg	4,317 mg
Reservoir capacity	25 mg	25 mg	28.79 mg	28.79 mg
Lineal feet of new water mains installed	85,000	142,506	155,000	157,000
Average number of service orders per month	1,103	1,996	2,190	2,409
Average number of work orders per month	63	68	127	194
Number of service leaks investigated per year	55	75	75	75
Number of water quality complaints received	18	10	10	10
Number of meters installed	3,329[a]	4,410[b]	2,475	3,000
Effectiveness Measures				
Reduction in peak day usage per person per day	1%	2.7%	1%	1%
Percentage of unaccounted water	6.5%	6.5%	5.5%	5%
Number of main breaks per mile of main line	0.05	0.02	0.01	0.01
Efficiency Measures				
Average number of service orders per employee per month	366	499	730	803

Source: City of Bend, Oregon, *Adopted Budget Fiscal Year 2006/07*, pp. 134-135, www.ci.bend.or.us/online_forms_and_documents/docs/FY_2006_07_Budget_for_CD.pdf.

a Includes conversion of un-metered services to metered service.

b Includes conversion of un-metered Juniper customers to metered service.

Performance measures for the Department of Human Resources of Fairfax County, Virginia, are shown in Table 2. Within this set are the following efficiency measures:

- Résumés reviewed for certification per recruitment analyst
- Cost per job class reviewed
- Benefit enrollments per staff-year equivalent
- Cost of training per employee.

Each of these efficiency measures relates outputs (that is, résumés reviewed, job class reviews, benefit enrollments, and employee training) to resources consumed to produce the output (that is, cost in dollars or in staff allocation).

Table 2. Key performance measures: Department of Human Resources of Fairfax County, Virginia.

Goal

Working in partnership with DHR customers to foster key communications and continuous improvement in attracting, retaining, and developing highly qualified employees to support a high performance organization.

Objectives

- To increase new hires who complete their probationary period to minimum of 78 percent.
- To maintain an average pay gap of no more than 15 percent between Fairfax County's pay range mid-points and comparable market midpoints in order to maintain a competitive pay structure.
- To maintain employee satisfaction in the variety and quality of benefit programs at 92 percent.
- To maintain the number of employees who indicate that DHR-sponsored training they receive will assist them in performing in their current role and prepare them for their career with Fairfax County government at 90 percent.

	Prior year actuals			Current estimate	Future estimate
Indicator	FY 2004 Actual	FY 2005 Actual	FY 2006 Estimate / Actual	FY 2007	FY 2008
Output					
Best qualified applicants forwarded to departments	17,777	20,207	19,593 / 23,850	22,278	23,837
Job classes benchmarked	142	124	104 / 175	125	167
Enrollments in benefit programs per year	46,767	52,270	47,250 / 48,168	50,000	53,000
Employees that attend DHR training events	NA	3,070	2,800 / 2,601	3,800	4,000
Efficiency ($)					
Resumes reviewed for certification per recruitment analyst	9,780	13,457	14,129 / 14,250	14,836	15,578
Cost per job class reviewed	$263	$230	$268 / $210	$232	$236
Benefit enrollments per staff-year equivalent (SYE)	5,196	5,807	5,250 / 5,352	5,556	5,889
Cost of training per employee	NA	$354	$431 / $312	$580	$650

(Continued on page 9)

(Continued from page 8)

| Indicator | Prior year actuals | | | Current estimate | Future estimate |
	FY 2004 Actual	FY 2005 Actual	FY 2006 Estimate / Actual	FY 2007	FY 2008
Service quality					
Percent customers satisfied with the applicants on certification list	97%	92%	98% / 98%	95%	97%
Work days between job closing date and publication of the centralized certification	8.5	8.0	8.0 / 8.0	8.0	8.0
Percent of benchmarked jobs that are between Fairfax County's pay range mid-points standard and comparable market mid-points	100%	100%	100% / 100%	100%	100%
Percent of employees indicating "satisfied or better" on customer service surveys or course assessments	NA	NA	NA / NA	90%	90%
Outcome (%)					
Percent of employees who complete their probationary period	79.12%	77.29%	78.00% / 71.34%	78.00%	78.00%
Average gap between Fairfax County's pay range mid-points and comparable range mid-points in the market for core classes	0%	5%	5% / 5%	5%	15%
Employee satisfaction with the variety and quality of benefit programs offered	92%	92%	92% / 92%	92%	92%
Percent of employees that indicated DHR-sponsored training assisted them in performing their jobs	NA	88%	90% / 90%	90%	90%

Source: *Fairfax County, Virginia, FY 2008 Adopted Budget Plan*, vol. 1, pp. 80–81, www.fairfaxcounty.gov/dmb/adopted/FY2008/pdf/Volume1/00111.pdf.

Outcome (effectiveness) measures

Outcome measures (also known as effectiveness measures) have considerable managerial and policy value. This category includes measures that gauge service quality, those that reflect service or program impact, and those that depict the extent to which program objectives are being met. (Note that in Table 2 Fairfax County placed service quality measures in their own separate category.) If trained observers at the city parks rate the condition of the turf to be in compliance with highest standards, this would be an effectiveness measure—as would a measure reporting the satisfaction of residents with county recreation programs. Also belonging in the effectiveness or outcome category would be program statistics showing the impact of public health programs designed to combat childhood obesity, teen pregnancy, or teen smoking. If police objectives emphasize responsiveness to emergencies and prescribe response times of five minutes or less to emergency calls, then a measure reflecting 92 percent compliance with that target would be an effectiveness measure and would belong in this category.

Among the various categories of measures displayed in Table 3 for the Information Technology Department of the city of Bellevue, Washington, are outcome or effectiveness measures addressing customer satisfaction with the department's consulting and support services, responsiveness to help desk repair calls, and the reliability of the phone system and servers maintained by the department. Overall, this department's set of measures focuses heavily on effectiveness.

Productivity measures

Although relatively rare, productivity measures occasionally are found in local government budgets and performance reports. One such measure, for instance, can be found in the set reported by the Office of the City Auditor in San José, California. The reporting format of the city of San José calls for departments to separate their measures into a "Performance Summary," consisting mostly of outcome measures, and an "Activity and Workload Highlights" section, consisting mostly of output measures. Among the measures reported in the performance summary for audit services is this productivity measure: "ratio of estimated audit benefits to audit costs" (Table 4).

Consider the distinctive feature that makes this benefit-to-cost ratio a productivity measure. Instead of this measure, the city could have inserted separate measures—one reporting the average benefit of an audit and the other reporting average cost. A measure focusing exclusively on the average benefit of an audit performed by this office would address effectiveness. A measure focusing strictly on the average cost of an audit would address efficiency. This measure, "ratio of estimated audit benefits to audit costs," combines efficiency and effectiveness in a single measure and thereby more fully addresses the dual dimensions of productivity.

Alignment with mission, goals, and objectives

To be meaningful, measures must address facets of performance that are important to an organization. In an organization that is serious about strategic planning and performance

Table 3.　Performance measures: Information technology in Bellevue, Washington.

Information Technology Department
Toni Cramer, Chief Information Officer　tel: (425) 452-2972
Annual Scorecard of Performance Measures

Key Performance Measures	2004 Actual	2005 Actual	2006 Actual	2006 Target	2006 Target Met or Exceeded
Program: Applications Services					$ 7,514,000
Effectiveness					
1. Percent of customers rating level of consulting services for business analysis and system design as good to excellent (a)	82%	74%	83%	80%	✓
2. Percent of customers rating the maintenance and support provided for their application(s) as good to excellent (a)	83%	90%	86%	80%	✓
Workload					
3. Number of Applications	183	91	95	170	
Program: Desktop Support Services					$ 2,458,000
Effectiveness					
4. Percentage of Help Desk repair calls resolved at the time of the call	87%	80%	70%	60%	✓
5. Percentage of Help Desk repair calls resolved within 4 hours	8%	9%	14%	11%	✓
6. Percentage of Help Desk repair calls resolved the next business day	2%	9%	5%	13%	
7. Percentage of customers rating satisfaction with Desktop Support Services as good to excellent	93%	93%	95%	85%	✓
Workload					
8. Number of PCs supported/number of technicians	1375/3.5	1388/3.5	1400/3.5	1400/ 4.5	
Program: Network & Systems Support Services					$ 4,680,000
Effectiveness					
9. Percent of time phone system fully functional during business hours	99.9%	99.9%	99.9%	99.9%	✓
10. .Percentage of time servers are fully functional during business hours	99.9%	99.7%	99.9%	99.9%	✓
Efficiency					
11. Cost of city phone line vs. phone company business line (City phone cost per month/phone company business line per month)	$17/$37	$17/$37	$17/$37	$16/$32	
Workload					
12. Number of servers supported (b)	98	114	120	106	
13. Number of phone line/number of technicians	1679	1679	1679	1761	

(a) Normal problems encountered in the implementation of new systems are expected to impact overall customer satisfaction;
(b) Includes virtual servers.

Source: City of Bellevue, Washington, *2006 Annual Performance Report,* June 2007, p. 81. www.ci.bellevue.wa.us/pdf/Finance/ 2006_Performance_Measures_Report_FINAL_Numbered.pdf.

Table 4. Performance measures: Audit services of the city of San José, California.

Office of the City Auditor

Audit Services Performance Summary	2005–2006 Actual	2006–2007 Target	2006–2007 Estimated	2007–2008 Target
Percentage of audit recommendations adopted by the City Council	100%	100%	100%	100%
Percentage of audit recommendations implemented within one year of adoption	57%	80%	80%	80%
Ratio estimated audit benefit to audit cost	$11 to 1	$4 to 1	$9 to 1	$4 to 1
Ratio actual to estimated audit benefit	$1 to 1	$1 to 1	$1 to 1	$1 to 1
Percentage of approved work plan completed or substantially completed during the fiscal year	100%	100%	100%	100%
Percentage of audits completed within 30 days of the projected completion date	100%	90%	92%	90%
Percentage of City Council members rating the reliability, timeliness, and value of audit services "good" or "excellent"	97%	95%	95%	95%
Percentage of auditees rating the reliability, timeliness, and value of audit services "good" or "excellent"	100%	95%	95%	95%
Activity & Workload Highlights	**2005–2006 Actual**	**2006–2007 Forecast**	**2006–2007 Estimated**	**2007–2008 Forecast**
Number of audit reports issued	22	22	24	20
Number of audit recommendations adopted	11	70	51	50
Number of audit reports per auditor	1.8 to 1	1.5 to 1	1.7 to 1	1.5 to 1
Estimated audit benefits (i.e., cost savings and revenue enhancements)	$24,523,448	$9,500,000	$19,184,872	$9,500,000
Actual audit benefits (i.e., cost savings and revenues received)	$24,688,977	$9,500,000	$19,132,211	$9,500,000

Source: *City of San José, California, 2007-2008 Adopted Operating Budget,* pp. VII-671-672, http://www.sanjoseca.gov/budget/FY0708/documents/VII-7b.MayorCouncilAppointeeSS.pdf.

management, the measures will be aligned with its long-range mission and goals, and even more specifically with its shorter-term objectives. These objectives express the more immediate intentions of the organization and thereby set its course toward fulfilling its aspirations, as reflected in the organization's mission and goals. Properly aligned with the mission and goals, objectives bring action that moves the organization toward its aspirations.

While mission statements and goals tend to be broad and imprecise, objectives are much narrower and more precise. Well-written objectives are said to be SMART, an acronym for specific, measurable, aggressive but attainable, results-oriented, and time-bound. For instance, a public health department might have a mission or goal of "ensuring the health and well-being of the citizens of the community" and a much more specific and measurable objective of "reducing the rate of infant mortality by three percentage points during the next two fiscal years." The objective *operationalizes* the goal and, by doing so, focuses the attention of the program staff on the problem of infant mortality and challenges it to strengthen projects already in place and, if needed, to devise new strategies . Performance measures aligned with objectives gauge progress toward achieving these objectives.

Should only those performance measures specifically tied to declared objectives be included in an organization's set of measures? No. In fact, some common measures—such as police response time to emergencies, the government's bond rating, and the circulation rate of library materials—are likely to be reported, whether or not a specific objective has been articulated for that particular dimension of service. In essence, there are *implied objectives* for some services. Nevertheless, proper alignment does suggest that there should be no "widows" among the declared objectives. Every objective should be accompanied by a performance measure that tracks progress toward its achievement.

Too often, local governments unveil impressive mission statements or announce broad goals but fail to develop objectives that would operationalize these goals and performance measures that would gauge progress toward the objectives. These governments inadvertently give themselves little chance of achieving the goals they desire. Effective systems of performance management—that is, systems designed to truly influence performance—are built upon the conscientious alignment of goals, objectives, and performance measures.

Why do it? Why do it right?

If the logic of performance measurement is compelling, the potential uses are many, and the concepts underlying the measurement process are simple, why then do some local governments choose not to measure performance? And why do so many of the local governments that *do* measure performance develop only poor sets of measures?

Those governments choosing not to measure performance offer a variety of reasons. Some government officials say that they intend to develop performance measures someday—perhaps soon, when they get a little spare time or when they hire a staff member with the skills to assist departmental officials in designing the measures. Others, however, show less interest in and perhaps even skepticism toward performance measurement. They doubt whether very many local government services can be measured adequately; they are suspicious of the reliability of the measures they have seen reported by other governments; and they are sure that their limited resources would be better spent delivering services rather than measuring and reporting on services. Some are also fearful that measures might reveal performance deficiencies, that performance measures would invite micromanagement by higher-level officials, and that performance measures could be misused by the media, political officials, and critics.

It would be inaccurate to allege that governments without performance measures are flying blind, for even without measures, government officials can assess performance on the basis of their own observations, the observations of trusted subordinates, the input of elected officials, and remarks from citizens. Sometimes these methods yield a reasonably accurate assessment that would be borne out by systematic measurement. At other times, however, assessments based on intermittent personal observations, anecdotal feedback, and intuition are inaccurate and can lead to ill-advised program adjustments, failure to make needed adjustments, or other poor decisions. Without performance measurement, gradual slippages in service quality and efficiency can go undetected by program officials, creating sizable deficiencies over time—unintended and escaping notice until a major problem brings unfavorable attention. The cumulative effect of gradual slippages renders a program vulnerable, perhaps to the threat of privatization and assuredly to a barrage of criticism. Without performance measurement, a program facing the threat of privatization will be ill-equipped to counter assertions that another entity could produce the service more efficiently and at higher quality. The threatened department simply will have no facts and figures upon which to mount its defense.

What about the assertion that limited resources would be better spent delivering services rather than measuring and reporting them? This contention is correct only if the gains in quality and efficiency of services derived from a more complete and accurate knowledge of an operation are of lesser value than the costs of acquiring that knowledge. If the slippage in quality and efficiency that is likely to occur in the absence of performance measurement is halted or even reversed by the availability of measures, then the resources devoted to measurement are a wise investment. In that light, the presumed savings from the choice to direct resources to service delivery rather than measurement could be a false economy.

Increasingly, local governments are choosing to measure performance (Poister and Streib 1999). Still, many of these governments persist in measuring performance only in the most rudimentary way, yielding poor sets of measures. Why do they take this minimalist approach? Perhaps officials in these governments share to a degree some of the sentiments expressed more openly by the nonadopters. Prompted by the bandwagon effect—"professional associations say that performance measurement is a good idea, and most of our more progressive neighbors seem to be doing it"—many minimal adopters feel compelled to develop performance measures and report them in their annual budget, but they share much of the skepticism about the value of performance measurement harbored by nonadopters. Given their skepticism, they prefer to keep their measurement system simple and inexpensive—a sentiment that almost invariably yields sets of measures relying overwhelmingly on raw counts of workload (output measures). After all, these are the easiest measures to develop, to track, and to report. Unfortunately, output measures have limited public relations value and even less performance management value. A set relying on output measures alone is suitable only for use with an undiscerning audience that can be impressed simply by *how much* activity has been undertaken and that does not follow up with an inquiry into the efficiency of service delivery or the quality or effect of services.

An even greater deficiency of a measurement system that relies only on output measures is the inability of these measures to inspire managerial thinking (Ammons 2002). Periodic feedback that alerts program officials and employees to changes in service efficiency and quality causes them to think about new strategies to improve results. Raw output measures, though cheaper to compile, simply do not produce that effect. This is why serious performance management efforts require measures of efficiency and effectiveness.

Summary

In this article we have focused only on the basics of performance measurement, leaving more advanced topics in this field to be addressed elsewhere. Our attention has been directed toward the rationale for performance measurement, the many uses of performance measures, and their relationship to goals and objectives. We also considered why some local governments measure performance well, some only minimally, and others not at all.

What are the key lessons we draw from this review of the basics? They are four:

- Several categories of performance measures exist, but the most relevant categories—those most deserving of the attention of local government supervisors and other officials—are few.

- Local governments at the forefront of the performance management movement rely on their performance measures not only for purposes of accountability and performance reporting but also as catalysts for performance improvement. These governments do not rest their aspirations on eloquent mission statements and broad goals alone. Instead, they proceed from articulating their mission and goals to developing more specific and immediate objectives and associated measures that will mark progress toward achievement of these objectives.

- To have managerial and policy value, a set of performance measures must include more than raw counts of activities or tasks performed. It must include measures that address efficiency, service quality, and results. By moving beyond output measures, local governments that are serious about influencing results ensure that program officials and employees have the kind of performance feedback that either provides reassurance that the program is performing as intended or, if not, inspires employees and supervisors to consider new strategies. Raw output numbers, standing alone, rarely inspire that kind of thinking.

- The careful alignment of goals, objectives, and performance measures sets the stage for performance management.

Endnote

1. The literature on performance measurement includes many more categories of measures than the four listed here. Some authorities have listed eight or ten types of performance measures; however, careful examination reveals many of these categories to be weak and some of the categories to overlap one another. By rejecting the weakest categories and collapsing the overlapping categories, the number can easily be reduced to four or five. The list of four types of measures in this article omits one commonly listed category: input measures. Input measures have been left off not because input is unimportant but because raw input alone, typically in the form of dollars or employees, does not measure performance. Only when depicted in relation to outputs do inputs reveal a dimension of performance—this, in the form of an efficiency measure.

References

Ammons, David N. 2002. "Performance Measurement and Managerial Thinking." *Public Performance and Management Review* 25, no. 4:344–347.

Behn, Robert D. 2003. "Why Measure Performance? Different Purposes Require Different Measures," *Public Administration Review* 63, no. 5:586–606.

Poister, Theodore H., and Gregory Streib. 1999. "Performance Measurement in Municipal Government: Assessing the State of the Practice." *Public Administration Review* 59, no. 4:325–335.

Ten Significant Observations about How People View Local Government

Barbara J. Cohn Berman

Since 1995 the Fund for the City of New York's Center on Municipal Government (CMGP) has studied how "everyday New Yorkers" evaluate local government performance. Lessons gleaned from a series of focus group sessions conducted in 1995 and 2001 are reported in this article.

As we listened to people talk about the way they judge specific areas of government performance, some clear, consistent themes emerged that, once noted, held true throughout their discussion of all government services. These observations are important because many of them fly in the face of assumptions we heard from people at various levels and in different branches of government when we were planning these studies. Moreover, once acknowledged and accepted, this information can help government have a better understanding of the public's needs and, in turn, can help government respond to these needs directly. The views noted here were expressed by people across neighborhoods, income levels and ethnicities, in both rounds of focus groups. They rang true for all of them, and probably will for all of us.

Observation 1 People are interested in local government and understanding of its complexities. Although people are firm about how they expect government to treat them, they are realistic in their expectations about what local government can do. They temper their aspirations for life in the city with realism and do not blame government for every problem. They know that resources are limited and that government cannot do everything.

They do not blame government for all urban ills. For example, they understand that an ambulance can be delayed because of heavy traffic; that the large demand for low income housing cannot be met easily, quickly or even fully; that supplying potable water to the entire city is an extraordinary feat as is government's ability to provide public transportation. They recognize and state that many of these services *"can't be perfect."*

They noted that actions by the public itself caused some problems. *("You can't really blame the ambulance on the delay time [when] cars do not move for those ambulances.")*

Observation 2   People's judgments about local government performance are formed primarily by their own personal experiences. Even when people read published reports about government or hear about them, they do not accept the reports blindly; they test them against their own experiences. For example, if the published crime rate is low but they feel threatened and unsafe on the street, or have been a victim of a crime and know of others who have been too, they question what data are included in the crime rate, and what is excluded. *("They don't include muggings in the crime report, to keep the rate down." "They say the air is clean, but I see a film of soot on my windowsill every morning. That can't be good. I wonder what it is that they are looking at.")*

There are two exceptions:

- Some people from the highest income groups cited newspapers and magazines as their source of information about government because they normally have little personal experience with many government services, such as public schools, public hospitals, social services; and

- The media influences people's judgments of services that are more distant from their daily lives. For example, if people have not been in a shelter for homeless persons, or visited a prison, or been involved with child protection, they are inclined to believe newspaper, radio and television reports.

Observation 3   The nature of the interactions with government employees and agencies is critical to the way people judge an agency and government itself. Often, the very first experience a person has with an agency—frequently with a person on the front line, or the gatekeeper—is decisive in people's judgment about the entire agency. *("The triage nurse was so rude and couldn't tell me how long I had to wait for my child to see a doctor. I know that there are good doctors in that hospital, but I will never go back there.")*

People were very clear about what they expect from all city employees and their agencies. Their expectations, once stated, sound both obvious and reasonable, yet they say they are not always met:

- Easy access to the office or person responsible for the service they need
- Easy access to information they need

- Courteous *and* respectful treatment
- Helpfulness and responsiveness
- Initiative
- A problem-solving attitude
- Compassion
- Reasonable, knowledgeable and timely responses
- Sensitivity to and respect for cultural differences among the population
- Even-handed treatment to all people.

When these expectations are not met, people judge government poorly.

Observation 4 People are clear and specific about what they do not want from government. That list includes:

- A run-around
- "Voice-mail jail"
- No response or very delayed response
- Rude, demeaning, unconcerned, or otherwise poor treatment.

Both good and unsatisfactory experiences are remembered for a long time.

Observation 5 People discuss and see government services differently from the way government is arranged and responds. Government is organized and delivers its services in departmental ways. Government employees' reference points are their own agencies. In their training they learn to see clear boundaries around their agency's responsibilities. They dissociate from functions and people in other agencies. *The general public, on the other hand, sees connections and relationships among functions.*

For example, when they are on the street, people observe the whole panoply of street level conditions, and if the street looks clean, feels safe, the lights work, the road is smooth, etc., they feel that government is working well. They do not say as they walk on the street that the environmental agency is doing a good job or the public works department is not performing well, and so on. Indeed, from the public's point of view, street level conditions, as a whole, are important indicators for judging local government performance. In New York and in our work with other cities, we see that at least ten government and other organizations are responsible for maintaining some aspect of the street environment. Yet there are no performance measures that cut across agency jurisdictions and report on the state of multiple street level conditions.

Similarly, people see connections among other functions that cut across agencies, such as:

- The full range of social services offered
- Crime, correction, probation, employment, homelessness, mental health
- Education, parks, out of school programs, child health, domestic violence, child protection
- Homelessness, health, mental health, public safety.

Observation 6   People recognize and acknowledge improvements in government performance. People noted with enthusiasm and specificity that some government services and performance had improved between the time of the first focus group sessions in 1995 and the second round in 2001. They singled out, in their discussions, improvements in:

- Public safety, noting that the city feels much safer;
- Public transportation, especially the subways that are *"cleaner, brighter, more reliable and safer"*;
- The extent of homelessness, which they assess by observing fewer homeless people on the streets.

Observation 7   People feel that *some*, but not all, governmental services are better in upscale neighborhoods. They single out public schools, police, parks, litter and snow removal, housing and health inspections of restaurants and grocery stores as examples of services they believe are better in upscale areas.

Observation 8   People want and like information from government. The public's desire and need for information spans a wide range. They want to know: what services are provided and by whom; how best to communicate with an agency; in advance, when roadwork or any other activity that affects their lives is scheduled and why; where after school and summer youth programs are available; which restaurants and food stores have health violations; how public schools in their neighborhood are rated; why one roadway is being repaved and another is not, etc. Many people in the focus groups use the Internet and like getting information from the city's website.

People seek information because it helps them control, plan and simplify their days and their lives. When government provides information, people conclude that government cares about them.

Observation 9   Interestingly, people rarely complain about taxes, but they express deep outrage and resentment when:

- They see "shoddy work"
- They see public employees goofing off
- They are treated with disrespect
- There is malfeasance and/or misfeasance.

Then they say: *"This is the public's (or my) money that is being wasted!"*

Observation 10   Despite their sophistication and interest in local government, people feel powerless and say that they cannot effect changes in how city services are delivered. Typical comments include: *"You can't fight city hall;" "You can't change the system."* Many attribute this sense of hopelessness to the rigidity of bureaucratic procedures, vested interests and unions. They also mention that there are no incentives for government employees to *"go out of their way to right a wrong."*

A critical issue for many was not having an effective feedback system in place so they could learn the effect of a complaint registered or a suggestion made.

Methods of Gathering Data

Harry P. Hatry

Local government officials wishing to expand or improve their sets of performance measures sometimes think they have only one or two options for gathering useful data. Often they actually have more choices than they realize, as described in this article.

The choice of collection procedures is key to getting valid, useful data. As the old saying goes: "Garbage in, garbage out." You cannot finalize performance indicators before deciding on data collection methods.

This chapter discusses five major alternatives for collecting quantitative performance indicator data:[1]

- Administrative data from program and/or agency records
- Customer surveys
- Trained observer ratings
- Role-playing ("testing")
- Special technical equipment.

Program and agency records

Most agencies and programs routinely record data on customers and/or transactions for administrative purposes.[2] This data collection procedure has been by far the most widely used for producing performance data. Agency records can be used to calculate perfor-

Adapted from Harry P. Hatry, "What Methods of Data Gathering Should Be Used?" pp. 83–117, in Harry P. Hatry, *Performance Measurement: Getting Results,* 2nd ed. (Washington, D.C.: Urban Institute Press, 2006). Copyright © Urban Institute Press, 2006. Used by permission.

mance indicators. Records may come from the program itself, from other programs within the agency, or from other agencies (including other levels of government). The relevant information needs to be extracted from those records and tabulated (if not already tabulated) in order to yield the desired outcome indicators.

Agency records are also the main data source on amounts of input (both dollars and employee time) and amounts of output produced by the program. This information is needed for output-based efficiency indicators. Records can also contain demographic characteristics of customers and other characteristics of the workload for breaking out outcome indicators.

Examples of outcome indicators for which agency records will be a source include the following:

- Data on timeliness and response times for police, fire, and emergency service calls or for any other customer requests for services or information.

- Number of complaints received, preferably broken out by the subject of the complaint and the severity of the problem. If the data are not already in the database, staff will have to develop a reliable procedure for producing the information. Number of *legitimate* complaints is the preferred indicator. Staff will also have to develop a way to assess which complaints are legitimate.

- Number of people who participated in services, such as for particular recreation, library, or social service programs. This information is needed in calculating customer success rates.

- Number of traffic accidents, injuries, and deaths.

- Number of reported crimes and fires.

- Clearance rates for each crime category.

- Incidence of various illnesses and deaths and their rates among program customers.

- Number of people receiving public assistance payments.

- Number and rates of low-weight births.

- Percent of clients employed and earnings levels after receiving employment and training assistance (from state unemployment insurance records).

- Recidivism rates.

Agency record data may be based in part on other procedures, such as trained observer ratings. For example, child welfare agency data on the number of children removed from unsafe homes may be based on staff members' observations of home conditions routinely tracked in agency records.

Advantages of agency records

- The data are readily available at low cost.

- Most program personnel are familiar with the procedures for transforming the data into indicators.

Disadvantages of agency records

- Agency records seldom contain enough service quality and outcome data to create an adequate set of performance indicators.

- Existing record collection processes often need modification to generate useful performance indicators. For example, though collecting data on program response times to requests is common for some types of services, others will need to modify their procedures to make sure that the following are provided:

  — Time of receipt of the service

  — Definition of what constitutes a completed response

  — Time of completion of response

  — Data-processing procedures to calculate and record the time between receipt of request and completion of response for individual requests

  — Data-processing procedures for combining the data on individual requests into aggregate response-time indicators

- Obtaining data from the records of other programs or agencies, which are sometimes needed to calculate an indicator, can be administratively difficult and can raise issues of confidentiality. For example,

  — indicators of the success rates of health and social service treatment programs may take the form of recidivism rates. Such data might need to be obtained from hospitals, police, courts, and other health and social service agencies where "failed" clients end up.

  — indicators on bringing criminals to justice need information from prosecutors and/or court systems on the dispositions of arrests (often difficult for other agencies to access).

Customer surveys

Customers—whether citizens, clients, or businesses—are an important source of information about service quality and outcomes. A major way to obtain reliable feedback from customers is through professionally prepared surveys.[3] Exhibit 1 lists the variety of information obtainable from such surveys.

Statistically valid surveys of customers, properly designed and implemented, are an excellent way to obtain information on such outcomes as customer condition, behavior, experiences, and satisfaction—especially after customers have completed services. Complaint data, while useful, do not cover the full range of information on service performance, because complainers are not likely to be representative of the full population of those served (only some people complain.) Focus groups are not designed to collect statistically representative data, though they are a very good way to help identify what outcomes should be measured and how to interpret data findings.

Exhibit 1.   Information obtainable from customer surveys.

1. Customer condition and attitudes after receiving services, as well as the results of those services
2. Customer action or behavior after receiving program services
3. Overall satisfaction with a service
4. Ratings of specific service quality characteristics
5. Extent of service use
6. Extent of awareness of services
7. Reasons for dissatisfaction with, or for not using, services
8. Suggestions for improving services
9. Demographic information on customers

Advantages of customer surveys

- Surveys are often the most feasible, if not the only, way to obtain data for some outcomes. Much of the information listed in Exhibit 1, for example, may be unavailable from other sources.
- Surveys provide direct input from the program's customers, adding not only valuable information but also credibility.

Disadvantages of customer surveys

- Surveys require special expertise, especially for development of the questionnaire and sampling plan and for training of interviewers.
- Surveys can require more time and are more costly than other forms of data collection, especially if the work is contracted out.
- Evidence based on respondents' perceptions and memory may be less convincing than data obtained from agency records.
- Some customers may not respond or will not be honest in their responses. This potential problem can be alleviated by well-worded questions and good interviewing. It is also alleviated with regularly repeated performance measurement, assuming the proportion of disaffected customers is likely to be about the same in each instance.

Content of customer surveys

The types of information listed in Exhibit 1 fall into five major categories:

Questions providing data on outcomes (items 1–4)   Responses to these questions provide the data for both end and intermediate outcome indicators. Questions can ask about specific service delivery characteristics (to help program personnel identify *specific* service problems) and *overall* service ratings.

Questions seeking information about the type and amount of the service used (item 5)   For some programs, amount of service can be used as an outcome indicator (such as to calculate the number and percent of families who used a park, library or public transit service at least once during the past month). These data can also be used to relate service outcomes to the types and amounts of services respondents received. (If the agency links the service information from its records to individual survey respondents, it can use data from agency records for this purpose. This option allows the survey questionnaire to be shorter and is presumably more accurate, since it does not rely on respondents' memories of services received.)

Diagnostic questions (items 6 and 7)   These questions ask why respondents gave particular answers or ratings, especially unfavorable ones.[4] In addition to being used in the performance measurement process, an edited list of such responses should be provided to program personnel, anonymously of course, to help them identify needed improvements. The information can also be used to construct more detailed outcome indicators, such as percentages of people who did not use the service in the past year for particular reasons.

Requests for suggestions on improving the service (item 8)   It is good practice to ask respondents at the end of the questionnaire for suggestions for improvement. These suggestions should also be provided, again anonymously, to program personnel.

Questions seeking demographic information (item 9)   Demographic information allows the program to tabulate responses by specific customer characteristics.

Survey all potential customers or only service users?

A program needs to decide what kind of survey to use: a survey of the full population in its jurisdiction (called here "household surveys"), a survey of its own customers only (called here "user surveys"), or both.

Household surveys include representative samples of all potential customers in a jurisdiction, regardless of whether they have used the services about which they are being asked. *User surveys* are administered to customers who have actually used the particular service. (User surveys can seek responses from all customers or a representative sample.)

Advantages of household surveys over user surveys

- Household surveys can obtain information about several services simultaneously.

- If surveys cover several services, their costs can be shared among agencies, reducing the costs to each.

- They can obtain information from and about nonusers, enabling programs to estimate *rates of participation* by different types of households.[5]

- They can obtain feedback from nonusers on reasons a service is not used.

- Since they are usually administered centrally, they are likely to have better quality control.

- They are less of a burden on individual agencies. In addition to being usually administered centrally, they do not require information on the addresses or telephone numbers of specific agency customers.

Advantages of user surveys over household surveys

- User surveys usually can provide more in-depth information on a particular service because users are familiar with it and do not need to be asked about other services.

- Sample selection is easier because addresses and/or telephone numbers of users are usually available to the agency. For household surveys, the sample needs to be drawn from some census of households or businesses.

- They can sometimes be conducted at the facilities customers use (such as parks, libraries, and public assistance offices).

- Higher response rates are likely because users have a personal interest in and knowledge of the service.

- They are likely to be less expensive because of the advantages cited above.

- The information is likely to be considerably more useful to program personal because it is more extensive and detailed.

Examples of customer survey questionnaires

- Exhibit 2 is a very simple questionnaire. This is an on-site, written user survey that has been used by the Long Beach, California, Community Development Agency. This questionnaire is about as short as one can be. It asks service users to provide comments and suggestions for improvement, but it does not ask about any end outcomes. Note that the questionnaire also calls for identification by the agency of any action taken.

- Exhibit 3 is an extract from a questionnaire for users of specific public facilities. Originally designed to obtain feedback on park and recreation facilities in Saint Petersburg, Florida, it asks about particular aspects of services, as well as an overall satisfaction rating. Such questions can be readily adapted to most types of services and facilities.

- For internal support activities, other government staff and departments are customers. Exhibit 4 is a written survey that Seattle, Washington's Fleet Services Division used for its motor pool. Seattle has also undertaken surveys for other internal services, such as its copy center, janitorial services, and personnel. All customers were given a copy of the survey when they obtained a vehicle and were asked to complete it and send it back. This survey was printed on heavy paper with the return address printed on the outside. To return it, the user had only to fold the form and put it in the interoffice mail. Similar fold-over forms can be used for brief mail surveys to citizens.

- Exhibit 5 shows three questions from a mail survey of customers of family counseling services, used by what was then called the Family Services Association of America.

Exhibit 2.   A simple user questionnaire.

How are we doing?

Date _____

The quality of service I received today was (please circle one):

		Unsatisfactory		Satisfactory		Excellent
1.	HELPFULNESS	1	2	3	4	5
2.	WAIT TIME	1	2	3	4	5

The primary reason for my visit was:

_____

Comments _____

_____

_____

_____

(Use reverse side for additional comments)

Optional _____   _____
         Name   Date

FOR STAFF USE ONLY

Action Taken _____

_____

_____

_____

_____   _____
Name   Date

Exhibit 3. Survey of facility users.

How would you rate the following?

		Excellent	Good	Fair	Poor
1.	Hours of operation	☐	☐	☐	☐
2.	Cleanliness	☐	☐	☐	☐
3.	Condition of equipment	☐	☐	☐	☐
4.	Crowdedness	☐	☐	☐	☐
5.	Safety conditions	☐	☐	☐	☐
6.	Physical attractiveness	☐	☐	☐	☐
7.	Variety of programs	☐	☐	☐	☐
8.	Helpfulness of personnel	☐	☐	☐	☐
9.	Overall	☐	☐	☐	☐

These questions illustrate the multiple types of information that can be obtained from surveys:

— The first question focuses only on satisfaction with the client's counselor. It does not ask about the results of the service, so it provides only information on an *intermediate outcome*.

— The second question asks for information about customer improvement, an *end outcome* indicator.

— The third question asks respondents to identify the extent to which the agency's service *contributed* to the improvement (as the respondents saw it). This is also an end outcome indicator, but it has the additional value of providing information on the extent to which the program has caused the outcome. The responses from questions 2 and 3 can be combined into the following end outcome indicator: "Percent of clients reporting [a particular level] of improvement AND reporting that agency services contributed to the changes reported."

By now, survey questionnaires have been prepared and administered on almost every public service. As a starting point for developing their own questionnaire, readers can search the Internet and various literature for questionnaires on the service in which they are interested.

Survey administration methods and their trade-offs

Mail surveys This is a low-cost method, including second and third mailings to secure response rates high enough to yield reliable information. Mail questionnaires are not,

Exhibit 4.   Department of Administrative Services Fleet Division motor pool customer service checklist.

1. How often do you use the pool?

    ☐ Daily   ☐ Weekly   ☐ Monthly   ☐ Other

2. For this trip, do you call to make a reservation?   ☐ Yes   ☐ No

3. Was a car available when you needed it?   ☐ Yes   ☐ No

4. If not, how long did you have to wait? _____

5. Have you ever been turned down when you wanted to use a car?   ☐ Yes   ☐ No

    If yes, what did you do?

    ☐ Waited until a car was available   ☐ Used a private car

    ☐ Other: _____

    _____

6. Was the car clean?   ☐ Yes   ☐ No

7. Was the car in good mechanical condition?   ☐ Yes   ☐ No

8. Were you treated courteously by motor pool staff?   ☐ Yes   ☐ No

9. Please rate our quality of service:

    ☐ Excellent   ☐ Good   ☐ Fair   ☐ Poor

Comments or suggestions: _____

_____

_____

_____

_____

_____

_____

Name: _____ Department: _____ Phone: _____

Please fold in half and send back to DAS in interoffice mail. This form is preaddressed. If you have any questions or need additional information, please call 684-0137. Thank you.

Source: City of Seattle.

Exhibit 5. Mail survey questions on family counseling.

1. How satisfied were you with the way you and your counselor got along with each other?
   - ☐ Very satisfied
   - ☐ Satisfied
   - ☐ No particular feelings one way or the other
   - ☐ Somewhat dissatisfied
   - ☐ Very dissatisfied

2. Since you started at the agency, has there been any change for better or worse in the way the members of your family get along with each other? Would you say you now get along:
   - ☐ Much better
   - ☐ Somewhat better
   - ☐ Same
   - ☐ Somewhat worse
   - ☐ Much worse

3. How do you feel the service provided by the agency influenced the changes you have reported?
   - ☐ Helped a great deal
   - ☐ Helped some
   - ☐ Made no difference
   - ☐ Made things somewhat worse
   - ☐ Made things much worse

---

of course, useful for respondents who cannot read them. (For people who do not speak English, the questionnaire would need to be translated into their native language.) To obtain satisfactory completion rates, mail questionnaires generally need to be short and simple. Cluttered, complex questionnaires and questionnaires that are longer than four to five pages are likely to yield excessively low response rates. Response rates are likely to be much higher among people who have used the particular service than among a general sample of households in the area. (See Exhibit 6 for ways to increase response rates to mail surveys.)

Telephone surveys   Telephone surveys can achieve good response rates from households at lower cost than the in-person alternative. They are more expensive than mail surveys because they require considerable interviewer time and training. They cannot cover populations without telephone access or people who do not speak English (but foreign

---

Exhibit 6.   Suggestions for increasing response rates to mail surveys.

- Include a transmittal letter signed by a respected, high-level official. Guarantee complete confidentiality of responses. Address the letter to a specific individual whenever feasible.

- Emphasize the need for information *from customers to improve future services.*

- Mail an advance postcard notifying recipients that they will soon receive a questionnaire and asking explicitly for their help.

- Keep the questionnaire short and easy to use. Make sure each question has a clear purpose and stick primarily to response categories that only require a check mark. Open-ended questions (requiring an answer in the respondent's own words), though rich in information, should be limited to a very small number.

- Keep skip patterns (instructions to respondents to skip certain questions depending on their response to a previous question) *to an absolute minimum.* When unavoidable *be sure skip patterns are crystal clear.*

- Go for a professional, polished look. Even if the questionnaire is prepared in-house, it should look typeset and be printed on high-quality, preferably colored paper. *Cutting corners by using low-quality copiers and so forth risks unacceptable response rates.*

- Enclose a stamped, self-addressed envelope in each questionnaire mailing.

- Use multiple mailings. One mailing is seldom enough. Postcard and telephone reminders can also be used.

---

language interviewers can be used if resources are available to translate the questionnaire and do the interviews).

Phone surveys have faced considerably lower response rates in recent years, due to such factors as increasing use of answering machines, people's greater resistance to phone surveys, and greater use of cell phones. Cell phones pose particular problems because their phone numbers may be unavailable for sampling, and cell phone providers may charge users for each call. These factors are less of a problem for user surveys, where the agency sponsoring the survey has contact information on those to be surveyed and has gained the trust and cooperation of its customers.

In-person surveys administered at the respondent's home or business   These surveys tend to yield high response rates and can provide detailed information since they can be longer and more complicated than mail questionnaires. However, they are the most costly to administer and are usually too expensive for repeatedly collecting the data needed for performance measurement.

In-person surveys administered at a service facility   In-person survey administration at a facility—such as a park, library, school, or social service agency—has the advantages of obtaining high response rates without the high cost of finding respondents at their homes or businesses.[6] This option is a good one if the primary purpose of the survey is to capture the quality of the person's immediate experience at the site. It cannot, by definition, be used for outcomes that occur after the customer leaves the facility. However, respondents can also be asked about previous experiences with the service.

Internet surveys   An emerging option is to tap the increasing access of organizations and families to personal computers. These surveys are increasingly being used for surveys of *organizations* (such as of government agencies and in surveys by government agencies of businesses) and for populations expected to have ready access to a computer.

When applicable, Internet surveys often can be done at low cost. They require effort to obtain adequate response rates, however, perhaps including advance or follow-up mailed postcards to encourage completion of the questionnaire.

The primary obstacles to widespread use of Internet surveys are many households' lack of ready access to computers and interest in using their computers, even if available. But access and interest are both growing, so Internet surveys are likely to become more widely used.

Combination of survey methods   A good option often is to use combinations of methods. For example, mailings can be supplemented with telephone calls to people who failed to respond to follow-up mailings, mail or telephone might be used to supplement online surveys, and so on.

Mixing survey methods raises the question of the accuracy of combining responses from more than one method. The studies to date are far from conclusive about whether this significantly distorts the findings. Compared with the other issues, such as potential sampling errors and nonresponse biases, combining methods appears to be less of a concern.

Choosing among methods   In choosing which method is best, an agency needs to weigh the trade-offs between higher response rates (providing greater confidence that the findings represent the views of the population surveyed), larger sample sizes (providing greater precision) and cost of administration. *Whichever method is used, agencies should seek at least a 50 percent response rate.* (Techniques such as enclosing questionnaires with all utility bills will seldom yield high enough returns to make the data credible.)

How many people to survey

Surprisingly, for user surveys, it may be much less of a hassle, and involve less total effort, if a program surveys all its customers. For some programs, it may be feasible to survey all customers, such as by routinely mailing questionnaires to each customer. (If all a program's customers are surveyed, the program will not have to worry about possible sampling errors. The major remaining source of survey error comes from the possibility that if a large proportion of customers does not respond to the survey then the findings will not be sufficiently representative of all customers.)

When very large numbers of citizens, businesses, or clients are the population of interest, a sampling of the population is likely needed. The program will then have to decide on the sample size. Larger samples are needed if the program wants higher rates of precision, but high rates of precision are seldom needed in a customer survey. Larger samples will be needed if the program wants separate outcome information on a number of population subgroups.

Tips on customer survey design and administration

- *Establish a working group to help develop content.* This group should include key service agency representatives, perhaps a representative of the chief administrative officer, a survey expert, and a spokesperson for program customers.

- *Beware of biased or muddled wording.* Always have a professional survey expert review final question wording and sequencing.

- *Always test a questionnaire on a small number of customers* before full implementation to catch (a) awkward, ambiguous, or redundant questions; (b) confusing or incorrect instructions; and (c) wording that sounds offensive or just plain foolish.

- *Translate questionnaires* if substantial numbers of the desired respondents are unlikely to speak English.

- *Use outside contractors for the administration of regular surveys if resources are available.* Contracting out is usually easier than in-house administration, even for a mail questionnaire. Suggestions about what to include in a survey contract are provided in Exhibit 7.

- *Keep to a minimum changes in questions and question wording from year to year.* Changes compromise the year-to-year comparability of the findings.

Ways to reduce survey costs

Survey costs depend on the number of people surveyed, the frequency of the survey, the mode of administration, and efforts to increase response (and completion rates). Here are suggested ways to cut survey costs:

- *If the population represented is large, sample it rather than surveying everyone.* When a program has only a small number of customers (perhaps no more than one or two hundred each year), it is likely easier to survey all of them. But when very large numbers of citizens, businesses, or clients are the customers, selecting a representative sample is an efficient way to go.

- *Reduce required sample size by avoiding excessive precision.* For most programs, 95 or 99 percent confidence limits are overkill. While 95 percent limits are the standard in the academic community, they are likely excessive for most performance measurement work. Ninety percent limits are likely sufficient. The required sample size, and cost, will increase as precision requirements increase.

- *Do not seek higher response rates than you really need.* Statisticians have often recommended achieving response rates of around 75 percent. A 50 percent response rate is

Exhibit 7. Elements to include in contracts for customer surveys.

- Number of *completed* questionnaires, including minimum sizes for each major category of customer for whom data are sought, and minimum acceptable response rates.
- Survey administration details, such as (a) whether mail, telephone, or both are to be used; (b) the number of mailing or number of follow-up telephone calls; and (c) the time between mailings and telephone follow-ups.
- Contractor's role in questionnaire development.
- The amount of testing of the questionnaire that the contractor will do.
- Provisions for maintaining respondent confidentiality.
- Any special coding to be done by the contractor (e.g., transforming location data provided by respondents into a more compact grouping of geographical areas).
- Specification of how tabulations are to be handled, such as whether "not applicables" and "don't knows" should be included in the denominators for the percents calculated.
- Products, and their formats, that will be provided to the agency. Products should include, at a minimum, (a) a detailed description of survey procedures used and (b) the resulting response data (with confidentiality preserved).
- Time frame for the work.
- Any restriction on release of the data to the media.
- Overall cost.

likely adequate for most outcome measurement work. Survey administration costs rise steeply as response rate requirements increase.

- *Use agency personnel when appropriate and possible.* However, do not use as interviewers staff who are delivering the service. This undermines survey credibility.

- *Use the mail to administer the survey if you have mailing addresses for most customers. If the sample size is small, administer the mail survey in house.*

- *Use or adapt questionnaires that are already available.* Surveys might, for example, be available through the Internet, from other agencies in other locations, or from universities. After a questionnaire has been developed, keep it reasonably stable from year to year. It should be used to obtain the same data on the same performance indicators in future reporting periods. This practice avoids the need to invest in major new questionnaire development efforts.

- *Shorten the questionnaire.* Agencies are tempted, once they have decided to survey citizens, to add more and more subject matter and details. Be firm and consider the potential usefulness of each question. Another procedure is to identify some questions that are less important or not likely to change much between questionnaire administrations. Rotate such questions, including them perhaps in every other administration.

- *Look for expert help within the agency* or other low-cost sources.

- *Use commercially available software for tabulations.*

- *Use volunteers to administer surveys whenever possible.* Be warned, however, that volunteers need extensive training and may not be dependable. They also need to be carefully monitored.

- *Do not attempt to cover every category of customer in the sample.* Consider dropping groups that (a) are extremely costly to survey, (b) are only a very small proportion of the population of interest, and (c) are not vital to the survey objectives. Be sure that all such omissions are clearly identified in survey reports.

- *Add questions to already scheduled surveys, such as those of other agencies or universities.* For example, city (or county) governments might collect questions from a number of their agencies into one community household survey. Programs with related functions (such as various public or private child development programs) might develop a joint questionnaire and questionnaire administration process.

Trained observer ratings

Trained observers are used to rate outcome conditions that can be perceived by the eyes or other physical senses of an observer.[7] The physical observation can be through any of the five senses (sight, hearing, smell, taste, touch). Since most public-sector applications use sight, the text discussion focuses primarily on visual ratings.

The key element for performance measurement is that the rating scales and procedures provide values that are reliable enough to withstand challenge. The goal is to ensure that different observers at different times give the same or similar ratings to similar conditions.

The following elements are needed to ensure a high degree of reliability:

- Systematic rating scales that provide well-defined yardsticks against which the observers can assess conditions

- Adequate training and supervision of the observers and the process

- Periodic checking of the quality of the ratings

For trained observer ratings to be a suitable performance measurement procedure, the outcome needs to be measurable by physical observation and reliable on a scale that identifies several variations of the condition to be measured.

Inspections have traditionally been used to assess health, fire, and food safety at various facilities. For the most part, however, these findings were not aggregated to provide regular condition assessment ratings. In recent years, trained observer procedures have been used to track systematically these and other conditions. Trained observer ratings have been used for assessing the cleanliness of streets, condition of roads, condition of parks and playgrounds, condition of facilities (such as schools, hospitals, and prisons), condition of traffic signals and signs, and quality of food served to customers.

New York City has what is probably the longest running trained observer operation in the world. Since 1974, it has undertaken regular (currently daily) cleanliness ratings of a large sample of city streets. Its "service inspectors" use a seven-point photographic rating scale and enter the data into handheld computers at the end of the day to provide current reports for each of the city's sanitation districts.

The Fund for the City of New York, a nonprofit organization, has also been regularly providing trained observer ratings on a large number of New York City "street-level" conditions. These conditions include such items as rubbish collection, traffic and street light maintenance, tree plantings, graffiti, abandoned cars, rodent control, and potholes. The findings are reported to the government agencies and other organizations responsible for correcting the problems.

New York City (for a number of years) and San Francisco (more recently) have both been using trained observer procedures to regularly assess ice condition of their parks. In New York, the rating scales include detailed written descriptions. San Francisco's scale uses a combination of photographs and written descriptions.[8]

Advantages of trained observer ratings

- Trained observer ratings can provide reliable, reasonably accurate ratings of conditions that are otherwise difficult to measure.

- Periodic ratings can be used to help allocate program resources throughout the year. *The findings can be used not only for periodic performance reporting but also to guide early fixes of problem conditions.* For example, the New York City Sanitation Department has for many years used trained observer ratings of street cleanliness to help allocate and reallocate its street cleaning crews over time. The information provided by the ratings could be used to establish work orders aimed at correcting problems identified by the ratings.

- If handheld computers are used to record the ratings in the field, the data can be uploaded by the end of each day and reports made available to supervisors very quickly.

- The data can be presented in an easy-to-understand format, which is important in reaching officials and the public.

Disadvantages of trained observer ratings

- They are labor-intensive procedures that require significant personnel time, including time for training observers.

- If the people doing the ratings are the same people delivering the service, the results will likely lack credibility. For example, some social service and mental health agencies have used caseworkers to rate their own clients' progress on selected condition scales. This rating does not require significant added expense and is appropriate for internal tracking of client progress. However, for external performance measurement purposes, using an agency's own caseworkers should be avoided because their potential self-interest in the ratings reduces the perceived, if not the actual, credibility of the results.

- Observers need to be checked periodically to ensure that they are adhering to the procedures. This adds costs.

Added operational use of trained observers: Identify needed early corrective action

As noted in the advantages, the trained observer process might be extended to provide corrective action information. Observers would be asked to suggest the needed corrective action and how soon action is needed. For example, observers rating streets, parks, or building conditions might be asked to rate each problem using a scale such as the following:

1. No action needed

2. Only minor improvement needed; no immediate action needed

3. Only minor, but immediate, action should be taken

4. Major, but not immediate, improvements are needed

5. Major action needed immediately (hazardous to health or safety)

   To determine the priorities for action, program officials would also need to consider such information as the number of people affected and the cost of correcting the problem. Where the trained observers are expected to be sufficiently knowledgeable, they might also be asked to estimate the time and resources needed to correct the problem.

Types of rating systems

Trained observers use three major types of rating systems:

- Written descriptions
- Photographs
- Other visual scales, such as drawings or videos

Written descriptions   This type of system, the simplest and most familiar type, depends entirely on specific written descriptions of each grade used in the rating scale.
   An abbreviated written scale for building or street cleanliness is the following:

- Rating 1: **Clean.** Building or street is completely or almost completely clean; a maximum of three pieces of litter per floor or block is present.
- Rating 2: **Moderately clean.** Building or street is largely clean; a few pieces of isolated litter or dirt are observable.
- Rating 3: **Moderately dirty.** Some scattered litter or dirt is present.
- Rating 4: **Dirty.** Heavy litter or dirt is present in several locations throughout the building or along the block.

The Metropolitan Transit Authority's New York City Transit and a citizen's group, the Straphangers campaign, have been providing annual scorecards that provide information on each of the 22 New York City subway lines.[9] Each line is rated on the reliability of its train service, the chance of getting a seat, and the quality of subway car announcements. The data are obtained from agency records and trained observer ratings by travelers who come from departments not directly affected by the findings.[10]

Assessing the need for repairs is an additional, very important use for outcome information from observer ratings. The city of Toronto used the information obtained from the scale in Exhibit 8 not only to help track road conditions but also to determine what repairs were needed in each location, as noted in the right-hand column comments. That is, the ratings were used for performance measurement and for determining needed actions.

Photographs Photographic scales can be more precise than written scales in clearly defining each rating grade. Generic photos are used to represent grades on the rating scale. Observers are given (and trained in the use of) a set of photos, with several representing

Exhibit 8. Condition rating.

Rating	Condition	Description	Comments
9	Excellent	No fault whatsoever	Recently constructed work
8	Good	No damage, normal wear, and small cracks	
7	Fair	Slight damage, crack, fill or minor leveling required	Average rating for City of Toronto pavements and sidewalks
6	Repair	10% of complete replacement cost	Pavement requires preventive overlay. Level of Tolerance for City of Toronto pavements
5	Repair	25% of complete replacement cost	Eligible for reconstruction programme. Condition Rating-4 Level
4	Repair	50% of complete replacement cost	of Tolerance for City of Toronto curbs and sidewalks
3	Repair	75% of complete replacement cost	Total reconstruction probably indicated
2	Repair	More than 75% of complete replacement cost	Requires complete reconstruction
1	Impossible to repair		

each grade on the rating scale. See Exhibit 9, which shows a photographic scale for street rideability conditions.

Implementing a trained observer process

Implementing a trained observer process requires the following steps:

- Decide what conditions should be rated.
- Develop a rating scale for each condition. If possible, adapt an existing scale. Use photographs and written guidelines as appropriate.
- Determine which facilities or areas should be rated, when, and how frequently. Ratings can be applied to all or selected facilities or areas. If resources are only available to rate a subset of locations, choose the subset by random sampling so the locations chosen will be representative.

Exhibit 9.   Examples of street rideability conditions.

Condition 1: Smooth

Condition 2: Slightly bumpy

Condition 3: Considerably bumpy

Condition 4: Safety Hazard

Source: Harry P. Hatry, Donald M. Fisk, John R. Hall, Jr., Philip S. Schaenman, and Louise Snyder, *How Effective Are Your Community Services? Procedures for Performance Measurement,* 3rd ed. (Washington, D.C.: ICMA and The Urban Institute), pp. 105-107. Copyright © 2006 by the International City/County Management Association and The Urban Institute. Reprinted by permission.

- Select and train observers, who might be program personnel, college or graduate school students, or volunteers. Technical ratings, such as safety hazards, will require observers with the requisite professional training.
- Test the scale and observers on a small number of sites in the facility or area to make sure reasonably trained observers give consistent ratings.
- Establish procedures for supervising the observers and for recording, transcribing, and processing the data they collect.
- Conduct the ratings regularly.
- Establish procedures for systematically checking the ratings of trained observers to provide quality control. One way to do this is for the supervisor to check periodically a small sample of each observer's ratings.
- Develop and disseminate reports on the findings from each set of ratings for the current period and changes from previous periods. The Reports should show the number and percent of locations that fell into particular rating categories. *Do not report only the average scores, which can hide very important distributional information.*

The following additional steps are needed for a photographic rating system:

- Take a large number of photographs in settings representative of the range of conditions to be rated. These photos should reflect the actual types of conditions the program wants to assess.
- Select a panel of judges made up of people with varied backgrounds who are not associated with the measurement activities. Select a set of familiar labels, each representing a condition that the program expects to find, such as clean, moderately clean, moderately dirty, and dirty. Ask the judges to sort the photographs into groups that represent each condition.
- For each condition, select the photographs (perhaps four or five) that the largest number of judges identified as representative. These photographs then become the rating scale.
- Develop written guidelines to accompany the photographs, if needed.
- Train observers in the use of the photographic scale and field-test it with those observers to determine the extent of agreement among them. Revise the ratings and procedures as needed.
- Develop the final scale. Package copies of the photographs selected for the final scale in a kit for each trained observer.

Automating trained observer ratings

Handheld computers, available at surprisingly low prices, can be programmed to record observational data. This can considerably ease the amount of clerical work needed and reduce errors introduced by manual recording. New York City has been using such handheld computers to report on the condition of city buildings (including schools), as required to meet a legislative mandate. The Fund for the City of New York (a public interest organization) has also used handheld computers to collect data on several physically observable conditions in sample locations within the city. The conditions observed include, among others, defective street signs, abandoned cars, the presence of rodents or other pests, and defective street lights.[11] This information is used to identify both summary and specific conditions. Data entry, tabulations, and reports can be done quickly.

Role-playing ("testing")

For some services, outcome information can be obtained by people acting as service customers. Using systematic guidelines, the role players assess the service organization's service delivery response. (This procedure can be considered a special form of trained observer procedures. However, it is sufficiently different to warrant its own discussion.)

This procedure is not widely used. It probably has been used more by performance audit agencies for ad hoc studies. But, role-playing also lends itself to regular performance measurement. Here are the two major types of applications for this procedure.[12]

- Assessing whether different citizen groups receive similar treatment or service from a public or private agency. For example, federal agencies, such as the departments of Labor, Housing and Urban Development, and Justice have used role-playing to assess the prevalence of discrimination, such as in employment, housing, and bank loans.

- Assessing the accuracy and quality of agency responses to requests for information, such as by the Internal Revenue Service, a state or local tourism agency, or any federal, state, or local agency.

  For example, the District of Columbia's Office of Customer Service Operations hires external personnel to regularly test the quality of contacts with its agencies. The contacts may be face to face or by telephone, voice mail, or correspondence. The tester completes a rating form that assesses helpfulness, courtesy, knowledge, and etiquette (such as answering the call within three rings of the contact and checking back frequently with customer if the customer was put on hold). The tester rates most elements on a scale of 1 to 5, based on definitions developed by the Customer Service Office. An extract of the rating sheet is provided in Exhibit 10. The Customer Service Office provides quarterly reports on the rating of each agency (and posts them on the Internet).

This procedure requires careful determination of what will be rated, instructions of what constitutes the various rating categories, and instructions on how the testers will do the ratings so similar circumstances will each be rated approximately the same by different testers.

For the more complex role playing, such as testing for discrimination, the role players need considerable training. (For discrimination applications, usually two players are paired. One plays the role of a minority, and one the majority, applicant. They would represent people with similar qualifications and be as similar as possible other than in the discrimination characteristic being assessed.)

Special technical equipment

Special equipment is needed to collect data for outcome indicators that require scientific measurement, such as

- noise levels,
- air pollution levels,
- water pollution levels, or
- road conditions (using road meters).

Many state transportation agencies have been using road meters for years. The Fund for the City of New York used a special car outfitted with a "profilometer" to measure street roughness on a sample of 12 percent of the city's blocks. Two outcome indicators were generated from these readings for each of the city's 59 community districts: a smoothness score (percent of blocks rated acceptable) and number of "significant jolts" encountered per mile.[13] (Acceptability was determined by correlating citizen ratings of sample blocks with the profilometer's readings.)

Exhibit 10. Example of a tester's rating scale.

Explanation of Numerical Ratings for Agency Tester Calls

1. The service given is unacceptable
   - Courtesy: Operators use speakerphone, chew gum or food, carry on other conversations, or display brazen rudeness.
   - Knowledge: Operators demonstrate a complete lack of knowledge.
   - Etiquette: Operators do not answer calls in three rings, check with you after being on hold, transfer you more than once or without reference information, identify themselves, thank you for calling.
   - Overall Impression: Voice mail is reached or operators provide inferior service in all three criteria of courtesy, knowledge, and etiquette.

2. The service given is below average
   - Courtesy: Operators show minor irritation.
   - Knowledge: Operators have difficulty in finding basic information.
   - Etiquette: Operators do not answer call in three rings, check with you after being on hold, transfer you more than once without reference information, identify themselves, thank you for calling.
   - Overall Impression: Inferior service in courtesy, knowledge, and etiquette.

3. The service given is average and unremarkable
   - Courtesy: Operators are neither rude nor cheerful.
   - Knowledge: Basic knowledge is accurately provided.

(Continued on page 45)

Advantages of technical equipment

- Appropriate technical equipment usually provides accurate, reliable data.
- It may be the only reasonable way to achieve fully credible information on important environmental outcomes such as those listed above. Programs can obtain subjective outcome data using trained observers or user Surveys to assess the quality of roads, water, air, and so on, but such information is likely to lack the credibility, and validity, provided by technical measurement.

Disadvantages of technical equipment

- The equipment can be expensive to procure, operate, and maintain.
- The information obtained must be interpreted to be useful to program personnel and outsiders. For example, vertical displacement measurements need to be converted into an excellent, good, fair, or poor ride scale or similarly self-explanatory grouping, and air pollution measurements need to be converted into overall air quality levels understandable to the public, such as good, moderate, approaching unhealthful, and unhealthful.

(Continued from page 44)

-   Etiquette: Without enthusiasm or cheerfulness, operators make none of the mistakes outlined in the etiquette category in score 2.
-   Overall Impression: Operators answer questions, but the service is average.

4. The service given is above average
    -   Courtesy: Operators are cheerful and friendly.
    -   Knowledge: Operators provide useful information.
    -   Etiquette: While maintaining a cheerful and friendly demeanor, operators make none of the mistakes outlined in the etiquette category in score 2.
    -   Overall Impression: Superior service in courtesy, knowledge, and etiquette.

5. The service given is excellent
    -   Courtesy: Operators show genuine concern and see call through to resolution.
    -   Knowledge: Operators know their respective agencies and resources very well.
    -   Etiquette: Operators maintain a cheerful and friendly demeanor, put you at ease, and take care of your needs. Operators make none of the mistakes outlined in the etiquette category in score 2.
    -   Overall Impression: Superior service in courtesy, knowledge, and etiquette; genuinely makes you feel good about your interaction.

Source: Government of the District of Columbia, Mayor's Office, "Telephone Tester Program," 2006.

Selecting appropriate data sources and data collection procedures

The following are criteria for selecting data collection procedures:

- *Cost.* This is always a primary concern. Sometimes bargain-basement procedures can be used effectively (such as mail rather than telephone surveys), depending on the response rates and types of data required. Also, some outcome indicators can ride the coattails of other procedures. For example, *data for several outcome indicators might be obtainable from a single customer survey; or, trained observers might be able to collect data simultaneously for a number of different outcome indicators,* such as street cleanliness, road bumpiness, and condition of traffic signs, with little added cost.

- *Feasibility.* This criterion covers identification of nonfinancial obstacles that are likely to make data collection very difficult or impossible. For example, if data are needed from other agencies, will they permit access to it?

- *Accuracy and reliability achievable with the procedure.*

- *Understandability.* The data should be understandable to program managers and people outside the program, including the public.

- *Credibility.* This includes the potential for data manipulation, especially by people with an interest in making the data look good (such as caseworkers assessing the results of their work with their own clients). Because of the potential for data manipulation, surveys by outside contractors are likely to be more credible than surveys administered by the agency itself. However, for cost reasons, many agencies will find it necessary to use their own resources to obtain outcome data, such as when surveying their clients or using trained observers. Such problems will be reduced if an agency uses agency personnel who are not delivering the service and has a data quality control process that is recognized as good.

Pilot-testing new data collection procedures

All new or substantially modified data collection procedures should be pilot-tested to identify and eliminate bugs before full implementation. The pilot test should approximate the conditions that will exist during full implementation, but it will usually test the procedures only on some segments of the program. For example, a pilot test might cover

- only outcome indicators that are new or require substantial modifications to existing data collection procedures,
- only some activities,
- only some locations or customers, or
- only some part of a year.

The group developing the performance measurement process should oversee this test if possible, working with program and project personnel to identify problems. Modifications should then be made to alleviate problems found in the pilot test—such as problems with the sampling plan, questionnaires and other data collection instruments, and individual outcome indicator definitions.

The program should keep track of the staff time and out-of-pocket costs required for the new procedures during the test and use this information to estimate the annual cost to the program. If this estimated cost is too high, the group should provide recommendations regarding possible elimination of particularly marginal outcome indicators, reduced sample sizes, shorter data collection instruments, and so on. The group should also be on the lookout for additional outcome indicators that should be tracked.

Other potential problems in data collection

These problems include the following:

- Definitions that are unclear to those responsible for collecting the information.
- Missing data. For example, an economic development program might not have a complete list of businesses served. If missing data are a major problem, the program may need to modify its record-keeping.
- Confidentiality requirements, such as permission from parents to survey their children. Such requirements can add considerably to the effort required to obtain data.

Resolutions may involve correcting the problem, deciding to delete an outcome indicator, or accepting less accuracy.

Frequency of data collection and reporting

Programs need to think hard about how frequently their performance measurement data should be collected. Frequent collection and reporting is important for making the data useful to operating managers. However, higher frequency typically leads to higher cost. Some data need to be collected less frequently than others. For example, some information obtained from customer surveys, such as victimization rates, might not be expected to change for relatively long periods. Other indicators, such as number of traffic accidents or crimes reported, are tabulated and reported perhaps weekly but at least monthly. At the other end of the frequency scale, some data might be collected every other year.

The drive for accountability and performance information for budget planning has led agencies to focus on annual reporting. But *for the basic performance measurement purposes of helping managers monitor and seek continual program improvement, data collection at least quarterly should be the goal.* Quarterly program reporting has been common in government agencies for many years, but until recent years little reporting has included systematically collected data on outcomes.

With careful planning, quarterly data collection does not need to add substantially to costs. With agency records, for example, once the data have been computerized, frequent tabulations are feasible at minimal additional cost. Routine follow-up questionnaires sent to customers a certain period after service receipt (say, nine months) also may yield year-round data at little added cost.

For customer surveys, if sampling is used, consider splitting the annual sample size—defined by a budget constraint—into, say, four quarterly subsamples. A questionnaire would be administered to one-quarter of the eligible population during each quarter. This would give managers *more timely feedback and seasonal information.* The annual cost of the survey work would increase somewhat, about 10 percent more than if one large survey were conducted. The findings for each calendar quarter would be statistically less precise because the samples are smaller, but accumulating the data would yield annual data as precise as if the whole sample had been surveyed at a single point in time.[14]

Some outcomes need to be measured at a specific time after service started or was completed, as is the case for many social service programs. In these situations, the programs will probably need to collect outcome data throughout the year. The data can be tabulated at any useful intervals, such as monthly, bimonthly, or quarterly.

Questions whose responses are not expected to change appreciably from quarter to quarter, or even year to year, need not be asked every time. Agencies and their programs may also want to reserve space on the questionnaire for a small number of especially timely questions that are asked only once. These need not be performance measurement questions: they might seek opinions from citizens on policy or program changes that the agency or program is considering.

Final comment

When choosing among data collection procedures by cost and accuracy, programs need to trade off a high degree of accuracy against less statistical precision. *It is better to be roughly right than precisely ignorant.*

Endnotes

1. Obtaining quantitative data is not always possible for all indicators. The program needs to be explicit about important outcomes for which there is no quantitative performance information and provide qualitative judgments about performance on those outcomes.

2. The term "archival data" is sometimes used to refer to the use of records.

3. Numerous reports are available that much more fully address the technical issues of surveys, such as sample size and selection, administrative procedures, data accuracy, and response rates.

4. In the authors' experience, questions asking for explanations for "good" ratings seldom yield much useful information. Every question is an added burden on respondents and requires added coding time by those processing the responses. Therefore, only asking respondents why they gave unfavorable responses is likely to be more practical.

5. Attendance counts are useful but do not indicate how many *different* people or households used the service during a particular reporting period unless the names of particular users are available and can be analyzed.

6. For administration at a facility that is not under the agency's immediate control, permission from the facility is required. For surveys of minors, parental permission may be required.

7. For further details on trained observer procedures, see John Greiner, "Trained Observer Ratings," chapter 8 in *Handbook of Practical Program Evaluation,* 2nd edition, edited by Joseph S. Wholey, Harry Hatry, and Kathryn Newcomer (San Francisco: Jossey-Bass Publishers, 2004); and Harry Hatry and others, *How Effective Are Your Community Services? Procedures for Measuring Their Quality,* 3rd edition (Washington, DC: International City/County Manager's Association and the Urban Institute, 2006), especially chapter 10 and appendix 6.

8. See New York City Department of Parks and Recreation, "Park Inspection Program Standards: Guide to the Parks Inspection Program and Official Inspection Standards," Office of Operations and Management Planning, March. Every two weeks upper-level management reviews the inspection-summary reports to discuss problem areas and what can be done to

improve them. Some of the data are also included in the annual Mayor's Management Reports to citizens. As of early 2006, the department was developing a similar trained observer process for its recreation centers. For San Francisco, see San Francisco Recreation and Park Department, "Park Maintenance Standards: The Manual and Evaluation Form," May 3, 2005.

9. See http://www.straphangers.org for a description of New York City's Straphangers Campaign scorecard.

10. The Straphangers Campaign web site (http://www.straphangers.org) describes the methodology.

11. Fund for the City of New York, *Computerized Neighborhood Environment Tracking* (New York: Fund for the City of New York, 1999).

12. For more extensive details on the procedures and their application, see Margery Turner and Wendy Zimmermann, "Role Playing," chapter 11 in *Handbook of Practical Program Evaluation*, 2nd edition, edited by Joseph Wholey et al. (San Francisco: Jossey-Bass, 2004).

13. Fund for the City of New York, Center on Municipal Government Performance, *How Smooth Are New York City's Streets?* (New York: Fund for the City of New York, September 1998).

14. For example, an annual sample of 1,000 customers might be split into quarterly samples of 250 each. At a 90 percent confidence level, the sample size of 250 would yield a confidence interval of approximately +5.4 percentage points, versus +2.7 percentage points for the full sample of 1,000. If 50 percent of those sampled gave a certain rating to a particular service characteristic, the confidence intervals would be 44.6 percent to 55.4 percent for the quarter and 47.3 percent to 52.7 percent for the combined four quarters. If the first two quarters are added together, giving a total sample of 500, the confidence interval would be +3.8 percentage points. Further data and information on the trade-offs among sample sizes, confidence intervals, and confidence levels are given in Harry Hatry et al., *Customer Surveys for Agency Managers: What Managers Need to Know* (Washington, D.C.: Urban Institute Press, 1997).

Developing a Municipal Performance–Measurement System

Reflections on the Atlanta Dashboard

David Edwards and John Clayton Thomas

Some performance measurement efforts begin at the program level with operating officials who wish to adopt professional techniques or simply desire good performance data. Others, like the initiative of the city of Atlanta, are initiated and are more directly influenced by the organization's leaders or its strategic plan. Once they have been collected, performance measures may be used in many different ways and reported in many different formats and venues. This article describes Atlanta's approach.

Under the leadership of Mayor Shirley Franklin, the City of Atlanta introduced a new operating model for municipal government in early 2002. A central component of that effort has been a performance-measurement system—the "Atlanta Dashboard" designed to assess various aspects of municipal performance and, through that assessment, to improve the efficiency and effectiveness of municipal services.

   This article describes the development and operation of the Atlanta Dashboard and compares it to similar systems in other cities. We offer this profile in the belief that the Dashboard may be of interest to other municipal governments, to other units of government and to academics concerned with performance measurement. Although the Dashboard is unlikely to fit perfectly the needs of other cities, an understanding of Atlanta's experience may be useful to other municipalities as they develop or modify their own performance-measurement systems.

Toward that end, this article first describes why the Atlanta Dashboard developed as it did and how it works. We then compare the Dashboard to other "balanced measures" systems that have recently been adopted by or recommended for municipal governments. This comparison will highlight the special challenges that municipalities face in developing performance-measurement systems and suggest how a system such as the Atlanta Dashboard can help to meet these challenges.

By way of full disclosure, this article draws from the different perspectives of its two authors. One of us, a member of Mayor Franklin's cabinet, was the principal architect of the Atlanta Dashboard. The other is a public administration professor who has a long-standing scholarly interest in the performance of municipal governments, as well as a personal interest in the success of his adoptive home of Atlanta. We do not claim to be wholly objective in our analysis, but we believe our different perspectives enable us to offer a balanced description of the Atlanta experience.

Background: The challenge to a new mayor

When Shirley Franklin was sworn in as Atlanta's mayor in early 2002, the plight of the city's government was widely perceived as dire. The administration of her predecessor, Bill Campbell, had been reputedly corrupt, with 11 former administrators under indictment or in prison. A climate of distrust contributed to the public perception that Atlanta's city government was detached from citizens and generally uninterested in delivering basic services in a quality manner.

Beneath these high-visibility problems, the mayor's new administrative team found serious underlying organizational problems as well. In particular, city hall had little idea how well its various units were performing. Little data were being collected and no standard operating reports were being produced. The lack of performance data was clearly going to frustrate any attempts to improve service (see box 1, "The pothole posse").

The scarcity of performance data was the most obvious manifestation of a more fundamental problem: the lack of a "performance culture," as Mayor Franklin described it. City employees had few performance targets to reach or goals to accomplish, and consequently they were uninspired. In the last year of the outgoing administration, only 33 of 8,000 employees had been rated "less than effective" on their personnel evaluations, meaning that neither departmental nor individual performance was being evaluated seriously.

Mayor Franklin was far from a novice in municipal government, having served as chief administrative officer during the 1980s under Mayors Maynard Jackson and Andrew Young. Aided by that experience, in the face of this difficult environment she was able to quickly articulate a set of principles that she charged her administrative team with pursuing:

- We serve citizens, and we care about outcomes as experienced by citizens.
- We will be open and transparent.
- We will be effective and efficient.

The search for a performance-measurement system

The centerpiece of the city's pursuit of these principles, the mayor's team agreed, needed to be a new performance-measurement system that could do the following:

- Provide accurate and timely information about the state of city services and operations
- Provide management with operating targets and a means of tracking progress toward those targets in order to increase management accountability
- Provide a public window into the city's operating environment in order to increase transparency, thereby regaining the public's confidence in the competence of the city government.

With these objectives in mind, the mayor's team began by examining the performance-measurement systems used by other governments and by private businesses. According to the Gartner Group, private sector companies spent over $1.5 billion on performance tracking tools in 2003, and cities such as Baltimore and Charlotte, among others, have developed their own systems (see Kaplan 1998), so the team had some examples to look at.

Some lessons learned

The private sector clearly has the deepest and richest set of experiences with performance-measurement systems. Still, while private-sector models may be instructive, particularly in terms of the processes used to develop and operate systems, the team concluded that some stark differences between the operating environments prevented those models from being fully applicable to the public sector.

1. Local government lacks a financial "roll up" One attribute shared by most private-sector performance-measurement systems is that, regardless of how many measures they employ, at the end of the day overall performance can be summarized with a financial

---

Box 1. The pothole posse.

Few city services are more basic than filling potholes. In fact, the number of potholes serves as a good barometer for the overall quality of city services—if you can't fill potholes, you probably can't do much else.

Within the first week of the administration, having heard many complaints about potholes, we asked for an estimate of how many potholes were in the streets. The commissioner for public works at the time replied there were 587. We were impressed that he had the number at his fingertips, and with that data in hand the mayor formed and launched her "Pothole Posse"—a small team dedicated exclusively to filling potholes. The posse filled 3,606 potholes in the next three months. Obviously, the pothole problem was significantly larger than anyone in city government had known.

The pothole experience revealed the importance of accurate performance data to effective management. The critical service issues facing the city could not be tackled without systems in place to capture and report on performance. If the pothole problem was so big, how many more surprises were in store for us?

metric. Private-sector organizations, even those encompassing a variety of businesses, share the common bottom-line denominator of profitability. This common denominator allows private firms to compare performance across different operating units using a single, neutral metric. Other metrics may also be used, but the single financial metric of profitability provides an effective means of evaluating performance across multiple entities.

A local government such as Atlanta's, by contrast, cannot roll up its operations into a single metric. As a consequence, a performance-measurement system that would fit Atlanta's situation needed to be looser and more federalist in structure than what a typical private business might use.

2. Local government lacks a unified culture   The review of performance-measurement systems used by private companies revealed a common desire to use a single scorecard across the entire enterprise. Companies generally are not interested in developing scorecards tailored to each operating division. Hilton Hotels, for instance, uses a single scorecard for all of its hotel properties.

In homogenous organizations that are focused on a single line of business, this works well. The management team has a philosophy regarding how best to run its business, and this philosophy dictates how the scorecard is structured and what is measured. One can generally discern how an organization views its key to success by the attributes it chooses to measure. In the hospitality industry, customer satisfaction measures take center stage. In manufacturing, measures that gauge business-process efficiency are critical. In services industries, measures involving human capital development are emphasized. In other words, the measures tend to be homogeneous within particular industries and reflect business strategies within individual companies.

Local governments, on the other hand, are heterogeneous enterprises. One could argue that the City of Atlanta, for example, is a conglomerate spanning at least 15 different lines of businesses. These businesses are relatively small but highly diversified in terms of the services they deliver, the business practices that support them, and, perhaps most importantly the culture underlying their operations. Police departments have a military culture that is hierarchical and focused on command and control. Planning departments have a culture akin to an academic institution with a loosely collegial atmosphere. Public works departments function more like a manufacturing operation, with a blue-collar mentality. This diversity of cultures complicates efforts to design performance-measurement systems because each unit has its own idiosyncratic views on the optimal balance among business process improvement, customer service delivery, technology innovation, and human capital development. Again, that reality points to the need for a more federalist structure in municipal performance-measurement systems.

3. Local government information is public   Public access to performance information and the resulting transparency are high priorities for municipal scorecards, but they create issues. With openness comes public scrutiny and accountability, issues the private sector need not confront. Public managers naturally hesitate to reveal all, thereby inviting micromanagement. As well, the more managers must expose to public scrutiny, the more they may be tempted to spin data to make departmental performance appear more positive than it is.

Recognizing these realities, the mayor's team saw the need for a performance-measurement system that could achieve internal management goals while also providing meaningful public access. Private-sector scorecards that are shielded from the public eye could not fully meet this need.

A local government scorecard

With these lessons in mind, the team undertook the building of a new performance-measurement system for the city. They began by posing a simple question: What do the citizens of Atlanta care about in regard to their local government? The team concluded that citizens have two major categories of concerns.

The first category involves citizens in their capacity as taxpayers and, as such, as owners or shareholders in city government. Like private-sector owners, taxpayers can change management (through elections), divest (by moving away), or change the mix of businesses through referenda or legislative action. Citizens as owners concern themselves with the efficiency of local government. They want lower taxes (that is, higher returns), and therefore they emphasize the productivity of the enterprise and the elimination of wasteful spending.

The second category involves citizens as customers or consumers of government services. In this role, citizens care about the scope and quality of the services being provided. In some cases, such as water and sanitation services, citizens can see a direct link between what they pay in user fees and what they receive in services. In the rest of government, such as public safety or public works, this link does not exist because these services are generally paid for from general tax receipts. In these cases, the city government's challenge is to deliver services at or above levels that citizens perceive they pay for, even though they do not know what portion of their tax bill goes to any given service. In either case, citizens demand effectiveness in service delivery, and the city should be concerned with how citizens perceive that effectiveness.

The team now had an approach for defining the outcomes of the new performance-measurement system: Those outcomes needed to reflect aspects of either efficiency or effectiveness. As a thought experiment, the team began to generate an inventory of potential measures, but team members quickly realized that, although the measures seemed appropriate (for instance, the quality of sidewalks, homicide rates, response time to fires, return on cash management), there were too many of them. They seemed endless.

To address this problem of abundance, the team returned to another criterion for the performance-measurement system: It should be tied to the mayor's strategic priorities. She was elected on the basis of a reform agenda, so the performance-measurement system should be able to track her success at implementing that agenda. The team revisited the mayor's four key strategic pillars:

- Improve public safety
- Improve public infrastructure

- Improve efficiency and effectiveness of city services
- Create financial stability.

For each pillar, department heads were engaged to focus on the "how" (see box 2, "Perceptions as outcomes"). That is, how did their departments' efforts link to the strategies, and what measures would those links imply? In addition, what strategies would they employ to advance these strategic priorities? What will actually be done?

From a series of conversations, strategy trees began to emerge (figure 1). For example, to improve public safety, the police chief explained that one of his department's strategies was to align the police force in geographic zones, then holding senior officers accountable for reducing crime in those zones. Success would be measured by tracking crime statistics in those zones, with success defined as the outcome of "reduced crime"—what interests the customer (citizens) as well as a solid effectiveness measure.

The same process held true for internal departments. For example, to reduce costs the city had launched an effort to improve energy efficiency in city-owned buildings. The team created an energy-usage measure for the major city buildings—a solid efficiency measure.

A philosophically neutral scorecard

The scorecard that emerged from this process focused on outcomes and was operationally agnostic. The team did not attach any organizational values to the strategy tree, and so the measures generally do not reflect any philosophy regarding which customer, internal process, or employee levers should be pulled. Although department heads presumably need to address these issues within their departments, the performance-measurement system itself says nothing about how to do so. It is up to the fire chief to determine how to reduce fires; the concern of the team is only that fires be reduced.

To the team's way of thinking, this approach was necessary. After conferring with both private- and public-sector users of scorecards, the team was wary of imposing an operational philosophy. Let managers manage. At the end of the day, citizens do not care whether crime is down because training has been increased, more officers are on the beat, or technology improvements have been made. It is the outcome that matters.

Even as the mayor's team sought transparency for the new scorecard, they saw no reason to provide public access to internal departmental operations, which would be the case if those operations were included in the scorecard. Omitting internal operations from the visible part of the city's scorecard focuses the system—and, it is hoped, the public's attention—on core municipal performance, not on the micromanagement of departmental affairs.

By focusing on outcomes, the team designed a performance-measurement system—subsequently dubbed the *Atlanta Dashboard*—that is relatively streamlined, yet with several useful attributes. For one, measures can be weighted to reflect their priority. In the area of public safety, for example, the components may include (1) reducing crime, (2) reducing fire loss, and (3) rehabilitating criminals, but reducing crime has a higher weight due to its greater importance in contributing to public safety. Moreover, within the area of crime reduction, specific crimes (such as homicide) may be weighted more heavily. Those weights may change over time, too, if the city's strategic priorities change. If, for example, auto thefts became of particular concern to citizens and the mayor, that measure's weight could be increased, thereby increasing the police department's focus on that measure.

Box 2. Perceptions as outcomes.

One of the challenges we faced in designing a performance-measurement system for Atlanta was the lack of metrics to assess success. Private companies use a mix of financial metrics—profitability, sales revenue, and market share—to understand the degree to which their customers are satisfied with their services; the public sector lacks those metrics. As a consequence, cities generally employ the "squeakiest wheel gets the grease" approach to customer satisfaction. If you complain enough, you get attention.

This approach is clearly inadequate and can lead to a serious misallocation of resources and management attention. Mayor Franklin insisted on a more scientific approach, and thus the Citizen Satisfaction Survey was born. Designed and executed by the Carl Vinson Institute of Government at the University of Georgia, this survey of 600 Atlanta residents is conducted every quarter and focuses on outcome measures: Are the streets clean? Do you feel safe in your neighborhood? Are there enough parks? We add the survey results to other performance measures of the relevant operating departments. As a result, not only is the police chief responsible for reducing the number of homicides and burglaries across the city, he is also responsible for ensuring that people feel safer. And the commissioner for public works is responsible not only for filling potholes, but also for ensuring that people feel the streets ore in good condition.

While this may sound straightforward, it actually represented a huge leap in governance for the City of Atlanta. Being held accountable for citizens' perceptions is very different from being held accountable for executing a business process. Departmental managers now have to reconsider the mix of services they are providing, how they should cooperate with third parties to maximize the impact of their own efforts, and how they should market their services.

For example, the quality of Atlanta's streets depends on the volume of construction, cabling, and utility activity being carried out by private companies. Historically, it was not unusual for the city to completely resurface a street, only to have it torn up by private construction activity shortly thereafter. If the Department of Public Works is being measured simply by the miles of streets it resurfaces, then who cares? The managers resurfaced the street; it's not their fault that someone tore it up. However, if the department is held accountable for how citizens perceive the quality of streets, then managers have a strong incentive to coordinate their efforts with local companies to ensure the city's repaving schedule does not conflict with other street-related construction.

Outputs such as sweeping streets and fixing sidewalks are what a city does, but those outputs are only useful if they improve citizens' quality of life. We decided that the only way to know for sure whether those outputs are leading to the right outcomes is to ask citizens. Private-sector companies expend up to 15 percent of their revenues to understand and market to their customers. The least cities can do is spend a fraction of that amount on understanding whether their customers are satisfied with the services they receive.

Another useful attribute is that the Dashboard can be expanded vertically. The obvious example comes again from the police department, where the geographic zones that interest the mayor can be divided and subdivided to allow the police chief to track measures in more discrete units. The Dashboard can, in fact, be driven down through the organization, perhaps ultimately to personalized dashboards for each employee.

The Dashboard also makes links and dependencies among departments far more visible to senior managers. Street cleaning provides a good example. Public works managers sometimes complain that streets are not clean because the street sweepers have not been repaired in a timely manner by the city's Department of Motor Transport Services. Department management counters that the vehicles are abused and therefore out of service more than they should be. Without a way of measuring the performance of either operation, a stalemate ensued.

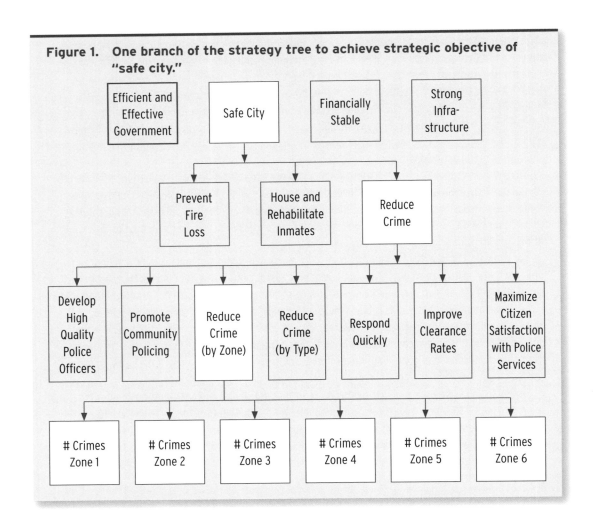

Figure 1. One branch of the strategy tree to achieve strategic objective of "safe city."

The Dashboard can resolve the issue. The relevant outcome goals include (1) reported citizen satisfaction with street cleanliness and (2) departmental records on miles of streets swept. Both are shaped by the availability of street sweepers, which in turn is driven in part by the maintenance and repair of the street sweeper fleet. Maintenance and repair link street sweeping to the Department of Motor Transport Services, which, in collaboration with the public works function, has developed the goals of (1) 100 percent turnaround within 24 hours of all street sweepers receiving preventive maintenance, and (2) 100 percent turnaround within two weeks of all street sweepers receiving major repairs. In turn, the department reports "abnormal failures" due to operator abuse or the failure to bring the vehicles in for preventative maintenance. The combination of these measures allows senior management on both sides to track performance and to hold everyone accountable.

But what if the performance goals at any given step in the process do not work for some reason? For example, what if the two-week maximum for major repairs on street sweepers proves excessive, so that street sweepers are insufficiently available? If so, the performance of street sweeping, measured by miles of streets swept and customer satisfaction, will presumably fall below desired expectations. That shortfall, in turn, should prompt departmental administrators to take another look at the system, perhaps identifying the need for quicker turnaround, triggering a renegotiation of performance targets.

The Atlanta Dashboard also uses weekly meetings of the mayor's cabinet to review performance reports. Each week the performance of selected departments is reviewed against the departmental plan, with programmatic changes formulated as necessary to address shortfalls. Those presentations and discussions help in interpreting the data, in targeting performance problems, and in refining the Dashboard (see box 3, "The mayor's cabinet discusses Dashboard data"). As that description suggests, the Dashboard remains a work in progress, with performance measures evolving as departments adapt to the system.

Overall, the Atlanta Dashboard embodies a number of characteristics that recommend its use. In particular, it is:

- *Strategic, not merely operational:* Measurement focuses on outcomes rather than inputs or outputs, and it links directly to the city's core business strategies.

- *Evolving and dynamic, not static:* As the city's strategic priorities change, so too can the measurement system.

- *Participatory and iterative, not top-down in development:* While the ultimate responsibility for what to measure resides with top management, input was and is solicited from all levels of the hierarchy, both to maximize information and to build ownership.

- *Tightly hierarchical, not loosely distributed in administration:* At the same time, the system is administered in a traditional hierarchical, pyramid format so that the work of individual supervisors and employees can be linked directly to performance expectations higher in the pyramid.

- *Transparent, not opaque:* The system is relatively easy to understand, even for someone with no knowledge of city government or its organization—for example, the average taxpayer or Atlanta resident.

The Atlanta Dashboard in comparative perspective

The Atlanta initiative represents only one of many recent initiatives by municipal governments and other public and private entities to develop comprehensive performance-measurement systems—what are sometimes termed "balanced measures" systems (Ho and Chan 2002; National Partnership for Reinventing Government 1999). The similarities and

---

Box 3.   The mayor's cabinet discusses Dashboard data.

At a recent meeting of the mayor's cabinet, we discussed the utility of the Dashboard in driving improvements in city services:

1. Providing a "heads up" for potential problems. The chief of corrections reported that daily housing of inmates was running 35 percent to 40 percent above target, posing a potential budget problem. Our chief operating officer asked, "At some point this will level off, but still at a higher level than projected, right?" "Yes," answered the corrections head, "and we have enough overtime to get through the year if this flattens out, but not if the figures go up further."

2. Highlighting and interpreting successes. The fire chief presented data showing the number of fires was substantially down over the average of the previous three years (which the city is using as an initial benchmark). Asked why, the chief initially credited increased training and inspections, but, in response to another question, he conceded that inspections focus on commercial buildings, whereas the decline in fires appeared to be mostly in private residences. It is also possible, he noted, that the decline was just part of a national trend toward declining fire rates.

3. Suggesting new initiatives. The police chief reported a spike in homicide rates–up more than 13 percent compared to 2002–but noted that murders tend to peak in July and August due to the heat. That prompted the chief operating officer to ask whether the city opens fire hydrants in the summer to cool people off. When the fire chief said no, the police chief suggested an economical sprinkler system approach he saw used in the city where he had worked previously. The fire chief indicated he would look into the possibility.

4. Refining measures. The human resources commissioner reported on the amount of comp time accumulated citywide and in the various departments. The chief operating officer voiced frustration with the measure as failing to reflect the city's true liability. "It would help," she suggested, "if you could overlay number of comp hours earned against number of comp hours used."

We also discussed the value of a practice the city had discontinued: requiring other department heads to listen to presentations by their peers. That practice was eliminated in the belief it took too much time for too little value, but the police-fire discussion about homicides and sprinkler systems, possible only because both departments were reviewed at the same meeting, illustrated that joint attendance can be useful. We decided that while requiring all department heads to attend is too onerous, there is value in scheduling related departments to be present at the same meeting, as the city did here by having police, fire, and corrections all presenting.

differences relative to those other systems warrant discussion to provide some perspective on the significance and value of the Atlanta approach.

The best-known of these other systems—and likely the inspiration for others—is the balanced scorecard approach, originally developed and popularized for the private sector by Robert Kaplan and David Norton (1992), then adapted for municipal use by cities such as Charlotte (Kaplan 1998). The balanced scorecard is designed to give "top managers a fast but comprehensive view of the business" by presenting in one place a broad range of indicators of finances, customer satisfaction, and other aspects of business performance. "Think of the balanced scorecard," Kaplan and Norton (1992, 71–72) argue, "as the dials and indicators in an airplane cockpit. For the complex task of navigating and flying an airplane, pilots need detailed information about many aspects of the flight.... Similarly, the complexity of managing an organization today requires that managers be able to view performance in several areas simultaneously." Those "several areas" reflect four important but distinct perspectives on the business:

- The customer perspective: How do customers see us?
- Internal business perspective: What must we excel at?
- Innovation and learning: Can we continue to improve and create value?
- Financial: How do we look to shareholders?

Together, the four perspectives provide a comprehensive view of organizational performance.

The balanced scorecard also holds the potential, Kaplan and Norton argue in a later article (1996), to "address a serious deficiency in traditional management systems: their inability to link a company's long-term strategy with its short-term actions" (75). That link could be achieved by developing four new management processes to complement the four measurement perspectives:

- *Translating the vision:* Building consensus around the vision among top management.
- *Communicating and linking:* Communicating the vision up and down the organization.
- *Business planning:* Making business plans that reflect the vision.
- *Feedback and learning:* Learning from data feedback to confirm or modify strategies.

The Atlanta Dashboard embodies some of the principles of the balanced scorecard. First, the Dashboard includes both owner/shareholder and customer perspectives, comparable to the balanced scorecard's financial and customer perspectives. In that regard, the balanced scorecard is superior to other private-sector approaches that focus only on profitability. Second, like the balanced scorecard, the Dashboard creates links to broader organizational strategies through its concern for how performance measures relate to the mayor's strategies. Third, the term "Dashboard" itself can be seen as derived from the scorecard metaphor.

The similarities end there because there is really nothing balanced about the Atlanta Dashboard. Where the balanced scorecard dictates the central administration's interest and ability to look closely at the internal workings of the various departments—the internal business and innovation and learning perspectives—the Dashboard ignores those perspectives entirely. Similarly with links to organizational strategy, the Dashboard concerns itself with translating and communicating the vision, but not with either business planning or feedback and learning.

The mayor's team in Atlanta chose not to extend the Dashboard's reach to these organizational dimensions for reasons suggested earlier. First, given the diversity of cultures across different municipal departments, team members felt that each department would have its own idiosyncratic views on the optimal mix of internal business and human resources practices, including employee training and development. Imposing a standardized system from above would force those different cultures to fit the same rigid system. Second, the mayor's team preferred to give departments maximum latitude to achieve performance targets. What is important, they felt, was that departments achieve the desired outcomes—less crime, cleaner streets, etc. Let departmental administrators operate their departments in whatever manner they think best, so long as they produce the promised outcomes. Third, even as the mayor's team wanted municipal performance to become transparent to the public, they did not necessarily want the public to have access to all internal departmental workings, as a balanced scorecard system would do. Finally, the mayor's team saw a sufficient challenge in the need to review all municipal outcomes without assuming the additional burden of examining internal departmental processes.

The experience of Charlotte, North Carolina, perhaps the highest-profile U.S. city to adopt a balanced scorecard, hints at some support for Atlanta's choices in this regard. While reporting an overall positive assessment of the system, Charlotte found adoption—and adaptation—of the balanced scorecard to be extremely time consuming, with one official saying that she had "underestimated the amount of change required to implement this strategic measurement approach" (Kaplan 1998, 8). Atlanta, of course, sidestepped some of that time commitment by focusing—at the top level anyway—only on outcome measures, not on internal business processes. Atlanta officials saw uncertain connections between some of the internal process and customer perspective outcome measures included in the Charlotte balanced scorecard. They also saw the potential for internal process perspectives to vary among departments.

The city of Baltimore, Maryland, offers an entirely different approach through its Citi-Stat program. In developing this system, Mayor Martin J. O'Malley "sought to build the kind of information management and control system that would enhance the capacity of city agencies to identify, respond to, and anticipate problems as they were emerging" (Henderson 2003, 12). CitiStat employs geographic mapping tools to track activity measures (for instance, animal carcasses collected, missed garbage pickups) across the city. In this sense, CitiStat—like its analogue CompStat used by police departments around the country—is an operations-management tool that provides managers with nearly real-time data on departmental activities. The utility of these systems rests largely in day-to-day operations management, where data can be used to respond to problems identified on the ground by rapidly redeploying resources. While these tools are useful for managers, they generally do not serve as true scorecards wherein targets for strategic outcomes are established and performance against those targets is tracked.

In looking at the various balanced measures systems that have proliferated in recent years (National Partnership for Reinventing Government 1999), a larger model for performance management begins to take shape. Although these systems use different approaches and achieve different goals, and each contributes in its own way to what might be a collective solution. Balanced scorecards, like the one used in Charlotte, tend to set strategic direction by tying together a loose set of management goals and philosophies (better employee development, focus on the customer, etc). Management dashboards, such as the Atlanta Dashboard, translate that strategic direction into a set of specific strategic outcomes that are tracked and monitored. Operations-assessment tools, like CitiStat, make sure day-to-day operations are functioning properly and are focused on achieving those strategic outcomes. In the end, cities need a combination of all three to truly achieve top-level performance.

Conclusion

Paralleling the efforts of many other municipalities, Mayor Shirley Franklin has undertaken the development of a new performance-measurement system, the Atlanta Dashboard. The Dashboard is designed to provide a vehicle for comprehensive reporting, review, and analysis of the how well the city's various operating agencies are performing. It is an essential element of Mayor Franklin's efforts to reform city government and to develop a new operating model for the city.

The Atlanta Dashboard resembles a number of other contemporary balanced measures systems (National Partnership for Reinventing Government 1999), but it is unique in many respects. Compared to the popular balanced scorecard approach, for example, the Dashboard omits all aspects of internal business processes in favor of the exclusive concern for outcomes. That choice gives departments more latitude in how to reach performance goals, while at the same time saving top management from having to scrutinize the internal operations of many different departments.

We believe the Atlanta Dashboard may be useful to other cities. To be sure, the uniqueness of every city means that no performance-measurement system is likely to fit without some adaptation, and other forms of balanced measures systems also merit attention. Still, many cities seem to have needs similar to those that drove Atlanta officials to develop the Dashboard. Cities that see themselves mirrored in Atlanta's needs may be well advised to examine the Atlanta Dashboard more closely.

References

Henderson, Lenneal J. 2003. *The Baltimore CitiStat Program: Performance and Accountability.* Washington, DC: IBM Endowment for the Business of Government.

Ho, Shih-Jen Kathy, and Yee-Ching Lilian Chan. 2002. Performance Measurement and the Implementation of Balanced Scorecards in Municipal Governments. *Journal of Government Financial Management* 51(4): 8–19.

Kaplan, Robert S. 1998. City of Charlotte (A), 9-199-036. Boston, MA: Harvard Business School.

Kaplan, Robert S., and David P. Norton. 1992. The Balanced Scorecard—Measures That Drive Performance. *Harvard Business Review* 70(1): 71–79.

———. 1996. Using the Balanced Scorecard as a Strategic Management System. *Harvard Business Review* 74(1): 75–85.

National Partnership for Reinventing Government. 1999. *Balancing Measures: Best Practices in Performance Management.* http://govinfo.library.unt.edu/npr/library/papers/bkgrd/balmeasure.html.

Section II:

From Performance Measurement to
Performance Management

Organizations Managing for Results

Paul D. Epstein, Paul M. Coates, Lyle D. Wray, with David Swain

The authors of this article consider performance management or "managing for results," as described on the following pages, to be one of four advanced governance practices. They reserve even higher praise for a variation that adds citizen engagement to performance management's emphasis on measuring results and getting things done. "Managing for results" and the other three advanced governance practices, all part of the "Effective Community Governance Model," are described in their book, *Results That Matter* (San Francisco: Jossey-Bass, 2006) and at the Web site effectivegovernance.net.

> You mean we clean only clean sewers?
> —*Wayne Tanda, former director of streets and traffic, City of San Jose*

In the mid-1990s in San Jose, Wayne Tanda, then director of streets and traffic, was surprised to learn that his sewer cleaning crews focused all scheduled operations on cleaning sewers that were already clean. Cleaning dirty sewers would slow productivity and cut down the miles of sewers they cleaned. Crew chiefs told him they were rated on how many miles of sewers they cleaned, and they were very proud of the high mileage they cleaned each year. But the purpose of cleaning sewers was to keep sewage from backing up into people's homes and businesses, not to rack up cleaning mileage. And it is the dirty sewers that clog and back up. Tanda told the sewer cleaning manager, "This is absolutely wrong. I could care less about how many miles of sewers you clean. What I care about is how many get clogged."

By questioning how his crews measured success, Tanda took the first step toward managing for results. This chapter focuses on how governments align measuring results with getting things done.

Managing for specific results or outcomes

Articulate and measure the results that best meet your purpose

The most basic requirement of managing for results is to measure results that are most important to accomplish. Put another way, be sure your measures meet your purpose. Infrastructure managers need to know the output of work done by maintenance crews, such as the miles of sewers cleaned. But if the measurement focus is too narrow—only on output, for example, and not on desired outcomes or results—the wrong things can be done to maximize that output at the expense of more important results, as happened in San Jose until Wayne Tanda questioned this approach. Then, instead of focusing only on miles of sewers cleaned, they began to measure success differently. Said Tanda, "We would measure how many sewers are clear and not clogged. The bigger the percentage, the better job you are doing... So with that, the miles of sewers actually cleaned using mechanical techniques stayed about the same or decreased. What increased was the use of enzymes to eat grease. What increased was education in the neighborhoods that would typically use a lot of grease in their cooking. What we saw was a better condition, a better outcome." The sewer cleaning strategy in San Jose switched from a goal of racking up a large output of work, to a goal of achieving discernible results—fewer clogged sewers—for the community. Because they articulated and measured their result, they could manage for it, and they changed their strategy to achieve better results for the community.

Managing for results as a performance feedback cycle

The essence of managing for results is to feed back measured performance information into decision making so operations can be adjusted or policies, priorities, or program designs can be changed to improve future measured results.[1] That feedback means that any managing for results process is really a cycle of measurement and assessment of results, planning and decision making, and implementation. The examples in this chapter progress from simple to more complex results management cycles.

San Jose's improved sewer cleaning approach follows the simple cycle in Figure 1. Once they articulated and measured what was most important, they could assess results by analyzing where sewers were clear and where they were clogged with grease. Then they planned a variety of actions to respond differently to varying conditions in different sewers and neighborhoods, unlike their previous one-size-fits-all approach. San Jose's sewer cleaning responses primarily varied geographically, but as noted in Figure 1, for other services an organization's responses to measured results may also vary based on other dimensions, such as different needs or outcomes of different demographic groups or different types or ages of facilities maintained.[2]

They complete the cycle by implementing their planned actions and measuring results again to determine progress and how to respond in the future to changes—or the lack of changes—in conditions in sewers across the city. In other words, they keep checking how results change, keep feeding that information back into their operational plans, and keep adjusting their services to improve results further in the future.

Accountability for outcomes

Too often, public sector managers complain that they do not control the things that most affect outcomes, defined here as conditions in the community or conditions of people. They do not control how much grease people pour down their drains, how much trash people drop on the street, whether people maintain healthy lifestyles, or millions of other factors that service providers often consider external to their work that affect people's health and welfare or the physical condition of the community and its living environment. Should service managers be held accountable for things they cannot control? Or can they influence and improve outcomes more than they think they can?

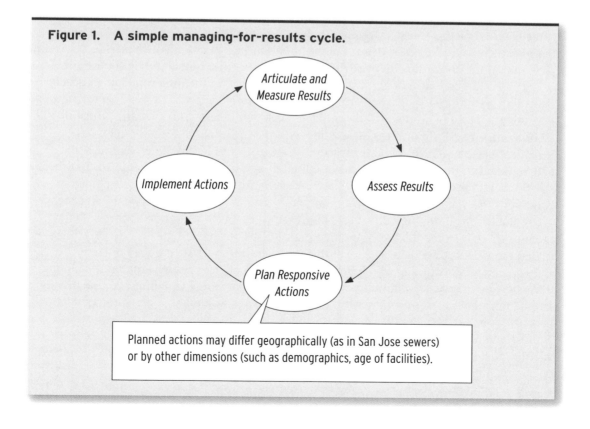

Figure 1.   A simple managing-for-results cycle.

Articulate and Measure Results

Assess Results

Implement Actions

Plan Responsive Actions

Planned actions may differ geographically (as in San Jose sewers) or by other dimensions (such as demographics, age of facilities).

Outcomes can be improved, when viewed as results to be accomplished Many public sector managers would rather have their performance measured based on the efforts they exert on activities to affect community conditions, the resources or "inputs" they dedicate to a problem, or how much of a service they provide ("outputs"), not on relevant outcomes—the actual conditions of people or the community their service is supposed to maintain or improve. But as Wayne Tanda proved with his sewer cleaning team, when you shift the focus to desired outcomes, people can get out of their standard service production mode and find a way to accomplish results. In San Jose, they not only applied their technical knowledge by using enzymes on greasy sewers, they showed extra creativity by doing something that public works operators are not especially known for: becoming engaged with people in targeted neighborhoods to educate them in proper ways to dispose of grease in order to reduce the size of the problem. In this case, San Jose staff engaged citizens in these neighborhoods as stakeholders and helped them become more than passive service customers to play a role as collaborators in improving their own neighborhood conditions: they helped them become coproducers in solving sewer backup problems. Often when service providers focus on desired outcomes, not just service activities or production, they find ways they can affect—if not totally control—some of those external factors and have a bigger impact on outcomes than they at first imagined.

Appropriate levels of outcome accountability In fairness to service providers, there are some external factors—severe weather including natural disasters, a major downturn in the regional economy, a new drug of choice flooding the street narcotics market, for example—that in the short run can overwhelm the positive impact local public service providers can have on certain human or community outcomes. In the long run, some decision makers in a community—particularly those at higher policy levels—should be accountable for anticipating some of these uncontrollable events or external factors, and adjusting to all of them, so performance results can move in the direction of desired outcomes.

If a service provider has a narrow scope of services and few flexible resources, the people who run that organization may be limited in what they can accomplish. But they should still do their best to change how they serve the community to reflect changing conditions, even if they can do only so much. It would not be appropriate to hold them accountable for improving outcomes communitywide, but it would be appropriate for them to show incremental gains in outcomes of just their immediate service customers or in just the neighborhoods or even just the blocks or buildings where they operate.

However, public officials who budget for services at all levels of government (including those beyond the local community, such as relevant state and federal officials) and private foundations that invest in community services should be accountable for learning whether the current mix of services they fund does not solve the problems they are intended to address and for adjusting their investment strategy to better achieve desired outcomes, whether that means providing more funds to services that work well but are overwhelmed, or finding more cost-effective—perhaps very different—approaches to solving problems and achieving outcomes. As is clear in the next example, Mayor Martin O'Malley believed in taking accountability for improving conditions in Baltimore and made sure his service managers were also held accountable as part of Baltimore's managing-for-results strategy.

Relentless management for results: City of Baltimore

When William Donald Schaefer was mayor of Baltimore from 1971 to 1987, he was famous for personally demanding that city agencies immediately fix service problems he encountered in daily travels around the city. He even spent parts of his weekends traveling through streets and alleys around town to make his own inspections for problems that city workers should know about and fix.[3] Service departments got the message that Mayor Schaefer had better not see that same derelict vehicle on the corner or a noticed pothole unrepaired the next time he passed that way. And they would respond quickly to the problems he reported. While the energetic mayor seemed as if he was everywhere, he really could not see everything in the city in a systematic way all the time and still do his job as chief executive. So service departments' responses to problems he reported did not, by themselves, represent a systematic approach to all major city service issues and were not necessarily representative of their responses to all Baltimore neighborhoods all the time.

Twelve years after Schaefer's last term as mayor, enter Mayor Martin O'Malley, who could take advantage of advances in geographic information systems (GIS) and advice from former New York City deputy police commissioner Jack Maple, to make city agencies' responsiveness to problems both relentless and systematic. Maple was an innovator behind the New York Police Department's much-heralded and much copied Compstat Program, the centerpiece of department strategies that led to rapid, sustained crime reduction. Compstat involved computer mapping of crime levels and patterns by location and time, and frequent review at police headquarters with precinct captains and district commanders who were held accountable for changes in results and for developing credible strategies for improvement. Compstat also involved wide sharing and use of timely, accurate data, and stimulated creative problem solving to enable the police department to manage for impressive results in reducing crime.[4]

In 1999, Jack Maple, by then a consultant to police departments across the country, gave Baltimore mayoral candidate O'Malley the idea that a Compstat approach could work for any city service agency.[5] O'Malley, acting on the idea, launched CitiStat on June 29, 2000, and over the next twelve months, all of the city of Baltimore's major operating departments became participants in the CitiStat program.[6]

High-frequency feedback of mapped results drives accountability and performance

Baltimore's CitiStat uses the same four precepts as the New York's Compstat: "Accurate and timely intelligence; rapid deployment; effective tactics; and relentless follow-up and assessment."[7] Managers of regularly participating agencies attend biweekly meetings that drive home their accountability for results. The meetings are held in a specially designed room in which up-to-date data on key agency service and cost issues are displayed on screens, and agency managers are questioned by members of the mayor's cabinet, with Mayor O'Malley often in attendance.[8] CitiStat operations and technical teams check and analyze the data, compare performance with previous periods, prepare briefing books, and code data for "computer pin maps."[9] Wherever a problem appears on a map, the mayor wants to know his agencies have a strategy to solve it. As Mayor O'Malley said, "The nice thing about maps is that the map doesn't know whether a neighborhood is black or white, rich or poor, Democrat or Republican. And a map doesn't know whether a judge lives there or a congressman lives there or a senator lives there. The map tells us where problems are; then we relentlessly attack those problems, and we abate those problems and the tide rises for everybody."[10] Baltimore finally had a mayor who really was "everywhere," at least virtually because of the high-frequency systematic, geographic-based performance data at his disposal.

The CitiStat story involves Baltimore's using performance information well to achieve financial gains by the city government, measurably more responsive services to citizens as service customers, and outcome improvements for the community as a whole. The city government credited CitiStat with leading to over $13 million in savings and revenue across agencies in its first year of operation.[11] Baltimore's relentless management for results, enabled by CitiStat, has also led to improved service performance. A common priority for many services has been speeding response to service requests, better meeting service frequency standards such as annual restaurant inspections, and reducing service backlogs. Response time standards, including a "forty-eight-hour pothole guarantee" (largely met, except after severe winter storms), were established for many kinds of service requests and tracked to determine overdue responses. Other significant timeliness and backlog reduction improvements reported have been in animal control, repair debris removal, cleaning clogged storm drains, food establishment inspection, design and construction of city projects, and street light repairs.[12] A key part of Baltimore's strategy to improve customer responsiveness was creation of a 3-1-1 call center for all non-public-safety-emergency service requests, which opened March 28, 2002.[13] Significant public health and safety outcomes have also been achieved, including steady reductions in violent crime[14] and in the number of cases of syphilis.[15]

Figure 2 depicts a managing-for-results cycle as driven by CitiStat, featuring high-frequency review and accountability, and geographic, strategic responses.

Frequent review of mapped results can clarify where strategic partnerships are needed
CitiStat has also stimulated improved cooperation to solve problems that cross city agency lines or require efforts by the city government and other entities, as noted by the references to strategic partnerships and collaborative responses in Figure 2. For example, the street light repair improvements came in cooperation with a private utility. When long-standing problems are exposed on maps and charts in CitiStat meetings, it quickly becomes clear when the reporting agency cannot solve the problem alone. In response, interagency (and sometimes intergovernmental) efforts have been initiated to focus on, for example, arson, lead poisoning ("LeadStat"), drug abuse ("DrugStat"), and coordination of inspection and enforcement functions.[16] Some of these collaborative efforts have led to impressive improvements in public outcomes. For example, in January 2003, Mayor O'Malley reported that Bal-

timore had the largest two-year drop in drug related hospital emergency department visits in the nation (18 percent decrease overall, 36 percent for heroin cases).[17] In June 2003, the mayor reported that his initiative on lead poisoning prevention led to 675 homes being made lead safe through a combination of grants for repairs and the first legal actions taken against property owners in a decade. Perhaps most impressive, child testing revealed a 50 percent reduction in children ages up to age three with lead poisoning from 1999 to 2002.[18]

Managing for results by design

CitiStat is part of Mayor O'Malley's design to achieve responsive improvements and better results for the many different services provided by the City of Baltimore. In San Jose, minimizing the number of clogged sewers is a small part of a big design by the city

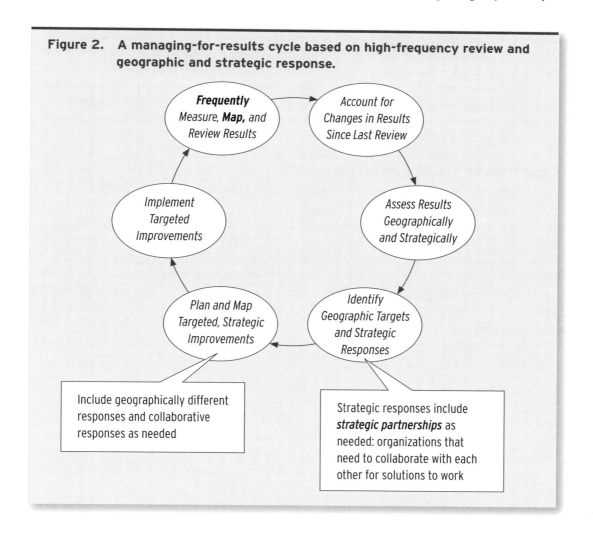

Figure 2.   A managing-for-results cycle based on high-frequency review and geographic and strategic response.

government to align the measured performance of operational services, in several strategic stages, with the mayor and city council's vision for the desired quality of life, part of a system San Jose calls "Investing in Results."[19]

Investing in results

Often one of the strongest representations of an organization's policies is seen in how the organization spends money, whether or not decision makers consciously relate spending decisions to policy Governments, foundations, and service providers that want their spending decisions not only to reflect policies, but to reflect successful policies that achieve results, have become more strategic in deciding what to fund and in considering the performance of services they support in their budgeting, grant making, or other resource allocation decisions. A shift from simply distributing money based on policy, to strategically targeting resources to achieve results, reflects a shift in mind-set from that of a "funder" to that of an "investor."[20] When a funding organization becomes a true "investor" in results, it does not simply make stock market-like bets in successful organizations, expecting their success to grow. Performance-informed investment can be more complex. When some results are lagging, a service provider may be under resourced and need an investment in more service capacity. Other useful capacity-building investments can be made in improving the productivity of service providers.[21]

Long-term strategic investing in results

A challenge for funders of community services, whether governments or foundations, is ensuring that investments make a difference for the long term. For a foundation, that can mean seeing its grants yield increasing measurable outcomes over time. For a local government, that can mean both improving service results and being able to afford to produce results most needed by the community for many years. To meet this challenge, funders must be strategic about their investments, which can sometimes mean not investing in even good programs if they do not meet a determined need or strategic focus or if funding cannot be sustained for the long term. It can also mean making hard decisions about whether a service that is not producing needed results should have its funding reduced or eliminated or should get extra investment in hopes of catching up with the need. The following examples explore these challenges.

Budgeting for strategic results   General-purpose local governments are often mandated to provide a wide range of public services, so they cannot focus their investments narrowly. Instead of narrowing funding to one or two fields, the challenge for multipurpose governments is to determine how to make shifts in allocating available funds from year to year to keep pace with strategic trends in the community (for example, regional economic trends, population changes, aging infrastructure) amid achieve outcomes people feel are important, while still meeting basic community needs with quality services. This is really two challenges: knowing what is strategic to the community and budgeting for results.[22] Prince William

County Virginia, meets these challenges by using both a multiyear strategic plan and mea-sured results of service performance as key drivers of its annual budget process. Citizens are engaged in major updates of the strategic plan every four years before it is approved by a newly elected board of county supervisors, giving the plan a high degree of credibility as a source for what is most important or strategic to emphasize in funding from year to year. Prince William County has used its strategic plans to make multimillion-dollar budget shifts to increase investment in the county's priority goals.[23] These investment choices, as well as an overall emphasis on performance measurement and improvement, have helped the county earn consistently high ratings in citizen satisfaction surveys.[24]

County executive Craig Gerhart has used the chart in Figure 3 to describe the county's approach to considering both strategic priorities and performance results in making budget decisions. According to Gerhart, while it is not a universal rule of county budgeting, programs with low strategic importance and poor performance results become targets for budget cuts, while programs with high strategic importance and poor performance results become targets for increased funding. In one 1990s example, the county police's clearance rates (percentage of crimes resolved or cases closed) were reported low compared with other local governments Prince William uses to benchmark its performance. That represented a measure of low perfor-mance related to a high-priority goal in the county strategic plan of improving public safety. Other comparative measures revealed that the Prince William County Police appeared under-

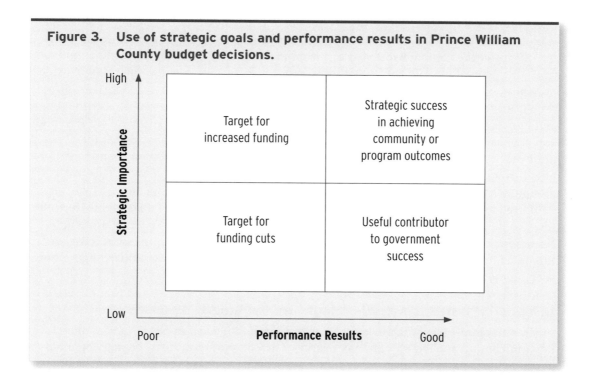

Figure 3.   Use of strategic goals and performance results in Prince William County budget decisions.

resourced compared with the benchmark jurisdictions, with Prince William having fewer officers per capita. A police department staffing plan was approved that increased the number of officers in order to improve results, as measured by increased clearance rates.[25]

Budgeting for performance and long-term fiscal impact Across the country from Prince William County and just northwest of San Jose, is the City of Sunnyvale, California, which has over twenty years' experience using performance measures in its city budget process to influence resource allocation decisions. Sunnyvale has achieved impressive results, broadly realized as high levels of citizen satisfaction with public services, as measured by sample population surveys, and increased government efficiency, as measured by reduced unit costs of services.[26] These results are achieved not only through the budget, but because performance-influenced budgeting is one part of an integrated managing-for-results process described later in this chapter.

As an example of using results data in budgeting, a Sunnyvale City Council member described citing long-term reductions in crime rates to resist calls for adding police officers, despite population growth. In other cases, Sunnyvale has used unit cost and demand data to determine whether a program's inability to meet customer demand is a result of inefficiency or of being under resourced. Where low unit costs indicated high efficiency but demand was higher than expected, funding was increased.[27]

In addition to rising performance measures in budgeting, Sunnyvale relates its budget decisions to long-range plans. It examines how proposed new or expanded services will affect municipal finances over a twenty-year period as part of the city's long-range financial plan. The city council does not just consider whether the city government can afford the service in the coming fiscal year but what the long-term fiscal impact will be. It may cause the council to scale back a proposed service expansion, look for other programs to reduce, or new future revenue sources, to ensure their desired service increase will be fiscally sustainable. As a recent council member described it, "Make certain assumptions and plug them into the spreadsheet and you can identify a problem really quick. Revenue and expense lines go upside down. It allows you to do something today rather than wait until year nine or fifteen and say, 'Oops! We have a major problem on our hands right now'!' Not only measuring things well, but also taking a long-term view."[28] This fiscal discipline has helped Sunnyvale avoid some of the fiscal volatility experienced by other California local governments, which have tended to add services in fat years only to suffer severe cutbacks in lean years,[29] and it has also influenced Sunnyvale's long-term emphasis on efficiency improvement as a way to improve services. So when services have been expanded to serve a growing population, they have often expanded at reduced unit costs, keeping the overall cost of city government affordable to Sunnyvale citizens.

Integrated enterprisewide results management systems

When Baltimore's Mayor O'Malley took an approach pioneered in New' York's Police Department and applied it to all major services as Baltimore's CitiStat, he made it an enterprisewide managing-for-results tool. Some governments have taken a systems approach to enterprisewide management by integrating long-range and short-range planning and decision processes, including budgeting, that affect all programs and services—at least all that are locally funded. These become enterprisewide managing-for-results systems when performance measurement and reporting is used as a key informational and accountability tool tying these processes together.[30]

The results-based budgeting approach of the City of Sunnyvale, California, was described above as being influenced by longer-range financial planning. Sunnyvale's success has depended not only on its planning and budgeting processes, but on how the city government has linked these and other processes in an enterprisewide, integrated system of managing for results, which Sunnyvale calls its Planning and Management System (PAMS). Like all true managing for results processes, PAMS is cyclical in nature. As illustrated in Figure 4, Sunnyvale's long-range financial plan and its state-mandated general plan influence shorter-range budgeting and performance planning. Performance targets included in the budget and service plans influence service delivery and figure prominently in managers' performance plans. As Figure 4 also shows, multiple results management cycles are

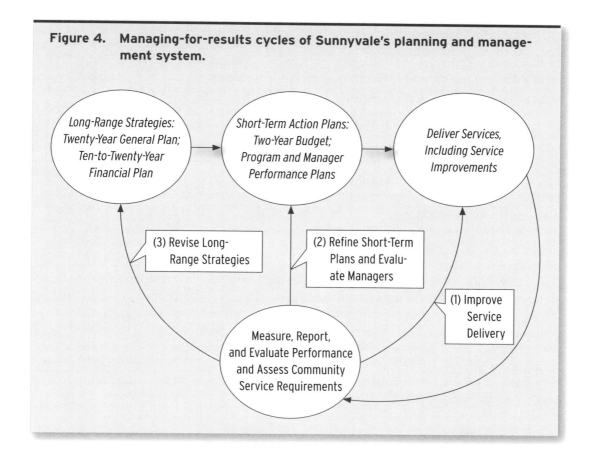

Figure 4. Managing-for-results cycles of Sunnyvale's planning and management system.

completed when measured results are fed back to inform (1) how managers improve service delivery on a day-to-day basis; (2) future short-term action planning including budgeting, and evaluation of managers against their performance plans; and (3) revisions of long-range goals and strategies.

As noted in the lower right of Figure 4, the service requirements of the community (for example, based on how the population and its needs change, the infrastructure ages, parts of the community are developed or redeveloped) are also fed back and considered in making long-range strategic plans and short-range action plans. Also, not only are services delivered to the community, but performance is reported back to the community as an additional level of accountability.[31]

While it is easy to draw conceptual pictures of systems like Sunnyvale's PAMS, the hard part is getting people in the organization to understand the system and use it. Sunnyvale has succeeded at that. The systemic connections in PAMS are apparent to city managers, as one remarked: "It is a very integrated system. Looking at it, you can see that the performance management piece ties very much into the budgeting piece, ties very much into the reporting and accountability pieces."[32]

The ties the manager was referring to represent the strong alignment of the parts of the integrated managing for results system. To help achieve alignment, Sunnyvale does not structure its budget by department, but by the twenty-six elements and supplements of its twenty-year general plan. California requires local governments to have general plans, mainly for land use purposes. However, Sunnyvale broadened the concept of a general plan to serve as a broader long-term strategic plan to drive service performance as well as land use policy. The seven main elements of Sunnyvale's General Plan are Land Use and Transportation, Community Development, Environmental Management, Public Safety Socio-Economic, Cultural, and Planning and Management. Performance measures are developed for programs and service delivery plans within the elements and sub-elements, and targeted based on amounts budgeted. The measures used for program performance evaluation can then be tracked back to priorities in the general plan. All Sunnyvale managerial employees are on performance based pay plans: their individual performance evaluations and pay levels are based in part on measured performance versus budget and service plan targets for the programs and services they manage, taking alignment down to a level of personal responsibility and accountability.[33]

On a personal level, alignment helps people working throughout the enterprise understand their contribution to the system. For elected officials and executive management, strong alignment means understanding the implications that broad community outcome goals have for narrower service accomplishments agency programs must achieve, so they can set service-level targets and budget for them appropriately. For line employees, alignment means understanding how their day-to-day work not only produces service outputs (say miles of sewers cleaned) but also contributes to high-level priority community goals (say an environmentally safe, healthy community).

Learning and improving how to manage for results over time

An important lesson from organizations that succeed at managing for results over many years is that they tend to change how they do it over time. Often the changes are minor adjustments that may go unnoticed to people outside the organization, but that keep performance measurement and improvement approaches relevant to managers and employees. But successful organizations do not shrink from making dramatic changes when needed.

Governments that have changed successful results management systems

The city of Charlotte, North Carolina began using performance measurement to manage for results in 1971, using performance feedback as part of a Management by Objectives system that tied measurable performance objectives to the budget process. The city government made gradual, evolutionary changes to its performance management approach over the years, such as adding performance auditing and contract evaluation, to ensure measurement leads to improvement.[34] In the 1990s, Charlotte was not afraid to make a major systemic change when it became the first general-purpose government to adopt the balanced scorecard approach to performance management on an enterprisewide basis.

The city of Sunnyvale has systematically used performance measures to manage for results for over twenty years, strongly integrated and aligned through the Planning and Management System (PAMS) since the early 1980s. Starting in 1996, following recommendations of the interdepartmental Committee on the Future of the Organization, the city began phasing in a major shift in its program structure and performance measures to outcomes, with an outcome management approach integrated into PAMS, especially in performance budgeting and management appraisal. The new approach emphasizes fewer, more results-based performance measures.

Recently as an extension of its new outcome focus, Sunnyvale added another level of performance measurement and reporting to its system: the Quality of Life Index, developed based on the work of two city council–appointed citizen task forces and a citizen participation process. The Quality of Life Index, intended to be more citizen friendly than Sunnyvale's detailed service plan and budget-related measures, covers a limited number of measures for eight strategic priorities similar to the seven main elements of the general plan, but formulated more to address priority citizen concerns directly. Each strategic priority has associated performance measures, some of which are existing measures in the program budget (an example is "community perception of safety") and some new measures (for example, "percent of houses and apartments that are affordable for households with median income"). By design, some goals and measures go beyond municipal services, reflecting citizen concerns that go beyond what the city government directly provides. For example, while a separate school district provides public education, "education" is one of the city's eight strategic priorities.[35] The Quality of Life Index will provide a new alignment challenge to Sunnyvale. The real challenge may not be for the city government to internally align this new measurement tool with its exquisitely aligned PAMS results-based management system, but to get other organizations, such as the school district and private housing developers, to collaborate in aligning their performance goals with the priorities in the Quality of Life Index. Sunnyvale completed its second Quality of Life Index Report in late 2003.[36]

Learning, changing, and improving as an organizational value

The city of Phoenix, Arizona, was a leader in performance measurement and improvement in the early 1970s, with its aggressive use of industrial engineering approaches, including stopwatch analysis and employee work standards; labor-saving mechanization such as single-staff trash collection trucks; detailed program and policy analyses; and its own version of a planning, program budgeting system. While the city documented tens of millions of dollars in savings from these approaches (by the 1980s, cumulative trash collection savings alone was over $25 million), it has not hesitated to try new approaches to performance management, and change or drop older ones that no longer seemed worth the investment needed to keep them going. A second wave of improvement approaches began in 1977, with a shift from industrial engineering to organization development approaches (for example, quality control circles and surveying and improving employee satisfaction), managerial performance based pay and less complex performance reporting. In 1979, Phoenix started a public-private competitive proposal process to reduce costs of selected services. By the 1980s, articles were being written emphasizing "evolution and change" as Phoenix's performance management theme.[37]

Through the 1980s, Phoenix kept adding and adjusting measurement and improvement approaches, especially emphasizing quality customer service and citizen satisfaction, and it has conducted community attitude surveys every two years since 1985. Into the 1990s, Phoenix kept reinvigorating its results management approaches, including, among other initiatives, a citywide strategic planning process, efforts in 1991 and again in the late 1990s to involve citizens in developing measures of results that were more relevant to citizen concerns and priorities, and a "seamless service" mission. Also, every two years the city auditor department has surveyed all city departments to assess their continued focus on results and provided the city manager with a comprehensive inventory of the organization's use of results data. It is not surprising, then, that when Phoenix managers and employees developed a "Vision and Values" statement in 1995, one of the core values was—and still is—"We learn, change, and improve."[38]

Phoenix did not invent most of the performance management approaches it has used over the years. Through several administrations, the city established a pattern of finding best practices in other organizations and adapting them to work in Phoenix, showing a remarkable openness to ideas from outside the organization. City Manager Frank Fairbanks once said, "We'll steal a practice from anyone if it will help us improve."

Perhaps the most extraordinary thing about Phoenix's history of frequently trying new performance management approaches is that the city seems to have avoided falling victim to the "fad of the month" syndrome, in which staff get jaded and show no enthusiasm for new approaches because they do not think they will last. That is probably because despite all the changes through the years, many results management approaches have lasted quite a while, at least in part. Phoenix has had a knack for keeping and improving those parts of older approaches that continue to add value—such as public-private competition, started in 1979, and the quality customer service emphasis, start in the 1980s, both still in use—while it keeps adapting new results management approaches for use by the organization.

Always learning to get better results, but what makes them results that matter?

Learning over many years by large organizations such as the city governments of Phoenix and Sunnyvale is impressive. But at any time scale—years, or just weeks at a time using high-frequency feedback—managing for results is about learning to get better results. Whether focusing on a single program or a large enterprise that manages many services, each step along the way of any managing-for-results cycle should be part of a learning process. As in the more complex cycles in this chapter, the learning is most effective when it takes place on several levels, including learning to:

- Improve results of current services, whether by targeting services better, tinkering with existing work practices, or significantly redesigning a program

- Determine what programs to invest in, how much to invest in each, and what performance and improvement targets should be met as a result of that investment, as with Prince William County and Sunnyvale

- Find better ways to articulate and measure results, for example, by changing the emphasis from outputs such as miles of sewers cleaned to outcomes such as percentage of sewers clear and not clogged

- Improve how to manage for results over time, as Charlotte, Sunnyvale, and Phoenix have

If learning through performance feedback is incorporated into regular management practice, organizations not only become better at improving results, they become better at holding themselves accountable for community outcomes. If they are always learning to better articulate, measure, and understand results, they will also better understand the broader community environment in which they perform and become better at adjusting to changes in that environment.

Of course, managing for results, while important, is not everything. If citizen engagement is added in ways that influence goals and decisions, managing for results becomes much more powerful and relevant to achieving the outcomes the community deems important, so the results achieved are results that matter.

Endnotes

1. A general approach to applying performance measures to developing and adjusting government policies and programs, including feedback on how well polices and programs are working, is provided in Brizius, J. A., and Campbell, M. D., *Getting Results: A Guide to Government Accountability* (Washington, D.C.: Council of Governors' Policy Advisors, 1991).

2. For a variety of ways to analyze reported performance information to identify improvement strategies and improve measured outcomes, based on a range of different kinds of comparisons, see Hatry, H. P., *Performance Measurement: Getting Results* (Washington, D.C.: Urban Institute Press, 1999), 131–145.

3. For example, see Weisskopf, M., "He Sells Baltimore; Baltimore: A Changing City Views Its Feisty Two-Term Mayor," *Washington Post*, Sept. 10, 1979, Cl.

4. Silverman, F., *NYPD Battles Crime: Innovative Strategies in Policing* (Boston: Northeastern University Press, 1999), esp. 97–124, 179–204. Silverman goes into great depth on the variety of improvement strategies used by the NYPD and how Compstat was the "informational cement" of reforming the department.

5. Swope, C., "Restless for Results," *Governing*, Apr. 2001.

6. "CitiStat: FY2001 Estimate of Financial Impact" [http://www.ci.baltimore.md.us/news/citistat/fiscal.html], Feb. 2005.

7. "CitiStat" [http://wwwci.baltimore.md.us/news/citistat/index.html], Feb. 2005.

8. Swope, "Restless for Results." The city posted views of the "CitiStat Room" [http://www.ci.baltimore.md.us/blank/citistattour/start.htm], Feb. 2005.

9. "CitiStat."

10. O'Malley, M., from a talk before former Vice President Al Gore's class at Tennessee State University, Nashville, Apr. 2002.

11. "CitiStat: FY2001 Estimate of Financial Impact."

12. As reported in the city of Baltimore's Neighborhood News Flashes [http://www.baltimorecity.gov/neighborhoods/nnf/index.html], and Taking Care of Business Bulletins [http://www.ci.baltimore.md.us/business/tcb], from Mar. 23, 2001, to May 9, 2003.

13. "Mayor's Press Advisory of March 28, 2002" [http://wwwci.baltimore.md.us/news/press/020328.html], Feb. 2005.

14. For example, "Baltimore Achieves Nation's Largest Two-Year Reduction in Violent Crime" reported for 1999–2001 on the Baltimore Police Department Web pages on crime data [http://www.baltimorecity.gov/government/police/ucr020624.html], Feb. 2005, with updates (for example, May 2002) [http://ww.baltimorecity.gov/government/police/stats020504.html], Feb. 2005.

15. As reported in the City of Baltimore's "Neighborhood News Flash of September 27, 2002" [http://www.ci.baltimore.md.us/neighborhoods/nnf/020927.html#citistat], Feb. 2005.

16. Linden, R. M., *Working Across Boundaries: Making Collaboration Work in Government and Nonprofit Organizations* (San Francisco: Jossey-Bass, 2002), 119–123, 245–247.

17. Office of the Mayor, "Three Year Accomplishments: Making Baltimore a Safer City," Jan. 2003 [http://www.baltimorecity.gov/mayor/3year/safer.html].

18. Office of the Mayor, Baltimore, "Mayor Martin O'Malley Announces the Success of Baltimore's Lead Poisoning Prevention Initiative," press release, June 4, 2003 [www.baltimorecity.gov/news/press/030604.html].

19. Epstein, P. D., Campbell, W., and Tucker, L., *Case Study: City of San Jose* (Norwalk, Conn.: Governmental Accounting Standards Board, Sept. 2002) [www.seagov.org/sea_gasb_project/case_studies.shtml], and Myrhe, B., Powell, D., and Turner, T., "Investing in Results: San Jose, California" (case study presented at ICMA University Best Practices 2003, Tacoma, Wash., Mar. 20–22, 2003). For this presentation and other documents on managing for results in San Jose, see the Publications page of the city government "Quest Partnership" [http://www.sanjoseca.gov/quest/publicat.htm].

20. For example, see Williams, H. S., Webb, A. Y., and Phillips, W. J., *Outcome Funding: A New Approach to Targeted Grantmaking* (Rensselaerville, N.Y.: The Rensselaerville Institute), 1996, 45–52. (Originally published 1991.)

21. For example, see Epstein, P., and Fass, S., "Build an Investment Portfolio in Government Productivity," *National Civic Review*, 1987, 76(2), 96–107.

22. For a thorough description of results-based budgeting as a process for encouraging improvements in service quality and outcomes, see Hatry, H. P., *Performance Measurement: Getting Results* (Washington, D.C.: Urban Institute Press, 1999), 179–214.

23. Epstein, P., Wray, L., Marshall, M., and Grifel, S., "Engaging Citizens in Achieving Results That Matter," in Newcomer, K., Jennings Jr., E. T., Broom, C., and Lomax, A. (eds.), *Meeting the Challenges of Performance-Oriented Government* (Washington, D.C.: American Society for Public Administration, 2002), 147.

24. For ten-year overall positive trends in citizen satisfaction, see Wood, K. F., and Guterbock, T. M., *Prince William County Citizen Satisfaction Survey: Report of Results* (Charlottesville: Center for Survey Research, University of Virginia, 2002), 8.

25. Bernstein, D. J., *GASB SEA Research Case Study: Prince William County, Virginia: Developing a Comprehensive Managing-for-Results Approach* (Norwalk, Conn.: Governmental Accounting Standards Board, Sept. 2002), 13–15. [www.seagov. org/sea_gasb_project/case_studies.shtml].

26. Osborne, D., and Gaebler, T., *Reinventing Government* (Reading, Mass.: Addison-Wesley, 1992), discuss Sunnyvale's efficiency gains (reduced unit costs of services) and Epstein, P. D., Campbell, W., and Tucker, L., *GASB SEA Research Case Study: City of Sunnyvale* (Norwalk, Conn.: Governmental Accounting Standards Board, Sept. 2002) [www. seagov.org/sea_gasb_project/case_studies.shtml], discuss both Sunnyvale's use of unit cost measures and high citizen satisfaction.

27. Epstein, Campbell, and Tucker, *GASB SEA Research Case Study: City of Sunnyvale*, 20.

28. Epstein, Campbell, and Tucker, *GASB SEA Research Case Study: City of Sunnyvale*, 18.

29. Epstein, Campbell, and Tucker, *GASB SEA Research Case Study: City of Sunnyvale*, 18.

30. For a basic description of how many planning and management processes can be part of an enterprisewide managing-for-results system, see Walters, J., Abrahams, M., and Fountain, J., "Managing for Results, an Overview" in Fountain, J., and others, *Special Report: Reporting Performance Information: Suggested Criteria for Effective Communication* (Norwalk, Conn.: Governmental Accounting Standards Board, Aug. 2003), 13–28 [http://www. seagov.org].

31. Figure 3.7 and this related discussion are based on the city of Sunnyvale's own depiction of the cycles involved in its planning and management system (in Epstein, Campbell, and Tucker, *GASB SEA Research Case Study: City of Sunnyvale*, 5), reformatted here to be consistent with the other managing-for-results cycles in this chapter.

32. Epstein, Campbell, and Tucker, *GASB SEA Research Case Study: City of Sunnyvale*, 4–5.

33. Epstein, Campbell, and Tucker, *GASB SEA Research Case Study: City of Sunnyvale*, 6–10.

34. Finnie, T., and Syfert, P., "Performance Measurement and Improvement in Charlotte, North Carolina," in Epstein, P. D., *Using Performance Measurement in Local Government* (Denver: National Civic League Press, 1988), 111–117.

35. Epstein, Campbell, and Tucker, *GASB SEA Research Case Study: City of Sunnyvale*, 4–12.

36. City of Sunnyvale, *Quality of Life Index Report for Fiscal Year 2002/2003* (Sunnyvale, Calif.: City of Sunnyvale, 2003).

37. For example, see Manion, P., "The Phoenix Experience: Evolution and Change," in Epstein, *Using Performance Measurement in Local Government*, 120–128, and Decker, L. L., and Manion, P., "Performance Measurement in Phoenix," *National Civic Review*, 1987, *76*(2), 119–129.

38. City of Phoenix, "Managing for Results" response to the *Governing* Magazine–Maxwell School (Syracuse University) Government Performance Project survey, 1999: "Managing for Results" under "Publications" from http://phoenix.gov/AUDITOR/index.html. Phoenix received a performance grade of A as the highest-rated city government in the United States in *Governing*'s "Grading the Cities" report in 2000. The Phoenix Vision and Values page on the Phoenix Web site is http://phoenix.gov/visvalue.html.

Implementing Results–Based Management in Local Government

James E. Swiss and Stephen K. Straus

Moving from performance measurement to performance management can be a big step. The authors of this article describe how constructing cause-and-effect chains can help local governments take this step to establish results-based management.

In recent years many local governments have started to track and report their performance using measures, often under such labels as "key indicators" or "balanced scorecards."[1] Because of the growing adoption of performance measurement, managers of numerous government agencies now better understand the results that their programs are producing.

Nonetheless, performance measurement will not produce greater effectiveness unless it consistently influences the decisions and the behaviors of agency workers. Accordingly, a number of agencies have begun to move to the next step, incorporating performance measurement into their day-to-day management decisions so that the resulting measures help drive planning, personnel assessment, process improvements, and budget. These performance-driven management systems have (confusingly) been given various names, including "performance-based management," "strategic management," and "results-based management." This chapter refers to all such systems as results-based management (RBM) systems.

Adapted from James E. Swiss and Stephen K. Straus, "Implementing Results-Based Management in Local Government," *Popular Government* 70, no. 3 (Spring/Summer 2005): 31-41. Reprinted with permission of the School of Government, copyright © 2005. This copyrighted material may not be reproduced in whole or in part without the express written permission of the School of Government, CB# 3330 UNC Chapel Hill, Chapel Hill, NC 27599–3330; www.sog.unc.edu.

Many agencies find it difficult to move from their traditional management approaches to RBM. This chapter provides some guidelines for agencies wishing to make the transition. It begins with an overview of RBM. It then discusses how government agencies can overcome common obstacles and successfully implement RBM. The chapter uses examples from the experiences of public agencies in the North Carolina communities of Greensboro and Wake Forest.

Benefits of results-based management

RBM asks an agency to define its most important results in a strategic planning process, to set annual objectives based on those results, and—most important—to use feedback about attainment of results in order to motivate agency members, improve internal processes, and guide personnel and budget decisions.

If an RBM system is well designed, implemented, and maintained, an agency can reap three substantial benefits:

- It can focus on its most important desired results. Often agency members work hard but become so caught up in day-to-day activities that they lose sight of their most important goals. An RBM system helps all agency members stay focused on outcomes, building a stronger, results-oriented organizational culture.

- It can become more proactive and agile. Too often, government agencies wait until a problem has become a crisis before acting.[2] Rather than slowly reacting to change, well-managed agencies proactively perceive upcoming challenges and take actions to meet them before they turn into crises. An RBM system facilitates this approach because its results-oriented strategic planning and annual goal-setting force managers to think ahead, proactively choosing new ways of reaching higher levels of performance.

- Its frontline staff will be empowered and accountable. Managers today hear a lot about the need to empower frontline staff so that their agencies can meet clients' needs more quickly. Empowerment of frontline staff can be an important step toward higher morale, greater organizational agility, and increased customer satisfaction. However, empowerment also can harm an agency if improperly implemented, with workers heading off in multiple and sometimes contradictory directions, all without clear accountability. An RBM system sets clear results-based goals, then gives staff great discretion in deciding how to reach them. Empowerment is thereby harnessed to an overarching organizational vision expressed in clear and measurable goals. This ensures results-based accountability as well.

Studies have shown that past management innovations, even useful ones, often have been accompanied by inflated claims that led to later disappointment.[3] An RBM system is far from a panacea for organizational ills. Nonetheless, an agency that correctly implements an RBM system can produce a noticeably more effective organization, which in turn produces more satisfied customers.[4]

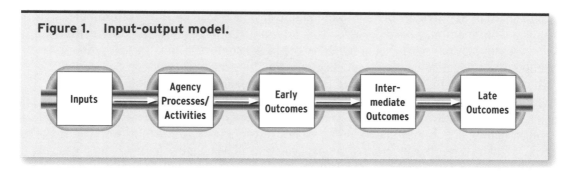

Figure 1. Input-output model.

Inputs → Agency Processes/ Activities → Early Outcomes → Inter- mediate Outcomes → Late Outcomes

Results as outcomes

An RBM system depends on agencies' focusing on, and then managing, their most important results. The most important results are outcomes, although agencies must track a few inputs and processes as well.

"Inputs" are the resources that an agency uses, such as money, time, and equipment. They are typically represented by the cost of programs or activities.

"Processes," or "activities," are the functions that take place within an agency. When the agency counts them, it produces activity measures that demonstrate how busy it is—number of police patrols conducted, food stamps distributed, babies immunized, mental health patients counseled, and so forth.

"Outcomes" are the effects of processes on stakeholders outside the agency, such as citizens or customers. For an urban health department, outcomes might include fewer cases of tuberculosis, fewer emergency room visits, and higher patient satisfaction; for a highway patrol, fewer cases of speeding, fewer accidents, and reduced highway fatalities; and for a school district, higher test scores, fewer dropouts, and higher earnings after graduation.

Outcomes are the reasons that public agencies exist. They do not exist to work hard or stay within their budget, although doing so is commendable. They exist to produce effects on the outside world, such as helping students get better jobs and helping patients recover from illnesses. Therefore management systems must focus on outcomes. There is a cause-and-effect relationship among inputs, processes, and outcomes (see Figure 1).

Process measures versus outcome measures

Outcomes often are difficult to define and measure. Therefore, government has traditionally emphasized (and measured) processes.[5] For example, human services organizations report on how many people they have served but not on how many people have become self-sufficient. Transportation departments report on the number of miles paved or maintained but typically not on the reduction in accidents or commuting time.

Process measures serve a useful role. They tell an agency how hard it is working (its workload). However, a near-exclusive focus on processes hurts an agency because it encourages goal displacement. Goal displacement occurs when agency members pursue goals that fail to provide a benefit to the public or other stakeholders.[6] For example, a police department may become so focused on running a large number of foot patrols (a process) that it does not focus on whether the patrols reduce crimes against property or people. Similarly a downtown revitalization committee may take pride in its frequent, well-attended meetings and its development of an elegant marketing plan, but those activities may not lead to more customers shopping downtown.

RBM, then, is outcomes-based management. An agency must track some inputs to keep its budget figures, and it must track some processes to determine how hard it is working. However, it should direct the attention of its managers and all its members primarily to outcomes.

Most complex public agencies generate many outcomes. How does an agency choose which outcomes it will track, and how does it use them to guide decisions and improve internal processes? Its primary tool is a cause-and-effect chain, often called a "logic model."[7]

Use of a cause-and-effect chain to choose the right results

Outcomes are the focus of an RBM system, but not all outcomes are the same. Depending on when they occur, outcomes may be classified as early, intermediate, and late.

"Early outcomes" are those that quickly result from activities. For instance, police foot patrols may directly lead to more arrests.

"Intermediate outcomes" are later effects, those that are caused by the early outcomes. For example, the increased arrests produced by foot patrols may lead to more convictions, lower crime rates in the next year or two, and an increased sense of security among citizens.

"Late outcomes" are long-term effects produced by the intermediate outcomes. For example, the reduced crime rate over the first year or two may produce sustained low rates of crime, more citizens walking at night, more businesses moving to town, and even increased property values.

(For cause-and-effect chains for a foot patrol operated by a police department, see Figure 2.)

Distinguishing between early, intermediate, and late outcomes has an important practical payoff for public managers. It helps them decide which outcomes to track, because each type of outcome measure has advantages and disadvantages.

Focusing entirely on processes will produce goal displacement. Therefore any focus on outcomes is an improvement. Nonetheless, if an agency focuses exclusively on measures of early outcomes, it may experience a milder form of goal displacement. A goal of increasing arrests (an early outcome) may not produce a safer city (a late outcome) if police respond to the new goal by increasing the number of arrests for very minor crimes. Similarly a goal of producing fewer high school dropouts (an early outcome) may not produce graduates with better job skills and higher incomes (later outcomes) if teachers and administrators respond to the early goal by dramatically decreasing the academic demands of high school in order to entice students to remain.

Although focusing on early outcomes is likely to result in some goal displacement, such a focus has advantages as well. Early outcomes are the ones most clearly controllable by the agency. For example, a police department controls the number of arrests much more completely than it controls increased feelings of public safety, a later outcome. Moreover, early outcomes are the easiest ones to measure, and they are apparent most quickly, allowing agencies to receive fast feedback and take remedial actions when an effort is going astray.

The primary advantage of focusing on late outcomes is that they represent the ultimate purpose of the agency. Therefore, goals based on them usually will not be displaced. For example, there is no goal displacement when the police department pursues the late outcome of "sustained low rates of crime," unlike the case when it pursues the early outcome of "increased arrests." Moreover, late outcomes are valuable when an agency performs a program evaluation to determine whether it is achieving its major missions in a cost-effective manner. Such evaluations are based on late outcomes: for a police department, sustained low rates of crime; for a communicable disease unit of a public health department, long-term drops in sexually transmitted diseases; and for a community college, students succeeding in four-year colleges and in jobs.

However, compared with early outcomes, late outcomes often are more difficult to measure, and they also are more affected by outside forces, making them farther outside

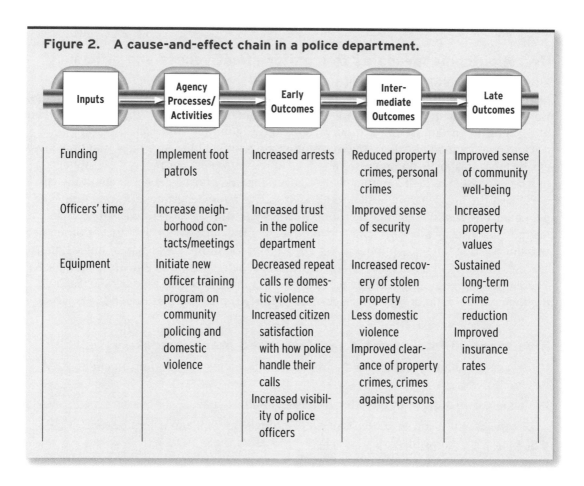

Figure 2.   A cause-and-effect chain in a police department.

Inputs	Agency Processes/ Activities	Early Outcomes	Inter- mediate Outcomes	Late Outcomes
Funding	Implement foot patrols	Increased arrests	Reduced property crimes, personal crimes	Improved sense of community well-being
Officers' time	Increase neighborhood contacts/meetings	Increased trust in the police department	Improved sense of security	Increased property values
Equipment	Initiate new officer training program on community policing and domestic violence	Decreased repeat calls re domestic violence Increased citizen satisfaction with how police handle their calls Increased visibility of police officers	Increased recovery of stolen property Less domestic violence Improved clearance of property crimes, crimes against persons	Sustained long-term crime reduction Improved insurance rates

the direct control of the agency. Moreover, late outcomes sometimes require so much time to achieve that they seem irrelevant to managers and to elected officials serving terms of only a few years.

Intermediate goals offer a useful balance between the advantages and disadvantages of early and late outcomes. They provide reasonably fast feedback—often in a year or so. They also provide a reasonable level of control: agencies usually have a large, but not total, influence over whether they are achieved.[8] For example, effective police departments can influence next year's crime rate, effective revitalization programs can help improve business downtown, and successful mental health agencies can enable their customers to become more self-sufficient.

The foregoing discussion suggests that a well-designed RBM system will use a combination of early, intermediate, and late outcomes in setting its goals. The measures of early outcomes will provide quick, step-by-step feedback. The measures of late outcomes will provide a long-term guide for strategic planning and program evaluation. However, the focus of an agency in setting up its RBM system usually should be on intermediate outcomes, and the agency usually should define its core mission in terms of them.

Use of outcome measures to monitor effectiveness and efficiency

Advocates of the RBM system often emphasize how such a system helps an agency monitor and manage its effectiveness—that is, achievement of its most important results. However, outcome measures also are useful for improving efficiency—that is, achievement of the most important results without wasting time, money, or other resources.

Outcome-oriented efficiency measures often are neglected because most traditional efficiency measures focus on processes and are expressed as cost per process. We are aware of a recent case in which a municipality's governing body raised concerns about the cost per call of the fire department. Responding to calls is a fire department process, and cost per call is one useful efficiency measure. However, as with all process measures, it can lead to goal displacement. No citizen would want a fire department that arrives promptly, without wasting time or equipment, yet does a poor job in fire suppression. Indeed, most citizens would want a fire department that enables them to avoid any fire loss at all. Therefore a more important efficiency measure would be based on an outcome, such as producing a low ratio of fire service costs to (adjusted) property loss due to fire.

Five steps to implement a results-based management system

Using a cause-and-effect chain as the unifying basis, an agency can implement an RBM system in five steps:

1. Define a core mission by applying a cause-and-effect chain.

2. Use the core mission to guide strategic planning's internal and external scans.

3. Set clear annual results-oriented goals.

4. Use backward mapping of the cause-and-effect chain to help develop new processes for achieving the goals.

5. Connect the RBM system to other organizational functions, including training, budget, and personnel evaluation.

All five steps are based on the recognition that performance measures are beneficial only if they are actually used. Therefore they must be linked to on-going organizational processes that encourage use. In other words, performance measurement must lead to performance management, with changes in organizational behavior and decisions that in turn lead to demonstrably better outcomes for program clients.

The following sections discuss each of the steps in greater detail, using two examples: Greensboro–High Point Training and Employment Services (G–TES) and, to a lesser extent, the Wake Forest Fleet Maintenance Department. G–TES is a local government program that provides training and employment services to people who are unemployed or underemployed. The Fleet Maintenance Department services all the town vehicles and equipment.

Step 1: Define a core mission by applying a cause-and-effect chain

Before an agency can define its desired results and then measure its progress toward those results, it must ask, What are the most important things we are trying to do? In other words, What are our core mission and values?

Defining a core mission and values, with its specific clients, is much more difficult in government than in business. A business can choose its niche. For example, IBM can target its top-of-the-line laptop computers at the affluent business executive. However, outsiders—interest groups, legislators, executive branch officials, and others—define the core mission of government agencies, and this mission often is broad because it must satisfy a large number of stakeholders.[9] Moreover, once an agency has chosen its core mission, it often has a difficult time measuring its effectiveness in achieving that mission, because it lacks a single measure of effectiveness, such as the profit measure for business.

These obstacles mean that top managers wishing to install an RBM system must define the core mission in terms of outcomes and recognize that their core mission will be far broader than that of the typical business.

G–TES example   To determine its primary mission, the G–TES Leadership Team developed a cause-and-effect chain (see Figure 3) and used it to consider which intermediate outcomes best captured the most important results. The discussion helped the team establish the primary outcomes—the core mission—by which G–TES should operate.[10] The team then concluded that the most significant of these outcomes was clients becoming self-sufficient.

Step 2: Use the core mission to guide strategic planning's scans

In step 2 the agency should use its core mission as the basis of internal and external scans. First it should ask, What internal and external opportunities exist to achieve that mission?

Figure 3.   Initial cause-and-effect chain for G-TES.

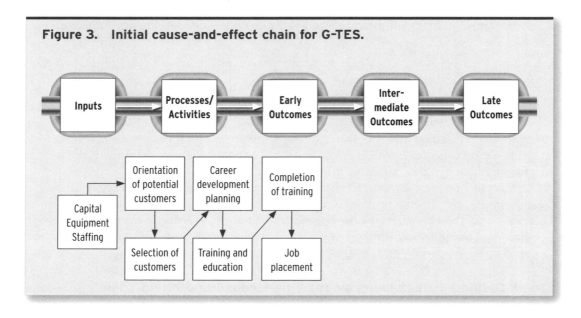

What internal and external threats to the mission loom? Then it should ask, What strengths and weaknesses do we have to meet those opportunities and threats and carry out our core mission? (Most managers know this analytic process by its acronym, SWOT, for strengths, weaknesses, opportunities, and threats.) As a product of this analysis, an agency usually identifies some long-term goals that will aid in achieving its core mission.

G–TES example   After determining its core mission, the G–TES Leadership Team conducted a SWOT analysis. One of G–TES's internal weaknesses, the team determined, was that it had fallen prey to goal displacement. It had been focusing on a combination of process and early outcome measures. The processes and, in parentheses, the corresponding measures were as follows:

- Orientation of potential customers (number of potential customers attending orientation)
- Selection of customers (number of customers in the program)
- Career development planning (number of customers completing career development planning)
- Training and education (number of customers in various training and education programs)
  The early outcomes (and measures) were these:
- Completion of training (number of customers completing training)
- Job placement (number of customers hired by local employers)

As is generally true with goal displacement, even when G–TES was successful in meeting its process and early outcome goals, it was not achieving its more important, broader mission. Many customers completed training and obtained jobs (thereby meeting the early outcome goals), yet they were not independent of government support or willing or able to hold their jobs for sustained periods, the desired immediate outcome. Many former customers, in fact, were returning to G–TES for training in new careers that could better sustain them and their families.

Fleet Maintenance Department example   The Wake Forest Fleet Maintenance Department provides another example of avoiding goal displacement. That department had a goal of repairing as many vehicles and pieces of equipment as possible. Obviously a fleet maintenance operation could exceed this goal and still be ineffective if its repairs were shoddy and repaired vehicles and equipment soon broke down again. Such a process-oriented goal might encourage the maintenance department to do fast but sloppy work. To overcome goal displacement, the Fleet Maintenance Department adopted a strategic goal of "minimizing the downtime of operating departments due to vehicle and equipment failure." This intermediate goal encouraged careful work and long-term maintenance, thereby better meeting the expectations of customers—the operating departments that rely on the Fleet Maintenance Department.

Step 3: Set clear annual results-oriented goals

An RBM system is proactive; it requires agencies and individuals to decide what they specifically wish to accomplish during a time period, such as a quarter, a year, or three years. Therefore the outcome measures shown on the cause-and-effect chain must be turned into agency and individual goals. To construct a goal, managers and workers must combine the outcome measure with a target—a measurable standard of performance—and a date. The outcome measure "reduced burglaries" becomes part of a goal when stated as "Burglaries will be reduced by 12 percent by June 30, 2006." Reduced burglaries is the measure; 12 percent is the target; and the end of the fiscal year is the date. Such goals often are set with the active involvement of both the manager and his or her team members. The desired goal is a stretch but also reasonable and attainable.

The importance of appropriate goals cannot be overemphasized. When measurement of results is actually used to track performance and to hold management and staff accountable for that performance, agency members will pursue those measures.

G–TES example   The G–TES Leadership Team understood the importance of determining goals for the agency. After a spirited discussion, the team reached consensus that it should define self-sufficiency as clients who are no longer in need of government support.

G–TES then developed two key goals based on this intermediate outcome:

- Sixty percent of the customers of G–TES will attain self-sufficiency one year after completing the program.

- Within one year after completing the program, customers will save taxpayers more money than G–TES invests in those customers.[11]

The first goal simply specifies the desired percentage of customers who will attain self-sufficiency. The second goal focuses on efficiency by employing a cost-benefit ratio.

The team also established twelve goals based on measures of processes and early outcomes. Many of these measures already were mandated by federal and state reporting requirements. Nevertheless, the leadership team wanted to have detailed information to assess the effectiveness of each part of the cause-and-effect chain and to test its validity over time.

Step 4: Use backward mapping of the cause-and-effect chain to help develop new processes for achieving the goals

Once an agency has chosen a series of annual results-oriented goals, it must ask, How do we achieve those goals? Here too, a cause-and-effect chain can help. Usually a cause-and-effect chain is constructed by working forward—by specifying a process, then the first result (outcome) it produces, then the second result it produces, and so on. However, when analyzing new processes, an agency builds the chain by working backward, usually called "backward mapping."[12] It starts from the desired outcomes, then asks, What outcomes or actions would produce the desired outcomes (and therefore precede them on the chain)? Once it has an answer, the team asks, What outcomes or actions would precede that?

Many local managers are familiar with the "balanced scorecard" approach to performance measurement.[13] Balanced scorecards often are a useful tool, but this step helps illustrate the two advantages of cause-and-effect chains over balanced scorecards. First, because they do not treat all outcomes as equivalent, cause-and-effect chains serve as an organizing and brainstorming device that allows managers to generate new, related measures for their programs. Chains help agencies generate a slate of management measures that does not just balance processes with outcomes, as balanced scorecards do, but also balances different types of outcomes: early, intermediate, and late.

Second, backward mapping, which helps suggest process improvements by asking which causes immediately precede desired outcomes, is far easier when using chains than when using scorecards. Even agencies that wish to retain scorecards often will find that chains provide a useful tool for building and analyzing their scorecards.

G–TES example   Spurred by a new perspective on its mission, the G–TES Leadership Team eagerly set to work on a new cause-and-effect chain that moved beyond the early outcomes of training completion and job placement and emphasized later outcomes such as increased wages and less use of government services, which are indicators of self-sufficiency. This reformulation generated new processes and outcomes and led the team to redesign old processes to promote self-sufficiency better. (For the redesigned cause-and-effect chain, see Figure 4.)

The G–TES Leadership Team and staff used the cause-and-effect chain to work backward, asking, What processes or earlier outcomes should precede these desired outcomes? For example, when they considered the desired outcome of "self-sufficiency," they recognized that it needed to be preceded by an outcome of "good understanding by clients of their own job possibilities." This necessary prerequisite often was missing. Unrealistic expectations kept numerous customers from becoming self-sufficient. Many were unaware of how changes in job market might limit certain options and pave the way for others. Also, a lot expressed interest in careers that were unsuitable for their aptitudes or skills, or were unattainable, given their education and work records. For customers to become self-sufficient, they needed to have a more realistic sense of their abilities, aptitudes, and potential relative to the opportunities available in a rapidly changing job market.

Figure 4. Redesigned cause-and-effect chain for G-TES.

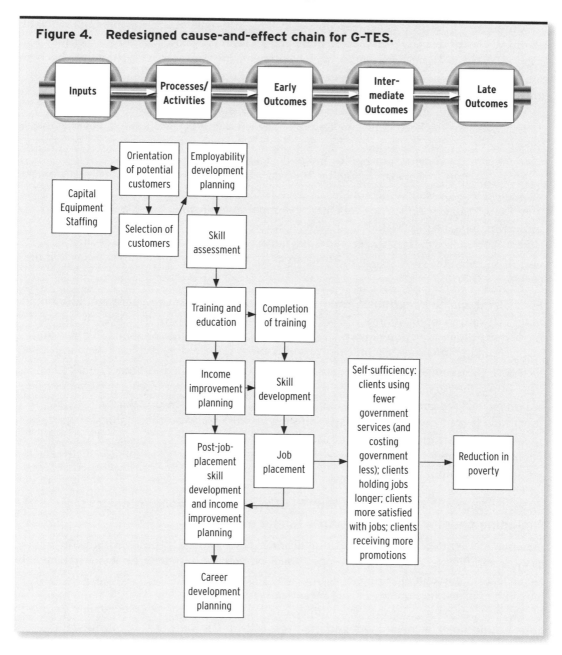

G–TES then designed new processes to produce this newly identified outcome of "good understanding by clients of their own job possibilities." One new process provided an intensive and valid battery of vocational and aptitude tests. A second one involved personal meetings with each customer to develop collaboratively an income improvement plan that matched the customer's test results with opportunities available in the local job market.

A third new process was called "continued skill development and income improvement planning." Its purpose was to help customers plan to improve their incomes after they had secured a position. Once employed, many customers still were not paid enough to become self-sufficient. Those customers needed to develop the skills, the motivation, and the attitude necessary to move from entry-level into higher-paying positions. Therefore the role of G–TES expanded from job attainment to continuous job advancement.

To achieve its longer-term results, G–TES changed other processes as well. For example, the career developers began to emphasize collaboration, rather than direction, in order to foster greater customer responsibility and understanding.

Also, the career developers learned to hold customers accountable. Previously, customers who failed to appear for appointments or were habitually late received no negative feedback from the staff. If self sufficiency was the most important outcome, the staff realized, they were reinforcing poor work habits and irresponsible behavior by tolerating these failures. Now G–TES makes clear its expectation that customers appear on time. If they do not, they may be dropped from the program. These are the same expectations and responses that the customers face on the job.

Fleet Maintenance Department example   The Fleet Maintenance Department also found that backward mapping improved its thinking about services. Given the goal of "reducing lost staff hours of town departments due to unavailable equipment or vehicles," staff began thinking differently about their services. They started by developing new processes to reduce the average turnaround time on repairs. They also tried to think "outside the box" about their operations: even with reduced turnaround time, town departments still would experience some lost hours due to unavailable equipment or vehicles. The department now is considering expanding or altering its work hours so that staff can complete repairs when operating departments are not using vehicles and equipment. They also are contemplating how they can improve their capacity to supply replacement vehicles and equipment to minimize downtime.

Step 5: Connect the RBM system to other organizational functions, including training, budget, and personnel evaluation

As noted earlier, outcome measures provide no value to an agency if they are gathered, reported, and then ignored. To encourage agency workers to base their decision making and behaviors on outcome-oriented goals, an agency should inextricably bind the measures to ongoing management processes and incentive systems.

Training, structure, rewards and budgets are central components of an agency's culture. Connections between them and the RBM system help shift the organizational culture toward a greater focus on results. For example, an appropriate outcome for a street department would be improvement in the safety of city streets. Such an outcome could be enhanced by partnering with the police department. Similarly, a fleet maintenance department could work more closely with operating departments to educate drivers and equipment operators about preventive maintenance. An agency also will tend to become somewhat decentralized, to make its budgets performance based, and to make its appraisal systems outcome based, with some group or team measures. These structural changes need not he made before initiating an RBM system, but they quite often ensue as a result of implementing one.

Some agencies choose to move to step 5 cautiously. Determining outcomes, measuring results, and developing systems to gather those measures typically demand ample commitment during the first year or so.

Nevertheless, once the measurement system is in place, an agency usually will wish to use measures to evaluate the effectiveness of individual units. Such accountability for results often is fostered by restructuring in a way that provides each subunit with a cross-functional capability to deliver some outcomes on its own. For instance, as part of community-based policing, a police department may enhance the capabilities of its local subunits (often called districts) and give them greater autonomy, but it then will evaluate how well the various districts are succeeding in reducing crime. This is a form of accountable decentralization.

Similarly, school districts may employ school-based accountability, which devolves many decisions to principals but holds the schools accountable for reaching defined academic and other goals. (Such decentralized structures often are called "results centers.")

An RBM system also allows legislatures and executive departments to loosen line-item restraints in their budgets but hold the program and agency subunits accountable for achieving longer-term results. These approaches, usually called "performance-based budgeting," are built on an RBM system.

Other connections can be made to training programs and to personnel appraisals, as G–TES illustrates.

G–TES example   Once it had established the new goals and processes, the G–TES Leadership Team was prepared to reassess the staff's training, structure, and performance appraisal system. The goal of customer self-sufficiency pinpointed the importance of the career developer position at G–TES. The team realized that customers would be better served by working directly with a single career developer than by being passed from one staff member to another. Such a full-service representative could better understand the total personal and professional needs of the customer and better hold that customer accountable for following through on commitments.

To enable career developers to adapt to their expanded roles, G–TES redesigned its training and clarified the values by which it should operate. For instance, the career developers needed to be trained in test interpretation so that they could share these results appropriately with customers. Moreover, career developer's needed to receive proper training in how to prepare their customers first to become more responsible, then to acquire an entry-level position, and finally to move up to higher and better positions that would allow them to achieve self sufficiency.

Obviously this commitment to client self-sufficiency transformed the job expectations of the career developer position. The job of the career developer no longer ended with the customer becoming employed. The relationship carried over for at least a year as the career developer worked with the employer and the customer to facilitate the advancement necessary for self-sufficiency. The career developers also needed to work effectively with employers to ensure proper support for customers and to build the confidence of the local business community in G–TES and its customers.

These new job expectations, coupled with the revised measurement system, enabled G–TES to develop precise performance appraisal criteria for its career developers and other staff. Most governments develop trait- or behavior-based personnel appraisal systems. All too often, these systems tend to be either too subjective or rife with goal displacement because they tend to measure processes rather than outcomes. G–TES was able to develop a performance-based appraisal system. The career developers are assessed according to a fully objective and quantifiable set of performance standards that tie directly into organizational outcomes (for excerpts from the appraisal instrument, see Figure 5). Therefore the performance appraisal system makes a clear connection between the goals of the agency and those of its members, encouraging goal alignment.

Evaluation of the success of results-based management at G-TES

Earlier this chapter discusses the three expected benefits of a well-designed RBM system. The advantages provide a useful checklist of system success at G–TES.

An agency can focus on its most important desired results Not only does the intermediate goal of enabling customers to become self-sufficient appropriately focus the actions of G–TES, but the measures of that success have enabled an objective evaluation, including an assessment of money saved. In fact, the measure of customers saving taxpayers more money than G–TES invests in its customers has provided a businesslike bottom line for the program. G–TES can build political support with elected officials by showing a return on the investment for the taxpayers.

This clarity of focus on results also has enabled G–TES to resolve some organizational issues. Before the implementation of the RBM system, management and staff were experiencing more than the usual tension. Management was frustrated with staff for not taking greater responsibility to ensure the success of customers, while staff were at odds with management for micromanaging their work. In addition, G–TES was adapting to new legal and reporting requirements as the Workforce Investment Act replaced the Job Training Partnership Act in 2000. Staff and management were in a state of confusion. The chaos has been resolved by the clear expectations provided by the RBM system. Both management and staff welcome the improved clarity after months of uncertainty.

After its first year of implementation of the RBM system, G–TES is not yet able to evaluate the impact on overall organizational performance. That first year was devoted to restructuring the agency, developing the measurement system, and establishing measurement baselines. Nevertheless, G–TES staff and managers have been pleased with the impact of the RBM system on their performance appraisals. For the first time in many years, no staff complained to management about their performance appraisal ratings, yet the ratings were lower than ever! Management and staff explain this paradox by pointing to the measures and the measurement system. Staff knew exactly what results were expected at the beginning of the year, and management was able to keep staff informed of their performance results on a monthly basis.

An agency can become more proactive and agile At the end of the first year of implementation, G–TES has acquired measures of its intermediate goals and a cause-and-effect model that enable it to make appropriate improvements in its programs. For instance,

---

Figure 5. Performance appraisal, G-TES position of: career developer.

Vision Statement: *"Every client of TES who is committed, has the potential to become self–sufficient. Commitment comes from within."*

Performance Factor #4: ACHIEVING SELF–SUFFICIENCY
Considers how the staff member enables customers to find placements that result in self–sufficiency.

RATING MEASURES	1 Fails to meet expectations	2 Partially meets expectations	3 Fully meets expectations	4 Exceeds expectations	5 Far exceeds expectations
Percent of exiters working in the occupational skill area in which they were trained	Less than 35%	35-39%	40-44%	45-49%	50%
Number of customers who have attained self–sufficiency as defined by the WDB standard	Less than 21%	21-25%	26-30	31-35%	36%
Percent of employed exiters still employed 12 months after exit	Less than 70%	70-74%	75-79%	80-84%	85%
Increase in average monthly income (adults and older youth) at point of entry compared to 6 months after exit	Less than $457	$457-$480	$481-$505	$506-$532	$533

Source: Excerpted from Greensboro-High Point Training and Employment Service, Performance Appraisal, G-TES Position of: Career Developer (Greensboro: G-TES, n.d.).

if customers are not adequately achieving self-sufficiency, G–TES adjusts its processes. Moreover, by rigorously evaluating results, the organization more scientifically tests what works and what does not.

Staff already have become more proactive. Despite staff knowing their exact performance results throughout the year, management found itself spending more time than ever discussing performance appraisals with them. The discussions did not involve quarrels about ratings, however. Instead, they focused on how performance results could be improved over the year. Staff fully accepted that their performance was not what it could have been. They took greater initiative to share their ideas for improvement with management. Moreover, they began to develop strategies to improve their results, especially by learning from staff who were performing at higher levels.

An agency's frontline staff will be empowered and accountable The new performance appraisal criteria have proven beneficial to both management and staff at G–TES. Management feels that it can hold staff fully accountable for results that have been clearly defined at the beginning of each rating period. Staff feel empowered to decide how to achieve the results. G–TES has the benefit of empowering its staff to make decisions, but it also holds them accountable for results.

A look to the future

The old saying, "There are no free lunches," holds true with an RBM system. Obviously, much time is required to design and maintain such a system. For example, G–TES now is devoting more time and resources to conducting customer service surveys both with its job-seeking customers and with the employers who hire those customers.

Nonetheless, the gains of an RBM system are clear. G–TES, like other agencies, now can build on this foundation by continuously measuring outcomes and proactively modifying services to improve on them. The RBM system provides a useful new approach to planning, staffing, and delivering government services.

Endnotes

1. David N. Ammons, "Performance Measurement in North Carolina Cities and Towns," *Popular Government,* Fall 2001, at 11.

2. Steven Cohen & William B. Eimicke, *The New Effective Public Manager* (San Francisco: Jossey-Bass, 1995).

3. Paul Light, *The Tides of Reform: Making Government Work, 1945–1995* (New Haven, Conn.: Yale Univ. Press, 1997).

4. Because RBM systems are still new, there are not enough studies to be conclusive about their effectiveness. There is some empirical support for them, however.

Studies suggest that strategic planning, which is essential for establishing RBM systems, can under some circumstances produce improvements. George Boyne, "Planning, Performance and Public Services," 79 *Public Administration* 73 (2001).

Studies also suggest that a results-based approach improves the validity of performance appraisal systems. Richard C. Grote, *The Complete Guide to Performance Appraisal* (New York: AMA-COM, 1996).

There is good evidence that process improvement techniques drawn from reengineering and Total Quality Management sometimes produce positive changes in internal activities. Bonnie G. Mani, "Old Wine in New Bottles Tastes Better: A

Case Study of TQM Implementation in the IRS," 55 *Public Administration Review* 147 (1995); Theodore H. Poister & Richard H. Harris, "Service Delivery Impacts of TQM: A Preliminary Investigation," 20 *Public Productivity & Management Review* 84 (1996); Theodore H. Poister & Richard H. Harris, "Building Quality Improvement over the Long Run: Approaches, Results and Lessons Learned from the PennDOT Experience," 24 *Public Productivity & Management Review* 161 (2000).

The evidence is best for management approaches based on target setting and feedback. A large number of studies show that setting goals face-to-face and tracking results often produce major gains in organizational outcomes. Three examples: Edwin A. Locke & Gary P. Latham, *A Theory of Goal Setting and Task Performance* (Englewood Cliffs, N.J.: Prentice Hall, 1990); Anne M. O'Leary-Kelly et al., "A Review of the Influence of Group Goals on Group Performance," 37 *Academy of Management Journal* 1285 (1994); Robert Rogers & John E. Hunter, "A Foundation of Good Management Practice in Government: Management by Objectives," 52 *Public Administration Review* 27 (1992).

5. *Creating High-Performance Government Organizations: A Practical Guide for Public Managers* (Mark G. Popovich ed., San Francisco: Jossey-Bass, 1998).

6. Michael L. Vasu et al., *Organizational Behavior and Public Management,* 291–297 (3d ed., New York: Marcell Dekker, 1998).

7. The underlying conceptual framework of cause-and-effect program linkages (that is, logic models) has a long history of development. One of the earliest discussions of the underlying concepts is in Edward A. Suchman, *Evaluative Research* 51–73 (New York: Russell Sage Found., 1967). Some of the earliest public management applications were developed in a number of works by Joseph Wholey (for example, "Evaluability Assessment: Developing Program Theory," in *Using Program Theory in Evaluation,* 77–92 (Leonard Bickman ed., San Francisco: Jossey-Bass, 1987). Michael Q. Patton, in his three editions of *Utilization-Focused Evaluation* (Beverly Hills, Cal.: Sage Publications), also has done much to popularize the concept.

8. Like all measures except those of late outcomes, intermediate outcome measures can cause goal displacement, but it is milder than that plaguing early outcome measures and far milder than that caused by measures of process goals.

9. Hal G. Raney, *Understanding and Managing Public Organizations,* 72–77 (2d ed., San Francisco: Jossey-Bass, 1997).

10. *Creating High-Performance Government Organizations.*

11. This latter goal bears some explanation. A typical customer who enrolls at G–TES depends on the government for income support, such as food stamps, unemployment compensation, or welfare. Once the customer becomes self-sufficient, he or she no longer depends on government support and begins to pay income taxes. For instance, a customer may be receiving $10,000 in support when he enrolls at G–TES. After completing the program, that customer becomes self-sufficient and pays taxes of $5,000. Therefore, taxpayers have realized a $15,000 benefit. If G–TES invests $5,000 in that customer, he has produced a 300 percent return on their investment.

12. Backward mapping was developed by Richard F. Elmore, who advanced the concept in a number of works, beginning with "Backward Mapping: Implementation Research and Policy Questions," 94 *Political Science Quarterly* 601 (Winter 1979–80).

13. Robert S. Kaplan & David P. Norton, *The Balanced Scorecard* (Boston: Harvard Univ. Press, 1996).

Factors Influencing the Use of Performance Data to Improve Municipal Services

Evidence from the North Carolina Benchmarking Project

David N. Ammons and William C. Rivenbark

Some local governments make greater use of performance measures for improving services than do others. Some barely use their measures at all for anything other than reporting about performance. What accounts for this difference among local governments in the use of performance measures for service improvements? This article identifies several performance-measurement-inspired initiatives among fifteen North Carolina cities engaged in a decade-long comparative performance measurement project. It examines some likely reasons for greater use of performance measures for service improvement decisions by this set of cities than by cities in general and also reasons for varying levels of use of measures among these fifteen cities.

For many years, professional associations and others have urged local government officials to measure performance for the sake of greater accountability and service improvement (for example, Governmental Accounting Standards Board 1989, International

Adapted from David N. Ammons and William C. Rivenbark, "Factors Influencing the Use of Performance Data to Improve Municipal Services: Evidence from the North Carolina Benchmarking Project," *Public Administration Review* 68, no. 2 (2008): 304-318. The authors gratefully acknowledge the assistance of Dale J. Roenigk, director of the North Carolina Benchmarking Project in helping compile the information for this article. Used with permission.

City/County Management Association 1991, National Academy of Public Administration 1991, American Society for Public Administration 1992). How, they have asked, can governments be truly accountable, unless they not only document their financial condition but also report about service levels and, ideally, about service effectiveness and the efficiency of service delivery? And how can officials manage departments and improve services without performance measures? Evidently, many officials saw the logic of the proponents' advice or succumbed to the pressure of the growing bandwagon for performance measurement.[1] Today, many local governments measure performance, although often at only the workload or output level. Typically, they report their measures in their budget or, perhaps, in a special report or on the government's Web site.

The record of local governments in the actual use of performance measures in managerial or policy decisions—beyond simply reporting the numbers—is much spottier. Noting the difference between the adoption of performance measures (i.e., the design and collection of measures) and implementation (i.e., actual use), Patria de Lancer Julnes and Marc Holzer (2001) have concluded that only a subset of the state and local governments that collect measures actually use them to improve decision making.[2] These authors and others who have attempted by means of broad surveys to gain information on the actual use of measures find only modest evidence of implementation and, even then, they acknowledge the possibility of overstatement when such information is self-reported and specific documentation substantiating respondents' claims is not required (Poister and Streib 1999, 332). Although a 1997 survey produced claims that performance measures had produced changes in program budgets, focus, and decisions of city governments, Ted Poister and Greg Streib detected a tendency for "favorable ratings of the effectiveness of these systems... to outstrip reported impacts.... [R]elatively few substantial effects were claimed" (1999, 334).

Many explanations are offered for the use or non-use of performance measures in local government. Some observers point to the support of top management as a crucial ingredient in performance measurement success (de Lancer Julnes and Holzer 2001; Page and Malinowski 2004). Some suggest that interest in performance measures among elected officials or citizen involvement in the development and even the collection of performance measures can be especially important or helpful (Ho and Coates 2004). Others contend that performance measurement is likely to have an influence on important managerial and policy decisions only when steps are intentionally taken to integrate measures into key management systems or decision processes—e.g., departmental objectives, work plans, budget proposals and decisions, and strategic planning (Poister and Streib 1999; Clay and Bass 2002).

Each of these explanations is plausible. Perhaps several others, not listed here, are too. To pass beyond mere conjecture, however, a possible explanation needs to be tested among multiple governments, ideally in a controlled or semi-controlled setting where comparisons can be made and claims can be confirmed. For this study, we examine characteristics and patterns of performance measurement use among 15 cities participating in the North Carolina Benchmarking Project (see sidebar). Through their experience we explore several factors that appear to distinguish those municipalities that present clear evidence of the use of performance measures in the making of important decisions from others that do not.

For our purposes, actual use excludes simply reporting measures or somewhat vaguely considering measures when monitoring operations.[3] For us, credible claims of actual use of performance measures require evidence of impact on decisions at some level of the organization.

North Carolina Benchmarking Project

Prompted by the desire among local government officials for better cost and performance data for comparing municipal services, the North Carolina Benchmarking Project was established in 1995 by a set of seven municipalities and the Institute of Government at the University of North Carolina. This project is similar in principle and motive to many other cooperative projects, but it is distinctive in at least three ways. First, the organizers of this project realized, more than organizers of most similar projects have, that their undertaking would be complex and they resisted the temptation to compare all service functions. Instead, they started small and only gradually have expanded to compare more than the original seven functions targeted at the outset. Second, the project has focused meticulously on cost accounting issues and the uniform application of cost accounting rules across participating municipalities. As a result, project participants exhibit a greater-than-typical degree of trust in efficiency measures, typically unit costs, developed through this project (Ammons, Coe, and Lombardo 2001). Third, the project has survived for more than a decade—and only a few undertakings of this sort can make that claim. The project's continuation is testimony to the project's value as perceived by the participating governments. By 2005 the North Carolina project had grown to include 15 cities and towns, herein referred to simply as cities, ranging in population from 24,357 to 599,771 residents.[1] The median population was 144,333.

In what ways is the project valuable to participating cities? Participants report a variety of benefits, both tangible and intangible. Among the intangibles cited are the importance of being among a group of cities engaged in something regarded as a progressive management initiative, increased awareness of the practices of other governments, and the project's stimulative effect in encouraging officials to consider service delivery options and to make data-driven decisions. Other reported benefits are more tangible and include improved performance measurement and reporting, handy access to better data for those instances when the governing body or chief executive requests comparisons, the ability to use project data in various reports and special studies, and improved service quality and efficiency. Perhaps the greatest test for a comparative performance measurement project, as well as for performance measurement in general, is whether the performance data are being used to influence operations. A few such examples appeared early in the project's history. Many more have emerged in recent years.

1. The 15 cities are Asheville, Cary, Charlotte, Concord, Durham, Gastonia, Greensboro, Hickory, High Point, Matthews, Raleigh, Salisbury, Wilmington, Wilson, and Winston-Salem, North Carolina. As a project participant, each city agrees to commit administrative resources necessary to compile its data in a timely manner and to pay an annual fee to offset costs borne by the university in managing the project. Any North Carolina municipality may join the project. For more information on this project, see www.sog.unc.edu/programs/perfmeas.

Research inquiry and methodology

Judging from the remarks of local government observers who report minimal use elsewhere, the record of performance data use by participants in the North Carolina project seems reasonably good and probably surpasses that of many other local governments. If cities participating in the project make greater use of performance measures, then why is this so? And why do some of the participants in the project use the data to influence operations more than other participants do?

In an attempt to answer these questions, the authors queried project officials in the 15 cities participating in the North Carolina Benchmarking Project in 2005 regarding their experiences and the various uses being made of project data. Unlike a random sample of cities, where claims of performance measurement use might be difficult to confirm, the participation of these cities in a coordinated project made confirmation of data use claims relatively easy. Officials in the 15 cities were queried by survey during the spring of 2005 and subsequently by on-site interviews, followed in some cases by telephone calls and email correspondence for clarification and further details. The survey questionnaire inquired about broad applications of performance measures (e.g., communication with elected officials and citizens, uses in support of long-range planning, use of measures in the budget process), preferences among measures and analytic techniques (e.g., staff reliance on outcome, efficiency, or output measures and the methods used to analyze the measures), and documented examples of performance data being used to alter performance to reduce costs or improve service quality. The responses and supporting material revealed extensive use in some cities, showed less use in others, and suggested possible factors influencing the difference.

The approach taken in this study has advantages over the two more common methods of performance measurement research: the single-city case study and the multi-city survey, usually without required documentation or follow-up to confirm respondent claims. The former typically lacks the breadth supplied by a multi-city study. The latter, usually in the form of fixed-response mail survey, often produces information of questionable reliability and relevance to performance measurement practice and has been criticized as "methodologically inappropriate" (Frank and D'Souza 2004, 704). Without the requirement of documentation or the promise of follow-up, many local officials responding to such surveys are tempted to overstate their organization's adoption and use of management techniques deemed to be progressive, such as performance measurement (Wang 1997). More intensive and thorough review on a case-by-case basis provides greater assurance of accurate reflection of conditions, as well as an opportunity to verify claims of performance measurement uses beyond reporting. This study's set of mini-case studies—less intensive individually than a full-scale case study, but much more intensive than a simple survey—has the advantages of modest breadth as well as relative depth and detail. This approach provided investigators the opportunity to confirm the assertions of municipal officials.

Using performance data for service improvement

The first instance of major impact from the use of data occurred early in the North Carolina project's history, when officials of one of the participating cities examined the efficiency measures for residential refuse collection in other cities and found their own measures to be far out of line. The measures indicated high unit costs and low worker productivity. After first challenging but eventually acknowledging the accuracy of their counterparts' figures, officials in this city realized that the measures revealed the underutilization of labor and equipment. Because a large section of this community was served by a private hauler whose contract would soon expire, the city was able to discontinue private refuse collection and extend its own operation into that area without adding equipment or labor. The annual savings totaled almost $400,000 (Jones 1997).

Another city used data from the benchmarking project to avoid a price hike from its residential refuse collection contractor. The contractor had insisted initially on a 10 percent increase in its new contract; however, the city used project data to argue convincingly that the contractor's efficiency was low and its record of complaints was high when compared to the residential refuse performance of other project participants. The contractor backed off its price hike. Still another participating city, using data from the benchmarking project to analyze service delivery options for refuse collection, switched to automated equipment and one-person crews. That city reduced its cost per ton for refuse collection by 30 percent from 1996 to 2004.

One of the participating cities was persuaded by project data to introduce changes in its recycling program that increased its waste diversion rate from 14 percent to 24 percent over a five-year period, thereby extending the life of its landfill. Another, alarmed by recycling inefficiencies relative to its counterparts, turned to privatization and reduced the cost per ton of recyclables collected by 24 percent, yielding a savings of approximately $75,000 per year (Ammons 2000). By 2004, the savings relative to the base year had grown from 24 percent to 58 percent per ton.

Project data prompted other analyses involving different departments and services in various cities. Fire service analysis in one case revealed underutilization of staff resources and led to the expansion of operations into emergency medical services. Relying on data from the project, a police study in one city revealed a level of staffing that was low relative to its counterparts and insufficient to meet the department's objectives regarding proactive patrols. This prompted the hiring of 33 new officers. Another study led to the establishment of a telephone response unit to deflect some of the burden placed on police officers, as documented by project data. Analyses in emergency communications and fleet maintenance in other cities revealed instances of overstaffing relative to actual service demand and led to staff reductions in these functions. Several cities used project data to help establish performance targets in various operations.

What factors have contributed to the use of performance data to improve operations in these cities? Coupled with information about performance measurement and performance management practices, the patterns of data use in these cities lead us to suggest three factors as being especially influential: the collection of and reliance on higher-order measures—outcome measures (effectiveness) and, especially, measures of efficiency—rather than simply output measures (workload); the willingness of officials to embrace comparison with other governments or service producers; and the incorporation of performance measures into key management systems.

Collection of and reliance on higher-order measures

As noted at the beginning of this chapter, the value of performance measurement can be divided into two broad categories. First it supports accountability—more specifically, performance reporting—and second, service improvement. Perhaps it is axiomatic that performance measurement systems designed strictly for the former (i.e., performance reporting), especially when a premium is placed on ease of data collection, are unlikely to yield much of the latter. Systems intended solely to assure elected officials, citizens, and the media that the government is busily engaged in a broad array of high-volume activities can be designed to achieve this aim while imposing minimal disruption and expense, if these systems focus only on workload measures. Unfortunately, such a system produces feedback having very little managerial or policy value to operating officials or government executives beyond merely documenting whether demand for a service is up, down, or relatively stable. Knowing that 45 citizens were enrolled in the art class at the civic center, that the library had 32,000 visitors, that the water department repaired 600 meters, or that the police department made 200 arrests probably inspires few managers, supervisors, and employees to consider strategies to improve services. Raw workload counts simply do not inspire much managerial thinking.

In contrast, measures focusing on service quality, effectiveness or efficiency can cause officials and employees to rethink service delivery strategies. For instance, measures revealing that persons signing up for a class at the civic center rarely re-enroll in another, that the local library's circulation-per-capita rate is among the lowest in the region, that the cost per repair is almost as much as the price of a new meter, and that the local home burglary rate has reached an historic high are measures of performance that are much more likely to prompt consideration of alternate strategies to achieve better results. Unlike workload measures, these measures of efficiency and effectiveness inspire managers, supervisors, and frontline employees to diagnose the problem, if one exists, and devise strategies to correct it. In short, they inspire managerial thinking.

Over the past few decades, the cities and counties that are considered leaders in local government performance measurement have supplemented their workload measures with measures of efficiency and effectiveness. These governments have invested in systems designed for accountability and service improvement (Halachmi 2002), and therefore are justified in expecting a higher return on their investment in a more advanced system of performance measurement. Good measures of efficiency and effectiveness are more likely than output measures to inspire managerial thinking for service improvement.

The importance of higher-order measures is amplified by a careful review of key distinctions among participants in the North Carolina project, including respondents' comments about where they focus their attention among the measures collected and how they use performance data. The project coordinators in some of the participating cities declared that their organization focuses its attention on one or both of the higher-order measures (efficiency and effectiveness); these officials did not even mention workload measures. By and large, these were the cities that accounted for most of the examples of application of performance measurement for service improvement. Their officials—the ones most often and most intensively engaged in the application of performance measures in key management systems and major management decisions—also appeared to be the ones who most fully grasped the value of good efficiency and effectiveness measures in these systems and decisions, and who most fully recognized the limited value of workload measures.

In contrast, coordinators who said that their city relies on all three types of measures, who said that it relies on workload and perhaps another type, or who were unable to say which types are most used tended to represent cities with average or less-than-average evidence of the actual application of performance measurement for service improvement. Their inability or unwillingness to discount the value of workload measures perhaps betrayed their limited attempts to apply performance measures in major management systems and decisions.

Focus on efficiency measures in particular

Ideally, measures of efficiency report with precision the relationship between production outputs and the resources consumed to produce these outputs (see, for example, Coplin and Dwyer 2000). Resources may be depicted as dollars or as some other representation of a major resource element—for example, $8 per application processed; 150 applications processed per $1,000; 2.2 applications processed per staff-hour; 4,400 applications processed per full-time equivalent (FTE) administrative clerk. Each of these examples relates outputs to the dollars or human energy required to produce them. Variations that also address efficiency include measures of utilization, depicting the extent to which equipment, facilities, and personnel are fully utilized, and measures that gauge only roughly the efficiency of production processes (e.g., turnaround time, average daily backlog, percent completed on schedule).

The pursuit of greater efficiency has a prominent place in the history of American government and public administration in the twentieth century, beginning with the "cult of efficiency" and extending to current insistence on accountability for productive use of resources (Haber 1964; Mosher 1968; Schiesl 1977; Comptroller General 1988; Schachter 1989; Hatry et al. 1989; GASB 1994). Typically, candidates for elective office promise to eliminate waste and administrators at all levels of government swear allegiance to the principles of efficiency. In reality, however, relatively few local governments are particularly adept at measuring their efficiency with much precision and those that are have been accorded something akin to celebrity status by counterparts and admirers—e.g., the cities of Sunnyvale, Indianapolis, Charlotte, and Phoenix.

Privatization and managed competition, the celebrated managing-for-results tactic in which municipal departments must compete with private companies or other producers for the opportunity to deliver services, have exposed vulnerabilities in many local government operations that perhaps have arisen in part because of the inadequate state of efficiency measurement in these governments. Unmeasured, untracked, and therefore often undetected, small inefficiencies can become large over a span of years and eventually cost-saving alternatives for these operations become understandably attractive.

Managed competition allows decision makers to skip past many of the intricacies and complexities of measuring efficiency at the various stages of the production process—stages and measures that should not be skipped if one is truly managing performance. All that officials need in order to make their managed competition decision are a few quality-of-service standards or measures and the bottom line costs for the various options. Managed competition is hardly a success story for efficiency measurement; instead, it signals a surrender to the reality that many local governments have not measured or managed their efficiency very well and now find themselves vulnerable if officials are ready to test the bottom line for selected operations.

Efficiency measurement is not easy, even if the concept seems simple. A measure that relates outputs to resources with precision requires the accurate measurement of outputs and inputs. The problem for most governments lies primarily in accounting for inputs. The cost accounting systems in many local governments, if they exist at all, fail to capture total costs. Perhaps they overlook overhead or other indirect costs, ignore the cost of employee benefits at least insofar as a particular program's costs are concerned, or fail to include annualized capital expenses. In such instances, if unit costs are calculated at all, they understate actual costs and mask inefficiency.

Some local governments desiring measures of efficiency cope with inadequate cost accounting systems by using staff hours, labor hours, or full-time equivalent (FTE) positions to reflect resources rather than dollars. This strategy dodges many cost accounting issues within their own system and has the additional advantage of permitting efficiency comparisons with other governments without worrying about differences in cost accounting rules from one government to another. Even this measure of efficiency becomes complex, however, when the time of a given employee must be divided among multiple duties and different outputs. While time-logging systems introduce complications that many operations resist, estimation techniques introduce imprecisions that can reduce the value of the measure as a diagnostic tool and as a reliable guide for performance management efforts.

In the face of these complexities, too many local governments resort to reporting "FTEs per 1,000 population" or "cost per capita" for services overall or for the services of a particular department. These are extremely crude measures of efficiency, if they can be called efficiency measures at all. Comparisons of "FTEs per 1,000 populations" are favorites of local governments that contract out one or more major functions; with fewer of their own employees, they look good in such comparisons, whether or not the privatization strategy improves services or saves money. "Costs per capita" for services overall typically are calculated by dividing the total budget by the current population and are compared with similar figures for neighboring jurisdictions or counterparts more broadly. These comparisons usually ignore differences in the quality and array of services provided by the listed governments. A city government that has no responsibility for parks or fire services because these are handled by a county government or special district will appear more efficient in a total-cost-per-capita comparison than its full-service counterparts that have responsibility for these costly functions. Per capita cost comparisons on a function-by-function basis reduce this problem but often are plagued by cost accounting variations from city to city.

Because of the inadequacies of efficiency measurement and lack of uniformity in cost accounting rules, most cities and counties wishing to compare their services with other jurisdictions are well advised to focus primarily on measures of effectiveness and quality, where cost accounting and the differentiation of multiple duties are not at issue, and only secondarily on measures of efficiency.

Participants in the North Carolina project tell a different story. In this project, which focuses a large portion of its attention on cost accounting rules and uniformity in reporting, participants claim to rely on efficiency measures as heavily or in some cases more heavily than on other categories of measures. The project has produced efficiency measures that participants consider to be reliable. Accordingly, project participants are less apt to ignore the messages they receive from these measures. Because they have expended so much effort on identifying costs precisely, when their efficiency measures suggest they are inefficient, they are unlikely to dismiss the warning. Instead, they are likely to focus on finding ways to correct the problem. The broad array of performance management initiatives reported in Table 1 reflects this tendency. Participating cities are arrayed from left to right roughly according to the level and significance of their use of project data to influence operations.

Among participants, some cities emphasize reliance on efficiency measures more than others do. Claims of reliance on efficiency measures appear to be necessary but insufficient as predictors of extensive use of performance measurement data. Some that claimed to use efficiency measures as much or more than workload or effectiveness measures were not among the project leaders in performance management applications; however, others making this claim were among the leaders. Participants who did not indicate use of efficiency measures tended not to be among the performance management leaders.

Comparison with others

Local governments in general exhibit different levels of enthusiasm for comparing their own performance statistics with the statistics of others. Some eschew interjurisdictional comparisons or engage in them only reluctantly; some are more receptive, but only if the comparisons are carefully controlled; and others appear to embrace comparisons wholeheartedly. For instance, the city of Portland, OR, and others voluntarily publishing "Service Efforts and Accomplishments Reports" at the urging of the Governmental Accounting Standards Board have featured performance comparisons prominently (Office of the City Auditor 2003). The

Table 1. Reported uses of performance data by cities participating in the North Carolina benchmarking project.

	City A	City B	City C	City D	City E	City F
"Claimed uses of project data, beyond reporting"						
Establishing performance targets	✓	✓	✓	✓	✓	
Contracting decision/ management	✓	✓	✓	✓		
Program evaluation	✓	✓	✓	✓	✓	✓
Budget proposal/review	✓	✓			✓	✓
Other [1]	✓	✓			✓	✓
Types of measures used						
Workload (output)		✓	✓	✓		✓
Efficiency	✓	✓	✓	✓	✓	✓
Effectiveness (outcome)	✓		✓	✓	✓	✓
Prefers comparison to cities of similar size?	Not necessarily–average, best, worst, all	✓	✓	State average and selected cities	✓	✓
Reported applications of project data	Used to negotiate price and establish performance standards for refuse contract; to project service costs for annexation; to review staff/ equipment requests; as gauge for redesign of service routes and monitoring performance; to monitor community policing performance and deployment results; influenced emergency communications work plans, leading to improved performance; influenced staffing decisions and development of work-order system in asphalt maintenance; incorporated into fire department goals and objectives, performance appraisals, analysis of station locations, and analysis for fire inspections; used for analysis of fleet maintenance, identifying opportunity for staff reduction and the need for revised vehicle replacement schedule; prompted review of HRM processes, goals, staffing, and employee benefits.	Data supported move to automated refuse trucks; used to monitor refuse collection efficiency and effectiveness, and waste diversion rate; to evaluate requests for additional police personnel; low ratio of calls per telecommunicator prompted analysis of emergency communication; to evaluate appropriate use of contractors in asphalt maintenance; to evaluate fleet maintenance operation, vehicle replacement policy, and set performance targets for mechanics; to consider comparative employee turnover rates in compensation deliberations.	Project data used to identify opportunities for more efficient deployment of refuse collection equipment and crews, yielding substantial budgetary savings; to assess the costs and benefits of backyard vs. curbside collection (leading to the introduction of voluntary curbside program).	Project data used to compare costs and workload in fire services, especially fire inspections.	Data confirmed benefits of automated refuse collection; data used to evaluate contract costs; to analyze effects of service delivery options on waste diversion rates; to evaluate use of seasonal vs. permanent staffing; to evaluate performance and set work levels in police/ emergency communications; to analyze equipment options for asphalt maintenance, improving efficiency; data analysis led to fire department taking role in EMS; influenced fleet maintenance performance targets.	Project data led to consideration of curbside collection and review of equipment type and crew configuration for recycling services; used in evaluating police deployment strategies; in assessing supervisory staff size in emergency communications (staff increased); in workforce planning for fire inspections; in monitoring fleet maintenance performance.

(1) "Other" uses noted by respondents included use of the project's measures in annexation studies and as a reference source for responding to manager and council requests.

City G	City H	City I	City J	City K	City L	City M	City N	City O
✓	✓	✓	✓					
		✓						
✓								
	✓			✓		✓		
		✓						
	✓		✓	✓	✓	✓		
✓	✓	✓		✓	✓	✓		
	✓				✓			
✓	✓	✓	✓	✓	✓	All and selected cities	All, keeping differences in mind	Yes; but departments prefer not to compare with others
Project data used to assess police staffing and deployment; to adjust fire department work plan; to focus improvement efforts and work planning in building inspections.	Project data prompted shift from rear loaders for refuse collection to side loaders and smaller crews; used to assess needs for support staff in police services.		Project data used to assess pros and cons of automated refuse collection; to push recycling vendor for improved performance reporting; to review asphalt maintenance strategies.	Data used to assess staffing and equipment needs in residential refuse and leaf and litter collection, including automation options; staffing needs in police and fire services and building inspection; identified and remedied inadequacies in performance information for emergency communication and asphalt maintenance; analysis of fleet services.	Project data used to assess conversion from backyard to curbside collection of residential refuse; provided impetus to analyze emergency communications.	Project data used to assess funding level for asphalt maintenance; comparative statistics for fire service prompted scrutiny.	Project data used in refuse collection contract negotiation; to review asphalt maintenance costs; to analyze HRM centralization.	

growth of the performance comparison project of the International City/County Management Association, which included 87 cities and counties in 2004 and more than 200 by 2007, is further evidence of an enthusiasm for comparison.[4] Representatives of each of the three groups—reluctant comparers, willing but cautious comparers, and enthusiastic comparers—are present among the 15 municipalities participating in the North Carolina project.

Some local governments engage in performance measurement, but insist that it is not for the purpose of interjurisdictional comparison. Officials of these governments, including one or two in the North Carolina project, contend that they are more interested in reviewing their own year-to-year performance than in comparing performance with others. While comparison with one's own performance at earlier periods of time is important, reluctance to embrace external comparison is odd for a participant in a project designed primarily for that purpose and may reveal an underlying distrust of performance measurement, anxiety about the numbers being produced and what they will suggest about relative standing, or lack of confidence in the organization's ability to improve performance. Representatives of one city (City L) have been outspoken from the start about their greater interest in year-to-year comparisons of their own performance data than in external comparisons, even if their official response to this study's inquiry indicated a willingness to compare with cities of similar size. This city's reticence about comparison with other local governments appears to extend also to its use of data for performance management. The concerns that inhibit the former apparently also inhibit the latter. These are the reluctant comparers.

A second group—the willing but cautious comparers—includes cities that are more open to external comparisons but strongly prefer comparisons only to cities of similar size, perhaps only including a select set of cities generally considered to be of a like nature by community leaders or citizens in general. Some officials are especially restrictive in their notions regarding suitable comparisons, preferring that the cities not only be similar in size, but also similar in other demographic characteristics and in mode of service delivery for whatever function is being compared.

The preference of these cities for comparison with other communities of similar size comes despite ambiguous evidence of population-related effects on service quality or unit costs within the project data.[5] This preference, even when efficiency measures are standardized as unit costs, reveals a latent belief in economies of scale stronger than the evidence of the existence and impact of such economies supports.

The desire to carefully control the comparison, not only by population but also by other factors to ensure similarity among the comparison group, suggests a sense of anxiety among officials over the possibility that the comparison will be used as a management report card—that is, as a gauge for assessing how well or how poorly department heads and other managers are doing their jobs. Unfortunately, this anxiety can completely displace the search for best practices and produce a benchmarking design that limits the likelihood of breakthrough discoveries.

Two characteristics of this group of officials hint at their concern that performance comparisons will be used as a management report card. First is their insistence on removing the population or economy-of-scale factor from the equation, even if scale economies are weak or nonexistent for a given function, rather than simply controlling for these effects. This suggests a preoccupation with having a "level playing field." When pressed, few local government officials will contend that all the best ideas for service delivery reside only in cities of their size and none would concede that larger municipalities are always more efficient than medium-sized or smaller ones. By insisting that their city be compared only with similarly sized municipalities, they willingly sacrifice the possibility of learning a valuable lesson from a larger city or a smaller city to the belief that comparison of like cities will be a fairer comparison.

Second, the preference of some that comparison units have the same mode of operation for the function being examined similarly emphasizes the importance of a level playing field. If, in fact, the comparison will be used simply to judge the performance of managers, then establishing a fair basis of comparison is indeed important. However, if the purpose is to find new ideas for improving operations, then omitting all but those operating in a similar fashion defeats this purpose.

Project participants in this second category, who are open mostly to comparison with "like" cities, occupied the broad middle range of participating municipalities. They varied in their performance management activities: some were among the project's leaders and others engaged in only a few data-driven management initiatives.

A third category, occupied consistently by only one project participant (City A) and intermittently by another (City C), includes local governments that embrace comparisons even when the initial results of these comparisons reveal local performance to be disappointing. These are the enthusiastic comparers. For them, the comparisons are the first in a series of steps that leads to performance improvement. The first step provides the impetus for the second and the third. These cities are more likely than others to use performance measures to improve operations. Their list of management initiatives tended to be longer or more significant in terms of documented service improvement or magnitude of budgetary impact.

Incorporating performance measurement into key management systems

Performance measurement has long been promoted as a method of achieving greater accountability in local government, but some officials have defined accountability more narrowly than others. For officials subscribing to the narrowest definition, accountability means performance reporting, plain and simple. They believe that an accountable city or county government will keep the governing body, media, and citizens informed about the government's financial condition and the performance of its major functions. These governments often report performance measures in their budget documents. Some produce separate performance reports or post performance measures on their Web site. Those perceiving accountability most narrowly may be inclined to view performance measurement as a necessary chore that must be done to fulfill their accountability obligation. In this view, expenditures of dollars, time, and energy to collect and report performance measures are a cost of doing business rather than an investment in service improvement, and as such this cost should be kept at a minimal level, if possible. Accordingly, many of these cities and counties load up their performance reports with raw counts of workload (outputs). After all, these are the simplest and cheapest measures to collect and tabulate—and perhaps the elected officials and citizens will be impressed by the number of transactions being processed or the tons of garbage being collected. The higher-order measures of efficiency and effectiveness are more difficult to compile and often are not attempted by officials taking a minimalist view of accountability.

A broader view of accountability includes the obligation for basic performance reporting but extends beyond the raw workload counts into dimensions of service efficiency, quality, and effectiveness. Accountable officials, in this view, are responsible stewards of the government's resources, who understand both their obligation to provide services that balance the community's desires for quality and efficiency and their obligation to produce evidence of their performance on this score. In order to conscientiously manage their operations, officials taking this broader view must be able to assure themselves and others that they are achieving reasonable levels of efficiency and service quality. For this they must have reliable measures of efficiency and effectiveness (outcomes) that will either alert them to problems and prompt the development of new management strategies or reassure them that they are meeting their performance targets.

Officials taking the narrow view of accountability are less likely to venture beyond workload measures and are unlikely to try to incorporate performance measures into key management systems. For them, it seems rational and prudent to collect only the simplest measures and to divert as few resources as possible from service delivery to the measurement of performance. Given their narrow view of accountability and the minimal value of raw workload counts for management or policy decisions, they are unlikely to use performance measures meaningfully in strategic planning or management systems, performance contracts, departmental or individual work plans, performance targets, performance audits, program evaluations, service improvement strategies, cost-benefit analyses, annexation and other special studies, or budget proposals. These uses are much more likely to be found in local governments where officials take the broader view of accountability, where performance measurement is considered an indispensable ingredient in performance management. In such governments, performance measurement is a tool that provides reassurance to the manager or supervisor when performance is on target and sounds an alarm when performance falls short of expectations, signaling the need for focused attention and perhaps a new strategy, and helping the organization fulfill its obligation for conscientious management that delivers quality services in an efficient manner.

Participating municipalities in the North Carolina project were questioned about their use of project data for four management purposes beyond reporting:

- establishing performance targets
- contracting and managed competition, including analysis of options as well as contract design and management

- program evaluation
- budget proposal and review.

Two of the cities (Cities A and B) reported all four uses. For instance, City A, the city mentioned previously for having used benchmarking project data to avoid a price hike from its refuse collection contractor, clearly benefited from having incorporated these data into its performance management, contract monitoring, and budgeting systems. Cities A and B are among the three or four in this set that have most fully adopted the broader definition of accountability. Not coincidentally, these two cities also provide some of the most extensive examples of the application of performance data to improve operations.

Two other cities (Cities D and G), recognized in other venues for the sophistication of their management systems and their use of performance data in general, have incorporated less of the data from this project into their systems and report fewer applications of the data from this project than do a few of their counterparts. Nevertheless, their level of use places them on the left side of Table 1. Two other cities that report three of the four uses beyond reporting (Cities C and E) are also among the project leaders in the tangible application of project data for operations improvement.

The incorporation of performance data into management systems is not a perfect predictor of the actual use of performance measurement to adjust operational processes or to improve the quality or efficiency of services. Nor is the failure to incorporate performance data into key management systems an absolute guarantee that the organization will not use its measures for service improvement. Some of the North Carolina cities that have been slow to incorporate project data into their management systems nevertheless have been able to report beneficial applications of project data. However, even among the small set of cities engaged in the North Carolina project, a positive relationship between the incorporation of performance data in key management systems and the application of these data for service improvement is evident.

Conclusions

As the collecting of performance measures by city and county governments has become more common, observers have increasingly noted with disappointment the meager use of these measures to improve the quality or efficiency of services. As researchers seek explanations for the use or nonuse of performance data in local government, they might look to the experience of the cities participating in the North Carolina Benchmarking Project for three possibilities. The experience of 15 participating municipalities suggests that the likelihood that performance data will be used to influence operations is enhanced by the collection of and reliance on higher-order measures, especially efficiency measures, rather than simply workload or output measures; the willingness of officials to embrace comparison with other governments or service producers; and the incorporation of performance measures into key management systems.

Endnotes

1. Although reviews of performance reporting documents have revealed the tendency of some local officials to overstate their government's measurement status in surveys (Hatry 1978; Usher and Cornia 1981; Ammons 1995), it is nevertheless safe to conclude that the practice of collecting basic measures—especially workload or output indicators—is widespread.

2. Common failure to use performance measurement for purposes beyond reporting is not confined to state and local governments. A National Academy of Public Administration panel examining early federal efforts to implement the Government Performance and Results Act found "little evidence in most plans that the performance information would be used to improve program performance" (NAPA 1994, 8).

3. While we readily acknowledge that reporting measures is an important use of performance measurement for the purpose of accountability, the focus of this study is the use of performance measures to influence decisions and improve services. Simply reporting measures does not necessarily reflect reliance on these measures for decisions. Similarly, while we agree that performance measures should be instrumental in the monitoring of operations, vague assertions of that use are easily overstated and therefore are dismissed in this study.

4. See information about ICMA's Center for Performance Measurement at www.icma.org.

5. While the challenges of service delivery and expectations of service recipients differ from community to community, the effects of scale economies are less clear than many who reject comparison across population ranges assume. Studies of economies of scale for local government services report different economy-of-scale rates and ceilings across various municipal functions and are sometimes contradictory in their findings (Hirsch 1964, 1965, 1968; Ahlbrandt 1973; DeBoer 1992; Deller, Chicoine, and Walzer 1988; Duncombe and Yinger 1993; Gyimah-Brempong 1987; Kitchen 1976; Walzer 1972; Ostrom, Bish, and Ostrom 1988; Savas 1977a, 1977b; Fox 1980; Newton 1982; Travers, Jones, and Burnham 1993; Boyne 1995).

References

Ahlbrandt, Jr., Roger S. 1973. Efficiency in the Provision of Fire Services. *Public Choice* 16 (Fall): 1–15.

American Society for Public Administration. 1992. *Resolution Encouraging the Use of Performance Measurement and Reporting by Government Organizations.* Washington, D.C.: ASPA.

Ammons, David N. 1995. Overcoming the Inadequacies of Performance Measurement in Local Government: The Case of Libraries and Leisure Services. *Public Administration Review* 55 (1): 37–47.

Ammons, David N. 2000. Benchmarking as a Performance Management Tool: Experiences Among Municipalities in North Carolina. *Journal of Public Budgeting, Accounting & Financial Management* 12 (1): 106–124.

Ammons, David N., Charles Coe, and Michael Lombardo. 2001. Performance-Comparison Projects in Local Government: Participants' Perspectives. *Public Administration Review* 61 (1) (January/February): 100–110.

Boyne, G. A. 1995. Population Size and Economies of Scale in Local Government. *Policy and Politics* 23 (3): 213–222.

Clay, Joy A., and Victoria Bass. 2002. Aligning Performance Measurement with Key Management Processes. *Government Finance Review* (April): 26–29.

Comptroller General of the United States. 1988. *Governmental Auditing Standards: Standards for Audit of Governmental Organizations, Programs, Activities, and Functions.* Rev. ed. Washington, D.C.: Government Printing Office.

Coplin, William D., and Carol Dwyer. 2000. *Does Your Government Measure Up? Basic Tools for Local Officials and Citizens.* Syracuse, NY: Syracuse University, Maxwell Community Benchmarks Program.

DeBoer, Larry. 1992. Economies of Scale and Input Substitution in Public Libraries. *Journal of Urban Economics* 32 (September): 257–268.

de Lancer Julnes, Patria, and Marc Holzer. 2001. Promoting the Utilization of Performance Measures in Public Organizations: An Empirical Study of Factors Affecting Adoption and Implementation. *Public Administration Review* 61 (6): 693–708.

Deller, Steven C., David L. Chicoine, and Norman Walzer. 1988. Economies of Size and Scope in Rural Low-Volume Roads. *Review of Economics and Statistics* 70 (August): 459–465.

Duncombe, William, and John Yinger. 1993. An Analysis of Returns to Scale in Public Production, with an Application to Fire Protection. *Journal of Public Economics* 52 (August): 49–72.

Fox, William F. 1980. *Size Economies in Local Government Services: A Review.* Rural Development Research Report No. 22. Washington, D.C.: U.S. Department of Agriculture.

Frank, Howard A., and Jayesh D'Souza. 2004. Twelve Years into the Performance Measurement Revolution: Where We Need to Go in Implementation Research. *International Journal of Public Administration* 27, Nos. 8 & 9: 701–718.

Governmental Accounting Standards Board. 1989. *Resolution on Service Efforts and Accomplishments Reporting.* Norwalk, CT: GASB.

Governmental Accounting Standards Board. 1994. *Concepts Statement No. 2 of the Governmental Accounting Standards Board on Concepts Related to Service Efforts and Accomplishments Reporting.* Norwalk, CT: GASB.

Gyimah-Brempong, Kwabana. 1987. Economies of Scale in Municipal Police Departments: The Case of Florida. *Review of Economics and Statistics* 69 (May): 352–356.

Haber, Samuel. 1964. *Efficiency and Uplift: Scientific Management in the Progressive Era 1890–1920.* Chicago: University of Chicago Press.

Halachmi, Arie. 2002. Performance Measurement, Accountability, and Improved Performance. *Public Performance and Management Review* 25 (4): 370–374.

Hatry, Harry P. 1978. The Status of Productivity Measurement in the Public Sector. *Public Administration Review* 38 (1): 28–33.

Hatry, Harry P., James R. Fountain, Jr., Jonathan M. Sullivan, and Lorraine Kremer. 1989. *Service Efforts and Accomplishments Reporting: Its Time Has Come.* Norwalk, CT: Governmental Accounting Standards Board, 1990.

Hirsch, Werner Z. 1964. Local vs. Areawide Urban Government Services. *National Tax Journal* 17 (4): 331–339.

Hirsch, Werner Z. 1965. Cost Functions of an Urban Government Service: Refuse Collection. *Review of Economics and Statistics* 47 (1): 87–93.

Hirsch, Werner Z. 1968. *The Supply of Urban Public Services. Issues in Urban Economics.* Baltimore, MD: The Johns Hopkins University Press.

Ho, Alfred, and Paul Coates. 2004. Citizen-Initiated Performance Assessment: The Initial Iowa Experience. *Public Performance and Management Review* 27 (3): 29–50.

International City/County Management Association. 1991. *Practices for Effective Local Government Management.* Washington, DC: ICMA. Revised version posted at www.icma.org July 6, 2006.

Jones, Ann. 1997. Winston-Salem's Participation in the North Carolina Performance Measurement Project. *Government Finance Review* 13 (4): 35–36.

Kitchen, Harry. 1976. A Statistical Estimation of an Operating Cost Function for Municipal Refuse Collection. *Public Finance Quarterly* 4 (January): 56–76.

Mosher, F. C. 1968. *Democracy and the Public Service.* New York: Oxford University Press.

National Academy of Public Administration. 1991. *Performance Monitoring and Reporting by Public Organizations.* Washington, DC: NAPA.

National Academy of Public Administration. 1994. *Toward Useful Performance Measurement: Lessons Learned from Initial Pilot Performance Plans Prepared under the Government Performance and Results Act.* Washington, DC: NAPA.

Newton, K. 1982. Is Small Really So Beautiful? Is Big Really So Ugly? Size, Effectiveness, and Democracy in Local Government. *Political Studies* 30 (2): 190–206.

Office of the City Auditor. 2003. *City of Portland Service Efforts and Accomplishments: 2002–03.* Portland, OR.

Ostrom, Vincent, Robert Bish, and Elinor Ostrom. 1988. *Local Government in the United States.* San Francisco, CA: Institute for Contemporary Studies.

Page, Sasha, and Chris Malinowski. 2004. Top 10 Performance Measurement Dos and Don'ts. *Government Finance Review* 20 (5): 28–32.

Poister, Theodore H., and Gregory Streib. 1999. Performance Measurement in Municipal Government: Assessing the State of the Practice. *Public Administration Review* 59 (4): 325–335.

Savas, E. S. 1977a. An Empirical Study of Competition in Municipal Service Delivery. *Public Administration Review* 37 (November–December): 717–724.

Savas, E. S. 1977b. *The Organization and Efficiency of Solid Waste Collection.* Lexington, MA.: Lexington Books.

Schachter, Hindy Lauer. 1989. *Frederick Taylor and the Public Administration Community: A Reevaluation.* Albany: State University of New York Press.

Schiesl, Martin J. 1977. *The Politics of Efficiency: Municipal Administration and Reform in America, 1880–1920.* Berkeley: University of California Press.

Travers, T., G. Jones, and J. Burnham. 1993. *The Impact of Population Size on Local Authority Costs and Effectiveness.* York, England: Joseph Rowntree Foundation.

Usher, Charles L., and Gary Cornia. 1981. Goal Setting and Performance Assessment in Municipal Budgeting. *Public Administration Review* 41 (2): 229–235.

Walzer, Norman. 1972. Economies of Scale and Municipal Police Services: The Illinois Experience. *Review of Economics and Statistics* 54 (November): 431–438.

Wang, XiaoHu. 1997. Local Officials' Preferences of Performance Measurements: A Study of Local Police Services. Dissertation. Florida International University.

Monitoring Quality and Productivity

Theodore H. Poister

Some sets of performance measures are compiled annually and consist of measures focused primarily on overall community conditions or progress toward the local government's overarching goals. The author of this article points out the importance of quality and efficiency measures directed toward the nuts and bolts of service delivery and compiled on a monthly, weekly, or even daily basis.

Performance measurement systems are indispensable for managing government agencies productively. Public administrators who are committed to results-oriented management need to (1) set goals and objectives, standards, or targets; (2) allocate resources accordingly and provide direction and control over people and programs so as to focus energy on attaining those goals; (3) monitor performance so as to identify strengths and weaknesses as well as measure overall success; and (4) stay on course or make midcourse corrections as indicated in order to improve performance. This is the sine qua non of effective management practice and applies to every level in an organization from top executives down to first-level supervisors.

To some extent performance measurement systems—tracking key indicators of agency or program performance at regular intervals over time—have been a staple in the public manager's toolkit for some time (Poister and Streib, 1989).

Attention focuses now more than ever on measuring *outcomes*, the end results or real impacts produced by public programs. This is obviously a very positive development, because it is impossible to know whether programs are effective or whether they are really making a difference if outcomes are not being measured. Such measures of outcomes or effectiveness are, or at least should be, the bottom line in assessing a public agency's

Adapted from Theodore H. Poister, "Monitoring Quality and Productivity in the Public Sector," in *Public Productivity Handbook,* 2nd ed. (New York: Marcel Dekker, 2004). Used with permission.

performance. However, there are a number of other criteria of program or agency performance that are also important to monitor although they are subordinate to effectiveness, precisely because they are linked to producing desired outcomes. This article, therefore, examines the use of performance measures focusing more specifically on quality and productivity in public sector operations.

Monitoring service quality

As the quality revolution has swept through government over the past fifteen years, it has made an indelible mark on the public management landscape (Carr and Littman, 1990; Berman and West, 1995; Hyde, 1997). Now more than ever, managers of public programs are challenged to improve the quality of the services they deliver as well as customer satisfaction with those services. From a performance measurement perspective this means tracking indicators of the quality of input, and especially the output produced and, as shown below, customer satisfaction. Typically, the dimensions of quality that are considered as being the most important in the quest for improving customer service include:

Timeliness, total time required, waiting time;

Accuracy, thoroughness, reliability, fairness;

Accessibility, hours of service, convenience;

Decor, cleanliness, and condition of facilities;

Personal safety and security; and

Courtesy, politeness, and professionalism.

Interestingly, these and other dimensions of service quality can usually be measured with quantitative indicators. This is usually a matter of defining what constitutes acceptable quality standards and then tracking the number or percentage of cases in which those standards are achieved or in which performance falls short of the standards. Looking at decentralized operations for renewing driver's licenses, for example, managers might want to monitor the (1) percentage of customers who have to wait in line for more than twenty minutes before being served, (2) the average time required for a customer to complete the license renewal process, and (3) the percentage of renewals that are processed correctly the first time.

Quality and productivity

In the past, managers often thought that quality improvement was antithetical to maintaining or increasing productivity. They felt that if they were forced to focus too much on achieving high-quality service, operations would slow down and productivity would necessarily suffer. More recently, though, advocates of the quality movement have pressed the argument that improving quality actually leads to greater productivity in the long run, largely by eliminating *rework,* or cases that have to be processed over again because they were done incorrectly the first time.

Thus quality and productivity are more often seen today as mutually supportive or complementary performance criteria. The Williamsport, Pennsylvania, Bureau of Transportation, for example, annually tracks the overall performance of its City Bus system through measures of quality and productivity, as well as overall utilization and cost effectiveness, as shown in Table 1. Actual performance is compared against predetermined

Table 1. Williamsport Bureau of Transportation city bus performance.

	WBT standard	WBT actual 1999	Statewide average for class 3 systems
Productivity standards			
Vehicle miles per employee	≥15,000	16,799	14,635
Vehicle miles per operator	≥22,000	24,190	N/A
Vehicle miles per maintenance employee	≥80,000	100,793	N/A
Vehicle hours per vehicle	≥2,000	2,232	1,903
Vehicle miles per vehicle	≥28,000	31,829	25,486
Service quality standards			
Percent trips +/- 5 minutes			
Nonpeak periods	≥95%	97.4%	N/A
Peak periods	≥90%	96.0%	N/A
Percent transfers	≤10%	17.6%	N/A
Collision accidents per 100,000 vehicle miles	≤3.0	0.7	N/A
Vehicle miles between road calls	≥3,500	6,171	N/A
Vehicle miles between service interruptions	≥25,000	60,756	N/A
Utilization standards			
Annual rides per capita	≥15	16.2	11.4
Passenger trips per vehicle mile	≥2	2.1	1.7
Passenger trips per vehicle hour	≥28.0	30.5	22.3
Passenger miles per vehicle mile	≥6.0	5.7	6.2
Cost effectiveness			
Cost per passenger trip	≤$1.85	$1.57	$2.14
Revenue per passenger trip	≥$0.70	$0.58	$1.04
Net cost per passenger trip	≤$1.15	$0.99	$1.10
Percent cost recovery	≥35%	37%	49%

Source: Williamsport Bureau of Transportation 1999-2000.

standards as well as statewide averages for other similar public transit systems in Pennsylvania. Labor productivity is measured by the number of vehicle miles per employee, per bus operator, and per maintenance employee, and vehicle productivity is measured by the number of miles and hours of service operated per vehicle.

Service quality is measured first of all in terms of schedule reliability, the percentage of bus trips that depart from identified bus stops within plus or minus five minutes of the times shown in printed schedules. This is tracked separately for both peak and nonpeak periods. WBT tracks the percentage of passenger trips that require transfers from one bus to another because this is an important indicator of convenience from the customer perspective. Safety is monitored by the number of collision accidents per 100,000 vehicle miles operated, and the overall reliability of the service is measured by the number of vehicle miles operated per road call required (instances in which a service truck must drive out to attend to an operating problem on a bus) and the number of vehicle miles between service interruptions, in which buses actually break down en route due to mechanical problems. These latter two measures are indicators of the quality of service provided by the maintenance department.

Overall utilization of the system is measured first by the number of passenger trips per capita per year, which is really a measure of the service area's usage of the transit system. Other measures of utilization relate the number of passenger trips served by the system to the number of vehicle miles or hours of service provided, along with the ratio of passenger miles traveled to vehicle miles operated. Finally, the operating cost per passenger trip, revenue per passenger trip, net cost per passenger trip, and percentage of total expenses recovered through the fare-box are all indicators of the system's overall cost effectiveness.

Disaggregated measures

Quality and productivity measures are often monitored in the aggregate but also broken down into the constituent elements of an operating system. Tracking such measures for individual work units or individual field offices delivering services, for example, provides much more detailed information regarding the strengths and weaknesses, or the locus of problems, within an overall operating system.

Continuing along the lines of the public transit illustration above, Table 2 shows some of the same productivity measures for individual routes in the City Bus system. Although the aggregate data for the system as a whole accumulate almost automatically over the course of a year from WBT's routine recordkeeping systems, obtaining some of the same measures for individual routes requires a special effort involving additional work on the part of the bus drivers. Thus these disaggregated data pertain to one particular week only.

Because many of the quality and efficiency indicators monitored in the aggregate above are a function of overall policies and procedures or the centralized maintenance function and are therefore truly measures of systemwide performance, the disaggregated data shown in Table 2 focus primarily on system productivity as influenced by ridership levels. And these measures vary substantially from route to route. The number of passenger trips per bus trip, for instance, ranges from 32.2 on the Newberry Route to only 5.4 on the

Market Street Route. In general, these comparisons show that in addition to the Newberry Route, the strongest performers are the Lycoming Mall Route, the Nightline West Route, and the PM Shuttle, and the Montoursville, Garden View, Loyalsock, West Third Street, Nightline East, and the Hill's Express Routes are fairly productive routes across this set of measures. The Market Street, South Side, East End, and Muncy/Mall Local Routes, on the other hand, are clearly the weak links in the system. These more detailed performance data provide greater insight as to where WBT might focus service enhancements and/or service trimming strategies in order to improve overall system productivity.

Quality and productivity improvement

As suggested by the example above, quality and Productivity measures are often monitored at fairly detailed levels. Whereas performance measures designed to track success in achieving an agency's strategic goals or monitor the overall performance of a major

Table 2.   City bus passenger statistics by route (December 8–13, 1997).

Route	Passenger trips per bus trip	Passenger trips per vehicle hour	Variable cost per passenger trip ($)	Revenue per passenger trip ($)	Net cost per passenger trip ($)	Variable cost per recovery (%)
Newberry	32.2	54.9	0.87	0.53	0.34	61
Montoursville	16.1	32.1	1.93	0.57	1.36	29
Garden view	18.3	33.9	1.55	0.55	1.00	35
Loyalsock	18.1	30.6	1.57	0.54	1.03	34
Market street	5.4	24.9	2.36	0.48	1.88	20
West third street	19.5	38.2	1.31	0.53	0.78	40
South side	6.6	15.2	2.93	0.56	2.37	19
East end	9.1	21.0	2.11	0.51	1.60	24
Nightline east	15.2	36.7	1.32	0.57	0.74	44
Nightline west	14.1	50.2	1.33	0.63	0.70	47
Hill's express	6.1	36.5	1.66	0.59	1.07	35
PM shuttle	19.8	49.5	0.83	0.43	0.40	52
Muncy/mall local	20.5	18.1	2.99	1.01	1.98	34
Lycoming mall	31.1	45.3	5.75	1.92	3.84	70
Total	15.9	33.0	1.56	$0.50	$1.00	32

program may tend to be more "global" and observed at a macro level, perhaps on an annual basis, quality and Productivity measures often tend to be analyzed at a more micro
level. What has become the conventional quality improvement process (which in practice
usually focuses on improving productivity as well as service quality) typically involves
analyzing work processes to identify problems and develop solutions to improve the
operation This work is necessarily carried out in some detail. Thus public agencies often
define quality and productivity indicators in detail, focusing on the operating level, and
observe them quite frequently.

Comparative measures

There is growing interest in the use of comparative performance measures (Coe, 1999;
Kopczynski and Lombardo, 1999; Morley et al., 2001), and this extends to customer satisfaction measures as well as other kinds of indicators. Comparing actual performance data
against the same measures for other agencies or programs provides a context for interpreting the results of performance measures and sometimes serves to identify leading edge
performers that might be helpful as benchmarking partners.

   Table 3 shows comparative data from passenger surveys conducted by the Williamsport
City Bus System and several other local public transit agencies with smaller and medium-
size service areas in Pennsylvania. Respondents were asked to rate their system on the
basis of five particular criteria as well as provide an overall rating of the service. These
comparative data exist because the state funding agency, PennDOT, requires each system
receiving state assistance to conduct such a survey once every three years, to contain at a
minimum items on these five specific elements. These common elements include vehicle
cleanliness, driver courtesy, fares, on-time performance, and personal safety. Table 3 compares the percentage of passengers on the City Bus system who indicated that they were
satisfied with each of these criteria against the range of the percentage satisfied in the
other eleven systems. Clearly WBT is at the top of the range in terms of overall passenger
satisfaction with the service provided, and it compares favorably with the other systems
in terms of vehicle cleanliness, driver courtesy, and personal safety. However, it is only in
the middle of the range—still a respectable rating—in terms of on-time performance, or
schedule reliability. Even though the passenger feedback on the City Bus System is obviously quite positive, comparing these ratings against those on other systems helps to put
these results into perspective.

Conclusions

This chapter has attempted to present the kinds of performance measures used most
frequently to monitor productivity and service quality in public agencies, and to illustrate how they are used. Rather than linking to overall program goals, policy objectives,
or substantive strategic initiatives, tracking quality and productivity measures tends to
focus more on the nuts and bolts of service delivery systems and ongoing operations. As
compared with performance measurement systems that are intended to support strategic

Table 3.   Percentage of customers satisfied with Pennsylvania public transit systems.

	Williamsport city bus (%)	Other systems (%)[a]
Vehicle cleanliness	89	64–93
Driver courtesy	92	75–94
Fares	88	45–95
On-time performance	84	63–94
Personal safety	91	74–97
Overall service	98	69–98

a Includes Harrisburg, Lancaster, Reading, Erie, Allentown/Bethlehem, State College, York, Wilkes-Barre, Scranton, Altoona, and Johnstown, Pennsylvania.
Source: On-board passenger surveys conducted by the participating transit systems.

management processes, or budgeting systems with annual data, for example, systems designed to monitor quality and productivity tend to focus on more detailed indicators of performance at the operating level, and often very frequently, perhaps on a monthly, weekly, or even daily basis.

The examples presented in this chapter also illustrate the importance of converting performance data into useful information through setting up comparisons of actual performance against standards or targets, trends over time, comparisons across operating units or programs, or benchmarking external comparisons against other agencies or programs. Assuming that the measures are designed deliberately for this purpose, and that the performance data are interpreted appropriately, such monitoring systems can indeed help managers improve both quality and productivity in public agencies and programs.

References

Berman, E. M., West, J. P. (1995). Municipal commitment to total quality management: a survey of recent progress. *Public Admin. Rev.* 55(1):57–66.

Carr, D. K., Littman, I. D. (1990). *Excellence in Government: Total Quality Management in the 1990s.* Arlington, VA: Coopers & Lybrand.

Coe, C. (1999). Local government benchmarking: lessons from two major multigovernment efforts. *Public Admin. Rev.* 59(2):111–115.

Hyde, A. (July 1997). A decade's worth of lessons in continuous improvement. *Govern. Exec.* 58–68.

Kopczynski, M., Lombardo, M. (1999). Comparative performance measurement: insights and lessons learned from a consortium effort. *Public Admin. Rev.* 59(2):124–134.

Morley, E., Bryant, S. P., Hatry, H. P. (2001). *Comparative Performance Measurement.* Washington, DC: Urban Institute.

Poister, T. H., Streib, G. (1989). Management tools in municipal government: trends over the past decade. *Public Admin. Rev.* 49(3):240–248.

Gainsharing in Local Government

David N. Ammons and William C. Rivenbark

Local governments with performance management systems often build in rewards of some kind for excellent performance. These rewards can be monetary or nonmonetary, and they can be directed toward the organization as a whole, the department, work unit, employee teams, or individuals. This article focuses on one type of monetary reward, called gainsharing.

Employee bonuses and other forms of rewards are standard practice in the private sector. When a company has a profitable year, employees hope to enjoy some of the fruits of the success. If the company has a profit-sharing plan, a formula prescribes the employee's share. Companies without formal profit-sharing systems may distribute bonuses in hopes that employees will appreciate their gesture of gratitude, will respond with loyalty, and will be motivated to expand profits in the future. Profit-sharing plans, whether formal or informal, help attract and retain talented employees and provide a personal incentive to increase the company's net revenues.

Profit-sharing and other incentive plans are hardly novel in the corporate world. They are regarded simply as good business—good for employees and good for the company and its shareholders.

The public sector is different. Profit sharing technically is impossible in the public sector, for governments have no profit to share. Nevertheless, governments do have budgets and balance sheets, and actions that trim costs without reducing service quality can improve the bottom line, even if the improvement is not called profit. Increasingly, governments across the nation are experimenting with a system called "gainsharing."[1]

This article describes gainsharing and distinguishes it from profit sharing. The article examines gainsharing as a performance management strategy and highlights examples of its use.

An explanation of gainsharing

Some people suggest simplistically that gainsharing is the public sector's version of profit sharing, as if the public sector exclusively owns gainsharing. Actually, gainsharing and profit sharing both originated in the private sector, and both are found there today.[2] A key distinction between the two systems is in their scope, profit sharing's being broad compared with the relatively narrow scope of gainsharing. Profit sharing focuses on a company's bottom line, which may seem far removed from the efforts of a single contributing unit. A host of factors and accounting maneuvers can influence the profit line on a company's income statement and may seem distant and unintelligible to most employees. Yet in profit-sharing systems, the employees' bonuses are tied to that line. Employees' rewards rise and fall with company fortunes, but executive decisions and outside forces may have a greater influence on company profits in a given year than the performance of rank-and-file workers. Sometimes workers have difficulty seeing how their ideas and efforts relate to their bonus checks.

Gainsharing narrows the scope from company profit and loss to a target that appears more concrete and manageable to employees of an organization, department, or program. Gainsharing challenges employees to reduce costs or expand revenues in their corner of the operation while maintaining or improving the quality of products and services. They must achieve these results through their ideas and energy, not through price or fee increases. If they succeed, they receive a share of the resulting gains. Good results by the gainsharing unit should contribute favorably to the company's bottom line, but the gainsharing bonus of a given unit does not depend on bottom-line profit. It depends instead on results more fully within the control of the gainsharing unit.

Model gainsharing programs exhibit three characteristics: (1) they focus on opportunities to reduce costs or increase revenues, and this allows them to be self-funded; (2) they feature meaningful employee participation, not simply in submitting suggestions but also in collaborating with other workers and management in brainstorming and decision making; and (3) employees receive bonuses based on group success in securing desired gains.[3]

Although many gainsharing programs have included all three characteristics, others have departed from the model, typically by incorporating less employee participation and relying instead on suggestion programs with management review, or on employee implementation of management strategies for cost reduction. Gainsharing experts advocate implementation of the full model, marshalling the motivating power of employee participation in combination with the motivating power of pay for performance.[4]

Consistency with current management thinking

Profit-sharing and gainsharing plans adhere to notions of employee motivation long accepted in the private sector.[5] Also, they coincide with current management thinking about the importance of encouraging employee initiative as organizations strive for continuous process improvement. Advocates of Total Quality Management and its variants argue that no process or pattern of service delivery is ever perfect or even good enough. Each deserves constant scrutiny, and employees should be encouraged to find better tools, better processes, and better options to meet the needs of customers and citizens.[6] Gainsharing is a method of providing this encouragement.

Furthermore, gainsharing is consistent with the management concepts associated with the reinvention movement, initiated by David Osborne and Ted Gaebler's *Reinventing Government* and developed further in subsequent books on the topic.[7] The reinvention philosophy emphasizes a focus not on effort, activities, or promises but on results. By methods embodied in a "consequences strategy," public officials are encouraged to raise the stakes for success and failure. They are encouraged not only to provide real incentives for achieving the desired results but also to raise the prospect of negative consequences for departments or programs that consistently fall short. Greater managerial flexibility as a reward for high achievers, the selection of service producers through managed competition, and gainsharing are among the featured tactics in the reinventor's arsenal.

Greater managerial flexibility may take the form of increased discretion in operating methods and limited freedom from bureaucratic rules governing budget procedures, hiring practices, and purchases. In some cases it even allows the carryover of budget savings from one year to the next and puts a stop to the yearend spending spree that a "spend-it-or-lose-it" budget rule often spurs. This flexibility comes to managers not as a gift but as a trade. In exchange they must promise results and deliver on the promise. Departments or programs agree to be accountable and to provide full documentation of the results that they achieve. In return, those that demonstrate the ability to achieve and sustain favorable results are freed from a few of the rules that many managers regard as bureaucratic straitjackets.

Another tactic in the consequences strategy is managed competition, which requires government departments to vie with private, nonprofit, and other government competitors for the privilege of delivering various government services. When a given service is subjected to managed competition, each competitor, including the government's own department, submits its bid for the service, and each bid is evaluated for service quantity, quality, and cost.[8] Local governments choosing this tactic do so not because they favor private-sector production of services but because they desire the best services at the best price, whether produced by contractors or the government's own employees. Employees in such governments recognize the importance of focusing on service quality, costs, and results, and they understand the consequences of failing to do so.

Government departments and programs that find themselves engaged in managed competition enjoy some advantages relative to their private competitors but also confront some disadvantages. Chief among the advantages are freedom from taxes, freedom from the necessity to make a profit, and favorable access to capital. Private competitors must build taxes, profit, and higher capital costs into their bids. On the other hand, private competitors are widely regarded to have the advantages of greater managerial flexibility, greater willingness to innovate, greater willingness to invest in new technology, and greater freedom to offer incentives that engage the creative energy, enthusiasm, and commitment of their employees. These private-sector advantages prompt public sector managers, especially those engaged in managed competition, to appeal for a level playing field.

Gainsharing is perceived to be a major leveler of the playing field. It allows government units to give their workers a personal stake in their unit's bottom-line success, an incentive akin to what vendors competing with a government unit might give their employees.

Typically, funds for gainsharing bonuses in local governments are drawn from savings during a given year. If a department just recently won with the low bid in a managed competition, that bid can serve as the baseline. Lower-than-expected expenditures would constitute savings and create a gainsharing pool. If no actual bid competition is involved, a local government that offers its employees a gainsharing incentive establishes its baseline (that is, the expected expenditure) through the budget process. The gainsharing award is drawn from the difference between the projected expenditure and the actual expenditure. The distribution to employees may include the entire amount, but more often it is a fixed proportion such as 50 percent. If, for example, total annual savings come to $100,000 and the gainsharing plan calls for a distribution of 50 percent, then $50,000 would be apportioned to employees, and the other $50,000 would be returned to the fund balance (equity in the case of enterprise funds). Typically, gainsharing payouts are conditioned not only on savings but also on the achievement of specified objectives or the continuation of services at previous levels or greater. Work units that fail to meet these standards forfeit their gainsharing payments.

Controversy over gainsharing

In some places, gainsharing plans are controversial. Opponents in some states have challenged their legality, arguing that they deviate from authorized forms of payment to public employees.[9] Even where they are legal, gainsharing plans have stirred negative as well as positive sentiment. Generally, detractors may be divided into two camps: those who oppose gainsharing on philosophical grounds and those who oppose it for practical reasons. Some detractors oppose gainsharing out of anxiety over how it will look to the public, though they usually express their opposition on philosophical or practical grounds.

Philosophical opposition often centers on the belief that the wages being paid to local government managers, supervisors, and other employees already oblige them to share their most creative ideas and contribute their most diligent efforts. In the view of these opponents, the local government should not have to pay a bonus to receive from employees what they were hired to do. Of course, the same could be said of private-sector employees with regard to profit-sharing gains.

Gainsharing proponents argue simply that the incentive works and that the stimulus for new ideas and government savings creates a win-win situation for taxpayers and employees.

People opposing gainsharing for practical reasons worry that resources intended for other purposes will be diverted to gainsharing payments and that the emphasis on cutting costs will interfere with efforts to sustain or even improve service quality. They also are concerned that undeserving employees will get a free ride on the coattails of others and receive gainsharing bonuses even when their contribution has been minimal.

In response, proponents point out that gainsharing bonuses do not come from budgeted funds; they come from savings. If there are no savings, there are no payments. If there are savings and if the payments are tied to a predetermined percentage less than 100 percent, then the ability of the local government to provide resources to priority programs is increased, not reduced.

Concern that service quality might suffer as workers cut expenditures—and corners—in hopes of creating a substantial gainsharing pool is countered by arguments that mechanisms can be put in place to hold any such tendencies in check. Chief among these mechanisms is an accountability system that ensures achievement of key objectives and maintenance of quality-of-service standards.

Gainsharing plans address the problem of free riders in various ways. Some disqualify employees who have unsatisfactory individual performance reports. Others tie awards to a combination of group and individual performance factors. An employee serving on a successful team receives a gainsharing bonus, but an employee with a mediocre individual performance rating receives a smaller bonus than one making a stronger contribution to the team's success. Still other local governments, though, base the award entirely on group achievement, insisting that the gains from developing team spirit and cooperation more than offset an occasional free-rider problem.

Bid to goal

Although managed competition brings the advantage of competitive prices for local services, it also carries risks. Engaging in managed competition can be threatening to local government employees and can jeopardize morale. When an outside contractor wins the bid, the displacement of employees must be handled with sensitivity and care to avoid long-term damage to the government's employee relations. Follow-through also is important. Contract management must be aggressive and thorough to ensure that contract promises are kept.

Local governments wishing to enjoy many of the benefits of managed competition without incurring the potential disruption and risks associated with it have begun to experiment with a process called "bid to goal." Coupled with gainsharing, this process can provide a powerful incentive for innovation and cost-effective service delivery.

The bid-to-goal process begins with the hiring of a consultant who is an expert in a given local government function. The consultant prepares a cost estimate for performing that function in the client's jurisdiction, based on his or her familiarity with companies that provide this service. In essence, this estimate is the consultant's prediction of a competitive contractor's bid, if bids were being sought.

Once the consultant's figure has been received and the government is satisfied as to its reasonableness, the department responsible for producing the service is invited to match or even beat the bid. If the department cannot do so, the local government is likely to seek outside bids. On the other hand, if the department streamlines its operations and beats the consultant's estimate, the department retains responsibility for producing the service. The department's bid becomes its budget, and if gainsharing is authorized, employees are encouraged to find additional savings with the promise of bonuses if expenditures come in below the budget. In fact, department managers facing the prospect of privatization often consider gainsharing to be an essential device in designing and delivering a competitive operation.[10]

Examples of gainsharing across the nation

Many local governments across the country have ventured successfully into gainsharing. For instance, in the late 1990s, a gainsharing plan for the wastewater treatment operation serving the Seattle area produced savings of $2.5 million over a four-year period, without a decline in effluent quality.[11] Under provisions of the plan, employees received half of the savings.

In 1997, using a bid-to-goal approach, San Diego's metropolitan wastewater department persuaded the union to agree to a set of operating revisions that promised to reduce cost by $78 million over a six-year period while achieving compliance with environmental standards. A gainsharing plan, distributing 50 percent of any savings beyond the target, to a maximum of $4,500 per employee annually, provided an additional incentive. By the sixth year, cumulative savings had surpassed $109 million, and employees had enjoyed gainsharing checks every year, ranging from a low of $1,500 to the $4,500 maximum.[12]

In 1997 a consultant hired by East Lansing, Michigan, concluded that the city's wastewater treatment facility could reduce costs by 20 percent if it eliminated eight positions and adopted best practices.[13] The department and its employees devised a plan to achieve these savings over a six-year period, relying on attrition rather than layoffs and introducing a gainsharing plan calling for the distribution of 25 percent of savings to employees. The targeted reduction was reached in just two years rather than six.

The managed-competition efforts of Indianapolis under Mayor Stephen Goldsmith earned national acclaim. Underlying Indianapolis's efforts was a gainsharing program that helped reverse union opposition and produced employee bonus checks as high as $1,750 a year. Osborne and Hutchinson report, "[U]nion officials were quietly approaching managers and suggesting functions that could be outsourced, to reduce costs. Since their members could now share in the savings, their interests were aligned with the mayor's."[14]

Other cost savings and program innovations have been credited to gainsharing programs in Baltimore County, Maryland, and College Station, Texas.[15]

Gainsharing in North Carolina local governments

At least four North Carolina local governments have introduced gainsharing plans: Charlotte, High Point, Pitt County, and Zebulon. Of this group, only Zebulon has chosen to discontinue the incentive.

Charlotte

Charlotte features two varieties of gainsharing. First, some departments, called "business units" in Charlotte, compete with the private sector in managed competition. When they win the bid, they can enjoy the benefits of gainsharing if they can find ways to spend even less than their bid amount. Employees share 50 percent of the additional savings, provided that performance objectives are met.

For example, in the mid-1990s, Charlotte-Mecklenburg Utility employees won the managed competition for the opportunity to operate a water treatment facility and a wastewater treatment facility. Gainsharing bonuses were conditioned not only on achieving additional savings but also on complying fully with all environmental standards and suffering no lost-time accidents.[16]

In managed competition the operating strategies of the public sector are subjected to the test of competition, and the risks to public-sector employees are significant. When municipal employees win the competition and subsequently find ways to reduce costs further, the gainsharing rewards—at 50 percent of additional savings in Charlotte—can be substantial.

When program officials in Charlotte come up with ideas for improving operations, sometimes gleaned from the lessons of competition, and proceed to implement these ideas without actually facing managed competition, the process is called "optimization." These optimization projects also can qualify for gainsharing bonuses, but because the ideas have not stood the test of actual managed competition, the gainsharing pool is established at a lesser rate, 33 percent of savings. Nevertheless, the savings and gainsharing payouts from these optimization projects can be substantial. (For gainsharing savings and payouts arising from managed competition and optimization projects in recent years, see Table 1.)

Table 1.   Charlotte's gainsharing program.

Fiscal Year	Savings	Gainsharing Distribution	Individual Gainsharing Awards
Managed-Competition Projects			
2000	$ 35,000	$ 17,359	$1,073–$1,690
2001	195,000	97,406	$282–$3,797
2002	387,000	193,253	$157–$1,113
2003	325,000	162,709	$322–$4,055
2004	5,000	2,551	$386–$1,380
2005	12,000	5,993	$205–$449
Optimization Projects (Cost Savings without Managed Competition)			
2000	$ 469,000	$154,770	$124–$3,822
2001	1,339,000	441,901	$28–$3,501
2002	2,170,000	715,267	$84–$6,497
2003	1,670,000	551,998	$177–$3,334
2004	2,000,000	660,283	$32–$5,610
2005	3,650,000	119,046	$205–$3,812

Source: Information provided by Kim Eagle, Eval. Manager, Budget & Eval. Dep't, City of Charlotte.

The second version of gainsharing in Charlotte has an even greater scale.[17] Each year the city manager sets a savings goal for the general fund. If the goal is met or surpassed, 50 percent of the savings becomes available in the gainsharing pool. Only half of this pool is distributed to all employees automatically. The distribution of the other half depends on whether or not a given employee's business unit meets its key objectives for the year. These objectives are called "incentive targets" and typically are tied to customer service, efficiency, quality, time standards, and safety. If the business unit meets four out of five incentive targets, employees receive an 80 percent share of this second component of the gainsharing pool. Employees in units meeting all their targets are eligible for a full share of both components—generally $300–$650.[18]

High Point

In 1999, High Point embraced gainsharing as part of its bid-to-goal initiative in the public services department.[19] The department submitted a bid for operation of the wastewater treatment plant that shaved 30 percent from its previous operating expenses and met the consultant's bid-to-goal target. A three-year contract then was signed, specifying performance and safety standards and authorizing gainsharing in the form of quarterly bonuses for cost savings beyond the department's bid. Half of any additional savings would be retained to increase fund equity. The other half would be distributed to employees as gainsharing bonuses.

High Point's bid-to-goal system has since been expanded from the wastewater treatment plant to other operations. Contracts based on the bid-to-goal methodology now are in place for other divisions of the public services department, including the water filtration plant, central lab services, the industrial pretreatment program, and maintenance services. (For savings and gainsharing distributions at the Westside Treatment Plant, see Table 2.)

Pitt County

The employee incentive program adopted by Pitt County in 2001 invited employee suggestions that would "save money [or] increase revenues without reducing services or increasing taxes or fees" and good ideas that would improve services or provide intangible benefits.[20] The awards have differed across these two categories. Employees whose suggestions provide benefits but produce no savings or additional revenues earn $250 and a certificate of appreciation. Awards in this category are limited to twenty-five per fiscal year. Employees whose suggestions produce savings or additional revenue receive 10 percent of the first year's savings, up to $10,000 per suggestion. (If a group of employees makes the suggestion, the award is shared equally among the group members.) These awards are not restricted in number because the savings create their own gainsharing pool.

Employees submit their suggestions to their immediate supervisors. The supervisors forward the suggestions to Pitt County's monetary awards review committee, which considers whether a given suggestion does one or more of the following:

- Identifies and reduces safety hazards
- Saves money or increases revenues
- Increases productivity or efficiency

- Improves conditions
- Improves services to the public
- Conserves resources
- Increases employee morale

Once approved, a suggestion is implemented and monitored for twelve months to confirm its value. If a team submits a suggestion, all team members must be identified at the time of the suggestion, and the monetary award is divided equally among them. (For savings and gainsharing distributions in recent years, see Table 3.)

Pitt County's approach to its larger monetary rewards requires monitoring and documentation of success. Through this single program, Pitt County has simultaneously encouraged employee suggestions, performance measurement, and program evaluation.

Zebulon

Gainsharing in Zebulon was initiated in 1992, when town officials sought an alternative to a merit-pay system that seemed driven less by merit considerations than by the need

Table 2.   Gainsharing at High Point's Westside Treatment Plant.

Fiscal Year	Bid-to-Goal Prescribed Savings	Actual Savings	Gainsharing Distribution	Individual Gainsharing Awards
1999–2000	$290,000	$336,142	$17,496	$1,458
2000–2001	290,000	303,229	5,568	464
2001–2002	290,000	255,960	0	0
2002–2003	290,000	362,874	1,164	97
2003–2004	355,744	514,556	6,768	564

Source: Information provided by Chip Vanderzee, Pub. Serv. Analyst, Pub. Serv. Dep't, City of High Point.

Table 3.   Gainsharing in Pitt County's employee suggestion program.

Fiscal Year	Savings	Gainsharing Distribution	Individual Gainsharing Awards
2001–2002	$95,678	$2,004	$250–$1,504
2002–2003	5,957	753	$250–$253
2003–2004	6,933	943	$154–$279
2004–2005	25,900	2,590	$2,590

Source: Information provided by Michael Taylor, Chief Info. Officer, Mgmt. Info. Sys., Pitt County.

for cost-of-living adjustments.[21] Gainsharing was introduced in hopes of encouraging and rewarding greater efficiency and excellent employee performance.

Zebulon's gainsharing pool was modest relative to others described in this chapter. Only 5 percent of any end-of-the-year savings went into the pool. The other 95 percent went to the fund balance.

Two factors determined employees' eligibility for gainsharing bonuses. One was performance on annual organizational goals set by the town council and the town manager, although exceptions were granted even when targets were not met. The other was satisfactory performance on individual employee performance appraisals, judged to be a performance rating of 2.95 or higher on a 5-point scale.

The town council eliminated the gainsharing initiative in Zebulon in 2000, following the recommendation of a new town manager to replace gainsharing with an annual contribution of 5 percent to 401(k)'s for all employees.[22] The gainsharing program was thought to have little employee support, and it was only loosely anchored in a set of organizational goals produced with little, if any, employee participation and little employee buy-in. With the establishment of 401(k) contributions from the city, the passing of the gainsharing program stirred little sentiment.

The rise and fall of gainsharing in Zebulon should not be regarded as especially unusual. Some private-sector management experts note that fewer than half of all gainsharing plans survive beyond five years and many appear to begin losing effectiveness after two or three years.[23] Some, however, exhibit much longer staying power.

Conclusion

Gainsharing has been shown to produce favorable results in local governments that are willing to establish a substantial gainsharing pool and are prepared to monitor the pool's distribution rigorously. Gainsharing programs that are self-funded by savings in local government operations offer the opportunity for a win-win result. That is, they produce bonuses for employees while expanding, rather than drawing down, local government resources.

Endnotes

1. Mark Michaels, The New Game of Motivation, 101 *American City & County* 36 (1986); Katherine C. Naff & Raymond Pomerleau, Productivity Gainsharing: A Federal Sector Case Study, 17 *Public Personnel Management* 403 (1988); U.S. General Accounting Office, *Gainsharing: DOD Efforts Highlight an Effective Tool for Enhancing Federal Productivity* (Washington, D.C.: USGAO, Sept. 1986), available at http://161.203.16.4/d4t4/131110.pdf; Scott Wilson, Counties Try Productivity Bonuses, *Washington Post*, Mar. 26, 1998, at M1.

2. Most management authorities trace gainsharing to the 1930s, the steel industry, and the introduction of the gainsharing Scanlon Plan, named for union official and subsequent Massachusetts Institute of Technology lecturer Joseph Scanlon. A few trace it back farther, to 1896, when Henry Towne coined the term "gainsharing." See Susan Hanlon et al., Consequences of Gainsharing: A Field Experiment Revisited, 19 *Group & Organization Management* 87 (1994); Kenneth Mericle & Dongone Kim, *Gainsharing and Goalsharing* (Westport, Conn.: Praeger, 2004); J. L. Zalusky, Labor's Collective Bargaining Experience with Gainsharing and Profit Sharing, in *Proceedings of the 39th Industrial Relations Research Association Annual Meeting* (Madison, Wisc.: IRRA, 1986).

3. Robert Masternak, *Gainsharing: A Team-based Approach to Driving Organizational Change* (Scottsdale, Ariz.: World at Work, 2003); Richard S. Saver,

Squandering the Gain: Gainsharing and the Continuing Dilemma of Physician Financial Incentives, 98 *Northwestern University Law Review* 145 (2003); Carl G. Thor, *Gainsharing: Creating and Sharing Success* (Menlo Park, Cal.: Crisp Publ'ns, 1999).

4. Brian E. Graham-Moore & Timothy L. Ross, Understanding Gainsharing, in *Gainsharing: Plans for Improving Performance* 3 (Graham-Moore & Ross eds., Washington, D.C.: Bureau of National Affairs, 1990); Saver, Squandering the Gain, at 149.

5. Corporations have regarded incentive plans as the positive side of a rewards-penalties coin. On the negative side of the coin are terminations for poor individual performance and broader layoffs for poor company performance. Although various limitations apply, governments have these negative options too, but typically have been less inclined and slower to exercise them.

6. Steven Cohen & Ronald Brand, *Total Quality Management in Government* (San Francisco: Jossey-Bass, 1993); Steven Cohen & William Eimicke, *Tools for Innovators: Creative Strategies for Managing Public Sector Organizations* (San Francisco: Jossey-Bass, 1998).

7. David Osborne & Ted Gaebler, *Reinventing Government: How the Entrepreneurial Spirit Is Transforming the Public Sector* (Reading, Mass.: Addison-Wesley, 1992); David Osborne & Peter Plastrik, *Banishing Bureaucracy: The Five Strategies for Reinventing Government* (Reading, Mass.: Addison-Wesley, 1997); David Osborne & Peter Plastrik, *The Reinventor's Fieldbook: Tools for Transforming Your Government* (San Francisco: Jossey-Bass, 2000); David Osborne & Peter Hutchinson, *The Price of Government: Getting the Results We Need in an Age OF Permanent Fiscal Crisis* (New York: Basic Books, 2004).

8. Pamela A. Syfert & David Cooke, Privatization and Competition in Charlotte, *Popular Government,* Winter 1997, at 12.

9. John M. Greiner et al., *Productivity and Motivation: A Review of State and Local Government Initiatives* (Washington, D.C.: Urban Inst. Press, 1981).

10. Barry M. Gullet & Douglas O. Bean, The Charlotte Model for Competition: A Case Study, *Popular Government,* Winter 1997, at 19.

11. Osborne & Hutchinson, *The Price of Government.*

12. *Id.*

13. *Id.*

14. *Id.* at 328.

15. See James Fox & Bruce Lawson, Gainsharing Program Lifts Baltimore Employees' Morale, 112 *American City & County* 93 (1997), and the following websites: www.cstx.gov and www.co.ba.md.us.

16. Gullet & Bean, The Charlotte Model.

17. Information on Charlotte's citywide gainsharing program is based on a telephone interview with Ann White, budget manager (Feb. 25, 2004).

18. Osborne & Hutchinson, *The Price of Government.*

19. Public Services Dep't, City of High Point, Bid-to-Goal Proposals (May 2000).

20. Pitt County, Pitt County Employee Incentive Program Policy (Nov. 2001).

21. Kevin R. Patton & Dennis M. Daley, Gainsharing in Zebulon: What Do Workers Want? 27 *Public Personnel Management* 117 (1998).

22. E-mail Correspondence with Rick Hardin, Town Manager, Town of Zebulon (Feb. 18, 2004).

23. Jeffrey B. Arthur & Lynda Aiman-Smith, Gainsharing and Organizational Learning: An Analysis of Employee Suggestions over Time, 44 *Academy of Management Journal* 737 (2001).

Section III:

The "Stat" Approach: Compstat, CitiStat, and Others

Performance Management in New York City

Compstat and the revolution in police management

Dennis C. Smith and William J. Bratton

Introduced in 1994 in the New York City Police Department, Compstat soon established itself as an important breakthrough in local government performance management. Credited with dramatic improvements in safety and crime reduction, this management system continues to be studied and emulated by others more than a decade later.

Scholars may argue about the effectiveness of the "reinvention movement" at the state and federal level. At the local level, the managers of urban police forces have in fact reinvented American police administration, and in doing so have contributed to dramatic reductions in crime all across the nation. The story of this reinvention is complex, but central to it is a radical shift in the way police organizations strategically use *information about performance* to achieve greater managerial accountability. Because these new performance management techniques were pioneered in New York City in the mid-1990s, the development and implementation of Compstat by the New York City Police Department (NYPD) is a valuable case study of this new approach to policing.

Excerpted from Dennis C. Smith and William J. Bratton, "Performance Management in New York City: Compstat and the Revolution in Police Management," pp. 453-482, in Dall W. Forsythe, ed., *Quicker Better Cheaper? Managing Performance in American Government* (Albany, N.Y.: Rockefeller Institute Press, 2001). Reprinted with permission of the Rockefeller Institute Press, Rockefeller Institute of Government, 411 State Street, Albany, NY 12203.

At the heart of the reinventing government movement that has flourished in the past decade is the idea of "managing for results." In New York City, a leading example of reinvention is the change in police management introduced by Police Commissioner William Bratton at the start of the administration of Mayor Rudolph Giuliani in 1994. In an institution long noted for its resistance to fundamental change, the introduction of a new system of management now known by the acronym for Computerized Statistics (Compstat) was remarkable for its scope, speed of implementation, and its impact on performance. The development of the Compstat system of police management involved not only a focus on measuring outcomes but also on managing for improved outcomes. Since the introduction of Compstat, various kinds of crime—the outcomes of policing—have plummeted to 1960s levels.

A 1996 article appearing in NYPD, published by the police department, entitled "Managing for Results: Building a Police Organization That Dramatically Reduces Crime, Disorder, and Fear," described Compstat in the following words:

> For the first time in its history, the NYPD is using crime statistics and regular meetings of key enforcement personnel to direct its enforcement efforts. In the past crime statistics often lagged events by months and so did the sense of whether crime control initiatives had succeeded or failed. Now there is a daily turnaround in the "Compstat" numbers, as crime statistics are called, and NYPD commanders watch weekly crime trends with the same hawk-like attention private corporations paid profits and loss. Crime statistics have become the department's bottom line, the best indicator of how police are doing precinct by precinct and citywide.

> At semi-weekly "Compstat" meetings the department's top executives meet in rotation with precinct commanders and detective squad commanders from different areas of the city. These are tough, probing sessions that review current crime trends, plan tactics, and allocate resources. Commanders are called back to present their results at the "Compstat" meetings at least every five weeks, creating a sense of immediate accountability that has energized the NYPD's widely scattered local commands. The meetings also provide the department's executive staff with a way of gauging the performance of precinct commanders, who have a better opportunity to be recognized for what they have accomplished in their commands and how effectively they are applying the NYPD strategies.

Since the introduction of Compstat in 1994 through fiscal 1999, major declines were reported in all categories of crime in New York City and *in all 76 precincts.*

In fact, New York City outperformed the nation in all categories, often by a wide margin, and was an early and leading contributor in the crime reductions reported nationally. The FBI's total crime index in New York City from 1993 to 1999 declined 50 percent compared with a drop of 17 percent in other major U.S. cities. Specifically, from 1993 to 1999 in New York:

- Murder and non-negligent manslaughter declined 66 percent (this crime rate for major cities in the United States, *excluding NYC,* dropped 34 percent);
- Larceny theft declined 40 percent (11 percent in the U.S.);
- Motor vehicle theft fell 66 percent (U.S.: 24 percent);
- Burglary dropped 59 percent (U.S.: 26 percent);
- Robbery declined 58 percent (U.S.: 35 percent);
- Grand larceny decreased 37 percent (U.S.: 6 percent);

- Aggravated assaults dropped 36 percent (U.S.: 19 percent);
- Forcible rape declined 40 percent (17 percent in the U.S.).

Moreover, New York City's relative crime rate ranking among the nearly 200 U.S. cities with populations of 100,000 or more also improved, dropping from 88th place to 165th. New York is now the safest large city in the country.

Police management reform: The Compstat model

Compstat was introduced in NYPD by the management team assembled by William Bratton when he became police commissioner at the start of Mayor Rudolf Giuliani's administration in 1994. After reaching a peak in the early 1990s, when homicides exceeded 2,000, and after a historic build-up in police personnel under Police Commissioners Lee Brown and Raymond Kelly,[1] funded by the 1991 Safe Streets, Safe City Act passed by the legislature at the insistence of Mayor Dinkins, index crime in New York had begun to decline. Nevertheless, in the 1993 mayoral election the incumbent David Dinkins had trouble winning credit for the success of his "community policing" approach to reduction in crime, and confronted a candidate who ran on the issue that public safety was still a leading problem.

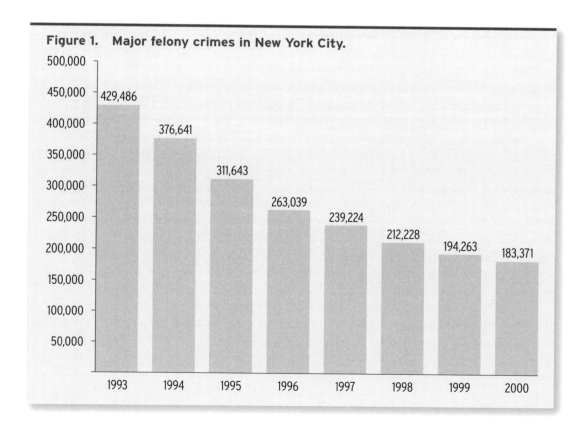

Figure 1. Major felony crimes in New York City.

Most analysts and certainly newly elected Mayor Giuliani believed that the voting public's continuing concern about crime and public safety were critical to his victory at the polls. However, Wayne Barrett, in his biography of Giuliani, takes pains to point out that candidate Giuliani had offered no specifics about how he would achieve his goal of reducing crime. Barrett also criticizes Dinkins's second Police Commissioner Raymond Kelly, under whose leadership index crime had declined, for attributing the crime wave to "family values...young people out there on the streets with no supervision...the out-of-wedlock birthrate," but failing to give credit for the decline to changes by the community (Barrett, 2000, p. 352).

By most accounts, Mayor Giuliani selected William Bratton as his police commissioner because Bratton believed the police could reduce crime. Commissioner Bratton had his own reasons to believe in the efficacy of police action. When he served as head of the New York City Transit Police, he had succeeded in dramatically reducing serious crime. The best example of his approach was the strategic enforcement of the laws against the minor criminal offense of "fare beating." The rationale was that persons entering the subways intent on robbery and other crimes were unlikely to pay to ride. By targeting stations where fare beating was most common, by using plainclothes officers to arrest and interrogate fare beaters, by checking for outstanding warrants, by searching those arrested for weapons, and by prosecuting those with weapons, the Transit Police reduced fare beating, but more importantly drove knives and guns out of the system. This kind of strategy-based law enforcement—more akin to "problem-solving policing" than community policing—became a cornerstone of Compstat.[2]

Police Commissioner Bratton's approach to management, which relied on computer-mapped crime statistics, departed from both the traditional model of a highly centralized, reactive bureaucracy and from the newer model of community policing. In fact, Compstat differs in philosophy, structure, and management process from its predecessors. Compstat is based on a complex set of interrelated assumptions about cause and effect in the production of public safety (Figure 2). The official police presentation of Compstat focused on only four factors: accurate and timely intelligence, rapid deployment, effective tactics, and relentless follow-up and assessment (Safir n.d.). Increased police personnel (provided by Safe Streets/Safe Cities), leadership (from the commissioner *and* the mayor), and the new role of precinct commanders (decentralization) are also critical inputs. The detailed tracking process cast a net around more than just index crimes. Compstat includes indicators believed to be warning markers, such as shooting incidents, shooting victims, and gun arrests, all displayed in geographically pinpointed detail for regular management review at every level.

The philosophical change entailed in this model rested on the belief that police action can affect crime and public safety. To the consternation of many of his police management colleagues and a chorus of disbelief among academic criminologists, Bratton began his tenure by setting a target of cutting crime by 10 percent the first year. (The actual drop was 12 percent.) The new philosophy was informed by the idea of "broken windows" articulated most clearly by George Kelling and James Q. Wilson who argued that effective crime control starts at the bottom of the scale of seriousness, not the top. However, Bratton

Figure 2.   The Compstat model of performance management.

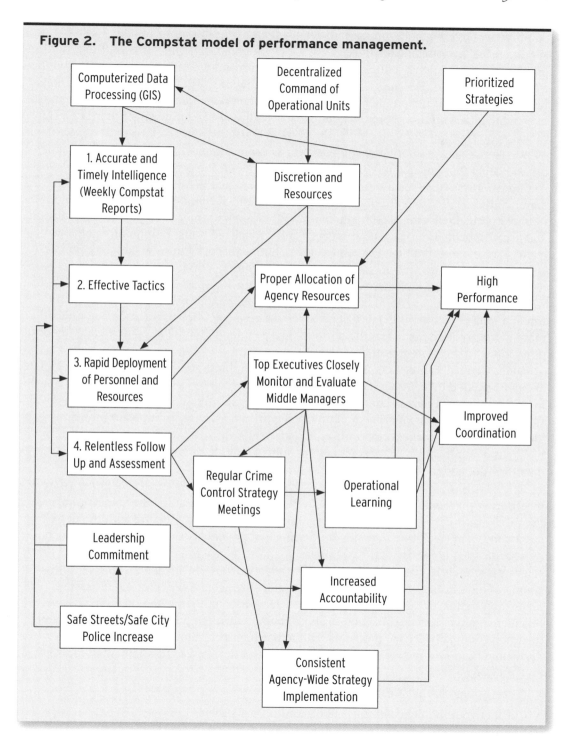

emphasized targeting both top (serious felonies) and bottom-ranked (quality-of-life) crimes simultaneously, winning back the city "block by block." Jack Maple, Bratton's deputy commissioner for operations, maintains that the "broken windows" idea actually formed only a limited part of the New York City intervention. He wrote, "While I applaud tactics that reduce disorder and the public's fear of crime, implementing quality-of-life tactics alone is like giving a face-lift to a cancer patient.... For quality-of-life enforcement to make a significant contribution to crime reduction, it has to be supported by a larger strategy" (Maple 1999). The key element of "broken windows" was not the specific focus of enforcement but the belief that police intervention could have a major impact on crime.

Compstat also includes a significant structural change: the identification of precinct commanders as the locus for operational authority and accountability, and community-oriented problem solving. The traditional NYPD structure centered command, information, and accountability on higher-level officials and specialized units. Community policing could have empowered precinct commanders, but as practiced in New York by Commissioners Ward and Brown it focused more on empowering individual police officers as problem solvers (McElroy, Cosgrove, and Sadd 1993; Ward 1988).

Also under the old system, the job of precinct commander was either the icing on the top of a long career at NYPD or a short stopover on a fast track in the career of upwardly mobile officers. In either case, the performance goal tended to be limited: escape the position before an incident or scandal marred the record.

Under Compstat, precincts became the locus of problem solving and performance management, guided by centrally devised strategies and aided by centrally deployed supplemental resources. Precinct commanders have been given the tools to analyze up-to-date statistics, find patterns of crime and police activity, and devise solutions to problems they identify within the context of priorities and strategies for reducing crime established by the central administration. Precinct commanders know that Compstat staff have the same data they do, and are analyzing it for review.

This change in management process is symbolized by the twice-weekly crime strategy meetings at the Command and Control Center at One Police Plaza. The leaders of one of the City's eight borough commands assemble for a three-hour meeting with the department's top managers to review the performance of precincts—originally one by one, now in adjacent clusters to facilitate awareness of and response to larger patterns. In the early stages these reviews were scheduled well in advance, but precincts now receive only a couple of days notice. The review process is aided by geographic information system (GIS) maps, and trends are presented on computer terminals and projected on large screens. Precinct commanders are questioned about their analyses of patterns and trends, about their actions to solve crime problems, and about their coordination with other police department units. A review session typically covers, in one way or another, all ten central police strategies:[3]

- Getting guns off the streets.
- Curbing youth violence in the schools and on the streets.

- Driving drug dealers out of New York City.
- Breaking the cycle of domestic violence.
- Reclaiming public spaces.
- Reducing auto related crime.
- Rooting out corruption.
- Reclaiming the roads.
- Fostering courtesy, professionalism, and respect.
- Bringing fugitives to justice.

In addition to sharpening the focus on accountability, Compstat sessions have become major vehicles for organizational learning. In the past, no mechanisms were in place to share lessons learned or advances in crime-fighting tactics. The evidence presented at Compstat meetings is intensely scrutinized for insights into what works—and does not work—in the fight against crime, with the results widely and rapidly disseminated within the department. Since commanders are often grilled in Compstat meetings about their familiarity with successful methods, they have strong incentives to be prepared.[4]

Community policing and problem-solving policing

Compstat had its roots in the rise of two sometimes-related reforms in managing public safety: community policing and problem-solving policing. Faced with the need for new approaches to urban public safety, many police departments in the 1980s experimented with new strategies based on two findings: police contributions to public safety were highly dependent on citizen inputs, and police efforts were oriented to apprehension more than prevention. From the first came "community policing" and a return to the idea of the cop on the beat who knows a neighborhood's people and places. From the second emerged "problem-solving policing," which suggests that police can reduce crime by focusing not just on incidents of crime but also on community problems which lead to those incidents.

Some departments combined the two. In New York City a version of problem-solving community policing began in 1984 under Police Commissioner Benjamin Ward and continued into the early 1990s. Since 1994 the city has changed the orientation of problem-solving policing and dropped the rhetoric of community policing almost completely. As will be shown, there has been some distance between rhetoric and reality both during the ascendance of community policing in New York and its apparent eclipse.

As Commissioner Ward was addressing how the department should deploy new officers in the early 1980s, James Q. Wilson and George Kelling (1982) published "Broken Windows." They argued that the neglect of quality-of-life crime enforcement in New York City in the late 1970s might be causally related to the rise in more serious crime in the early 1980s.[5] In 1984, after an extensive study of the needs of the department by the Vera Institute of Justice, the Community Patrol Officer Program (CPOP) was launched to test problem-solving, community-oriented policing in one precinct. CPOP started in Brooklyn with a 10-officer unit, supervised by a sergeant. The officers were assigned to work alone in fixed beat assignments, following a flexible schedule based on the needs of the beat. They were not responding to routine (911) calls for service, but learning neighborhood norms and folkways, identifying patterns of incidents ("problems"), and developing various strategies to address them. While community patrol officers were supposed to act on the information they obtained, they were also expected to serve as a communication link between the neighborhood and the department.

Before much testing of the model could occur, the idea grew wings and took off with a commitment in 1985 to extend it to every precinct in the city. [However] in his campaign for mayor in 1993, challenger Rudolph Giuliani characterized [Mayor David] Dinkins's community policing as "social work." A former federal prosecutor, he claimed to be a "real crime fighter." A "student" of George Kelling,[6] he also promised to pay more attention to quality-of-life offenses, symbolized by the "squeegee men" jaywalking city streets at intersections to try to clean the windows of often reluctant and even frightened drivers.[7]

William J. Bratton, who became police commissioner in January of 1994 and directed the departmental reengineering effort, was recognized nationally as a proponent of community policing. A number of his closest advisors while he led the Boston Police, such as George Kelling of Northeastern University and Robert Wasserman,[8] are considered founders of the community policing movement.

But New York in 1994 was a different story. Community policing was associated in the public mind with the Dinkins administration. In his book (1998, pp. 198–9), Bratton explains his view of community policing as practiced in New York City:

> Beat cops are important in maintaining contact with the public and offering them a sense of security. They can identify the communities' concerns and sometimes prevent crime simply by their visibility. Giving cops more individual power to make decisions is a good idea. But the community-policing plan as it was originally focused was not going to work because there was no focus on crime. The connection between having more cops on the street and the crime rate falling was implicit. There was no plan to deploy these officers in specifically hard-hit areas...and there were no concrete means by which they were supposed to address crime when they got there. They were simply supposed to go out on their beats and somehow improve their communities.

But did community policing disappear with the introduction of Compstat? Problem solving, its lesser-known twin, was infused into many parts of the new plan. While the operationalization of problem solving as a street-level police behavior remained problematic, it emerged in Bratton's 1994 *Plan of Action* for NYPD as a key to high performance reviews, favorable assignments, and promotions. However, the new version of problem solving centered on the precinct, and the primary accountable official was the precinct commander, not the individual community police officer.

Precinct commanders could design their own operating strategies and draw on the department's resources in making those strategies work, and were evaluated on their success in "reducing dramatically crime, disorder, and fear." Precinct commanders who had been trained in and believed in the efficacy of community policing almost inevitably relied on a partnership between their police and the community to achieve significant crime reduction. Thus, community policing has played a role in New York City's crime reduction success story.

The case for Compstat

It was probably inevitable, given the central place of crime-fighting strategies in the campaign that ousted the City's first African-American mayor and brought Rudy Giuliani into office, that the subject of crime and police performance in New York would be highly politicized. Mayor Giuliani did not acknowledge as significant the fact that crime had declined each year under his predecessor, nor credit the Safe Streets/Safe City legislation achieved under Mayor Dinkins for creating a much larger police force with which to pursue the fight against crime. Returning the favor, opponents and critics of the mayor are reluctant to find any merit in the claim that the NYPD under his leadership has played a central role in reducing crime. Most critics are content to offer alternative explanations, but one recent book goes to great if sometimes tortured lengths to challenge even the basic facts of crime reduction.[9]

The case we make here is that, while crime statistics are flawed in well-established ways, there is no evidence that the credibility of crime statistics changed during the Giuliani administration. If anything, crime statistics have been more carefully scrutinized in the last decade than at any time in history. Statisticians recommend the use of multiple measures of almost any complex phenomenon as an antidote to biases. An unprecedented number of police performance indicators are available, and those statistics tell the same story: crime in virtually all categories and in all sub-areas of the City is dramatically down. Not only are homicides now at 1960s levels, but reports of shots fired, gun incidents, and gunshot injuries are also dramatically down. And some of those numbers come from agencies other than the police.

The key point is that there is a remarkably close link between the introduction of the new approach to police management and a dramatic drop in crime, and that other possible explanations do not fit the pattern of crime reduction as closely.[10]

Applying the model to other public services

The claim that the new Compstat approach to police management can reduce crime, disorder, and fear is not limited to the experience of NYPD. Compstat received a Ford Foundation Innovations in Government award, and has been replicated in a number of other cities both in the United States and abroad. The extent to which these communities adhere to the New York City model has not been systematically documented, nor have the results. In *Crime Fighter*, former NYPD Deputy Police Commissioner Jack Maple recounts successful use of the Compstat approach in a number of American cities that had not been part of the general downward trend. After introducing a Compstat-like approach, each of these cities saw significant declines in crime.

Two New York City departments that have attempted to follow the NYPD model in areas other than policing provide additional evidence of the effectiveness of public-sector performance management. At the Department of Correction, the elements of accurate and timely intelligence combined with effective tactics, rapid deployment, relentless follow-up and assessment, and decentralized accountability produced a major turnaround in prisoner safety and drop in overtime expenses. From 1995, when the department introduced its Compstat-like management reform, through 2000, the number of violent incidents dropped from 593 to 54. The Rikers Island Jail, among the more dangerous facilities in the nation, became one of the safest (Smith 1997).

Using the principles of Compstat, the New York City Department of Parks and Recreation created PARKSTAT, which converted a very good systematic method of annually measuring park safety and cleanliness into a system for intensively managing those conditions. The department reported declining performance for two consecutive years after introducing the measurement tool. After using Compstat principles to convert its measurement system into a management system in 1996, the department more than doubled the percentage of park facilities rated as safe and clean, from 39 to 87 percent (Smith 1997).

That these successes occurred immediately after the introduction of Compstat management principles provides additional weight to the argument that a change in police management deserves significant credit for the greater safety of New York City. These experiences suggest that performance management can significantly improve complex urban services.[11]

Endnotes

1. Bratton notes in his book *Turnaround* that only a fraction of the more than 6,000 additional officers funded by Safe Streets legislation were on the streets of New York during the critical summer before the fall election of 1993 (1998, p. 198).

2. Maple emphasizes these follow-on actions in what he calls the "quality-of-life-plus" strategy (1999, p. 155).

3. During the first several years, there were only eight strategies; the last two were added by Commissioner Howard Safir.

4. The positive effect of this rapid transmission of "lessons learned" depends on the quality of the learning.

5. This neglect was exacerbated in New York City by NYPD's response to the 25 percent cut in uniform staff that occurred in the wake of the 1975 fiscal crisis. In a form of triage, NYPD significantly reduced its attention to "lesser crimes" to focus on "real police work"—index crimes (see Smith 1981).

6. Both Andrew Kirtzman (2000) and Wayne Barrett's biographies of Mayor Giuliani recount that he met with and was influenced by Professor Kelling during the period between his first unsuccessful and his second successful run for mayor. Both authors of this article participated in the candidate's policy "seminars" organized by Richard Schwartz.

7. The disappearance of "squeegee men" is often cited as an early success of the Giuliani quality-of-life law enforcement. However, William Bratton notes that in the summer of 1993, before the election, Commissioner Raymond Kelly used problem-solving methods to remove the squeegee men from intersections (Bratton and Knobler, 1998). One might concede that candidate Giuliani set this agenda as Mayor Dinkins's compassion for people who were washing car windows on the streets of New York was a matter of public record.

8. Robert Wasserman also played a central role in NYPD as a consultant to former Commissioner Lee Brown, who made community policing "the dominant operational philosophy of the Department."

9. In a chapter entitled "These Statistics Are Crime," Wayne Barrett (2000) argues: 1) that crime statistics clearly show that police efforts under Mayor Dinkins deserve credit for reducing crime, 2) that crime reductions during the Giuliani administration were the result of other factors, such as a changing drug culture, 3) that any reduction in crime that did occur is the work of Police Commissioner Bratton and his management, not the mayor, and 4) that crime statistics supporting the credit claims of Mayor Giuliani are not to be believed. (The same statistics, if issued during the Dinkins adminis-

tration or other jurisdictions apparently can be believed.) Even after he conjures every manner of challenge, Barrett's bottom line is not that crime has increased, nor that it has not declined, but rather that it has gone down less than claimed, and that other factors deserve credit besides the police.

10. *Editor's note:* In the lengthier, original version of this article appearing in Dall W. Forsythe, ed., *Quicker Better Cheaper? Managing Performance in American Government* (Albany, N.Y.: Rockefeller Institute Press, 2001), the authors include a section

addressing and rejecting alternate explanations tied to demographics, drugs, gun control, the economy, and incarcerations.

11. The City of Baltimore has introduced CitiStat, a Compstat-inspired approach to performance management, for all city agencies. See Francis X. Cline, "Baltimore Uses Data Bank to Wake Up City Workers," *New York Times,* June 10, 2001, p. 24. See also Christopher Swope, "Restless for Results, " *Governing,* April 2001.

References

Barrett, Wayne. 2000. *Rudy! An Investigative Biography of Rudolph Giuliani.* New York: Basic Books.

Bayley, David. 1994. *Police for the Future.* New York: Oxford University Press.

Bratton, William. 1995. "Measuring What Matters." A presentation at a conference convened by the National Institute of Justice Policing Research Institute. Washington, DC. November 28, 1995.

Bratton, William. 1998. "Crime Is Down in New York City: Blame the Police." In Norman Dennis, ed., *Zero Tolerance: Policing a Free Society,* 2nd ed. London: IEA Health and Welfare Unit.

Bratton, William with Peter Knobler. 1998. *Turnaround: How America's Top Cop Reversed the Crime Epidemic.* New York: Random House.

Brown, Lee P. 1991. "Policing New York City in the 1990s: The Strategy for Community Policing." New York City Police Department, January.

Brown, Lee P. and Elsie L. Scott. 1992. *Executive Session Training Implications of Community Policing.* New York City Police Department.

Citizens Budget Commission. *Making More Effective Use of New York State Prisons: A Report of the Citizens Budget Commission,* May 25, 2000.

Cline, Francis X. 2001. "Baltimore Uses Data Bank to Wake Up City Workers." *New York Times,* June 10, p. 24.

Eck, John. 1982. *Solving Crimes: The Investigation of Burglary and Robbery.* Washington, DC: Police Executive Research Forum.

Eck, John E., and William Spellman. 1987. *Problem Solving: Problem-Oriented Policing in Newport News.* Washington, DC: Police Executive Research Forum.

Goldstein, Herman. 1990. *Problem-Oriented Policing.* Philadelphia: Temple University Press.

Greene, Jack R., and Stephen D. Mastrofski. 1986. *Community Policing: Rhetoric or Reality?* New York: Praeger.

Greenwood, Peter, Joan Petersilia, and Jan Chaiken. 1977. *The Criminal Investigative Process.* Lexington, MA: D.C. Heath.

Kelling, George L. 1974. *The Kansas City Preventive Patrol Experiment: A Summary.* Washington, DC: The Police Foundation.

Kelling, George L., Tony Pate, Duane Dieckman, and Charles E. Brown. 1977. *The Kansas City Preventive Patrol Experiment: A Summary Report.* Washington, DC: The Police Foundation.

Kirtzman, Andrew. 2000. *Rudy Giuliani: Emperor of the City.* New York: William Morrow.

Lawrence, Paul, and Jay Lorsch. 1967; 2nd ed. 1986. *Organizations and Their Environments.* Cambridge, MA: Harvard University Press.

Maple, Jack, with Chris Mitchell. 1999. *The Crime Fighter: Putting the Bad Guys Out of Business.* New York: Doubleday.

Mc Elroy, Jerome, et al. 1993. *Community Policing: The CPOP in New York.* Newbury Park, CA: Sage.

New York City Mayor's Office of Operations. 2000. *Mayor's Management Report.* September.

Safir, Howard. Office of the Commissioner, New York City Police Department, Compstat, n.d.

Silverman, Eli B. 1999. *NYPD Battles Crime: Innovative Strategies in Policing.* Boston: Northeastern University Press.

Skogan, Wesley G. 1990. *Disorder and Decline: Crime and the Spiral of Decay in American Neighborhoods.* New York: Free Press.

Smith, Dennis C., and Robin Barnes. 1998. "Making Management Count: Toward Theory-Based Performance Management." Paper prepared for the annual research conference of the Association of Public Policy and Management. New York, October.

Smith, Dennis C. 1981. "Police." In *Setting Municipal Priorities, 1982.* Charles Brecher and Raymond Horton, eds. New York: Russell Sage Foundation.

Smith, Dennis C. 1993. "Performance Management in New York City: The Mayor's Management Plan and Report System in the Koch Administration." Paper prepared for the annual meeting of the Association of Public Policy and Management. Washington, DC, October.

Smith, Dennis C. 1997. "What Can Public Managers Learn from Police Reform in New York? Compstat and the Promise of Performance Management." Paper prepared for the annual meeting of the Association of Public Policy and Management. Washington, DC, November.

Sparrow, Malcolm K., Mark H. Moore, and David M. Kennedy. 1990. *Beyond 911: A New Era for Policing.* New York: Basis Books.

Swope, Christopher. 2001. "Restless for Results." *Governing.* April.

Thompson, James D. 1967. *Organizations in Action.* New York: McGraw-Hill.

Tracy, Paul E., Marvin E. Wolfgang, and Robert M. Figlio. 1990. *Delinquency Careers in Two Birth Cohorts.* New York: Plenum.

Ward, Benjamin. 1988. *Community Patrol Officer Program: Problem-Solving Guide.* New York City Police Department City. New York, September.

Wilson, James Q. 1967. *Varieties of Police Behavior.* Cambridge, MA: Harvard University Press.

Wilson, James Q. and Richard J. Herrnstein. 1985. *Crime and Human Nature: The Definitive Study of the Causes of Crime.* New York: Simon & Schuster.

Wilson, James Q., and George Kelling. 1982. "Broken Windows: The Police and Neighborhood Safety." *Atlantic Monthly,* March, pp. 29–38.

Wolfgang, Marvin E., Robert M. Figlio, and Thorsten Sellin. 1972. *Delinquency in a Birth Cohort.* Chicago: University of Chicago Press.

The Core Drivers of CitiStat

It's not just about the meetings and the maps

Robert D. Behn

In 2000 then-mayor Martin O'Malley introduced in Baltimore a management system modeled on New York City's Compstat. Called CitiStat, his new system included many of the features of Compstat but was designed to cover a broader array of municipal functions. CitiStat thrived under O'Malley's leadership and continues to function in Baltimore as a key management tool in the administration of his successor, Mayor Sheila Dixon. Meanwhile, O'Malley, now governor of Maryland, has launched StateStat in state government in hopes of achieving similar results there.

CitiStat is the new hot thing. Journalists have portrayed it as "a Baltimore success story" (Branch-Brioso 2001), "as a pioneering innovation in across-the-board, eye-on-the-sparrow management" (Clines 2001), as a program that "may represent the most significant local government management innovation of this decade" (Peirce 2004).

Of course, these journalists have emphasized different aspects of CitiStat: *The Baltimore Sun* labeled it a "statistics-driven concept," a "new high-tech program for government efficiency" (Shields 2004). *The Daily Standard* termed it "a computerized accountability program" (DiCarlo 2004). *The Irish Times* called it an effort "to replace a culture of delay and avoidance with a culture of accountability and results, monitored by technology" (Scales 2004, 13).

Robert D. Behn, "The Core Drivers of CitiStat: It's Not Just About the Meetings and the Maps," *International Public Management Journal* 8, no. 3 (2005), pp. 295-319. Copyright © 2005 Taylor & Francis. Reprinted by permission. The Web site of *International Public Management Journal* may be found at www.informaworld.com.

Many journalists have emphasized this accountability theme. *The Guardian* of London described CitiStat as a way "to allow politicians to put non-performing officials on the spot" (Cross 2004), while to *The Times* of London, "CitiStat is based on a specially designed performance-review meeting" in "a special 'confrontation room" ("How to torture your contractors," 2004). "The managers who are forced to go through these inquisitions are less than thrilled," reported *Governing;* they "often emerge from the sessions red-faced and embarrassed before their peers" (Swope 2001, 22).

Scholars have also examined CitiStat. Lenneal Henderson of the University of Baltimore called it "a bold and unprecedented effort to raise the performance of Baltimore City agencies," "a highly successful innovation in the management of city government," an effort "to immediately improve the performance and accountability of city agencies" (2003, 7, 6, 12). In *City Journal,* Fred Siegel and Van Smith, wrote that CitiStat "applies rapid data-gathering and analysis to all city agencies" and "introduces transparency and accountability into a city notoriously unfamiliar with either" (2001, 74).

All this attention has brought public officials from across the country—indeed, from around the world—to Baltimore to talk with Mayor Martin O'Malley and his CitiStat team and to observe CitiStat in action. Numerous municipal governments have copied the concept. Somerville, Massachusetts has SomerStat; Providence, Rhode Island has ProvStat; Syracuse, New York has SyraStat; St. Louis has CitiView, San Francisco has SFStat, and Atlanta has ATLStat.

What, however, is CitiStat? Is it all that new? Does it deserve to be hot—to be copied? What is the core of the CitiStat concept? What makes it work? Indeed, does it work? If so, what does this working accomplish?[1]

The six visible features of CitiStat

CitiStat is Compstat applied to an entire city. In the early 1990s, the New York City Police Department created Compstat to improve its performance (Bratton 1998, 225–239; Giuliani 2002, 71–91; Maple 1999; Silverman 1999, 97–145); in the early 2000s, Baltimore created CitiStat to improve the performance of all city agencies. Indeed, Jack Maple, who was instrumental in creating Compstat in the New York Police Department, helped O'Malley adapt the concept to Baltimore. Thus, anyone who has learned a little about Compstat will not be surprised that the most conspicuous features of CitiStat are similar to those of Compstat. These visible, obvious features are the room, the meetings, the data, the maps, the technology to project the data and the maps onto the wall, and the questioning of key executive with operational responsibilities. When people visit CitiStat, they see these six visible features.

The room

Baltimore has created a special room (see Figure 1) in which it holds every CitiStat meeting. The room itself is nothing fancy, though it does come with some technology for displaying data. The director of a city agency stands at a podium facing the top leadership of the city: the mayor, the first deputy mayor, and a variety of key resource managers (such

Figure 1.   The CitiStat room in Baltimore's city hall.

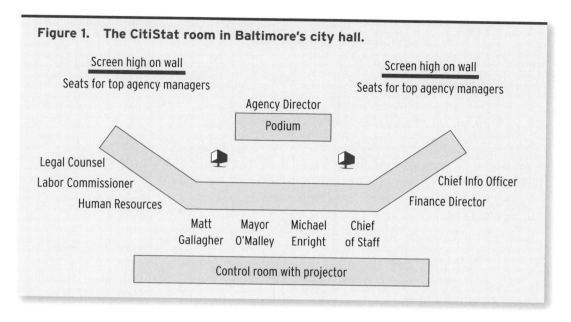

as the city's directors for finance and human resources). On the wall behind the agency director are two large screens onto which staff in the control room can project tables, charts, maps, and pictures. Sitting behind the director (under the two screens) are a dozen of the agency's top managers; in addition, in the wings to the left and the right sit other agency officials—as many as 20 or 30 in total.

The meetings

The CitiStat meetings in the CitiStat room occur on a regular schedule—either bi-weekly or monthly. For example, the director of the Bureau of Water & Wastewater takes the podium at 8:30 every other Thursday. Indeed, the list of CitiStat sessions that Baltimore conducts is long and varied:

Biweekly: Bureau of Water & Wastewater

Bureau of Solid Waste

Bureau of General Services

Fire Department

Police Department

Capital Projects (ProjectStat)

Department of Transportation

Department of Recreation & Parks

Mayor's Office of Information Technology

Department of Housing & Community Development, and Housing Authority
of Baltimore City

Baltimore City Public Schools (SchoolStat covers the department's administrative operations, not education issues)

Monthly: Health Department

Homeless

Office of Finance

Minority Business & Women's Business

In any given week, Baltimore conducts between six and eight CitiStat sessions.

Moreover, CitiStat meetings do not just happen at city hall. Different agencies also conduct their own similar sessions, for which I have coined the generic word "AgencyStat." For example, the Housing Authority of Baltimore City and the Department of Housing and Community Development have built their own room (similar to the CitiStat room, complete with podium, screen, and projector) in which they hold their own HousingStat meetings. The Health Department has created a number of different internal meetings (including DrugStat, LeadStat, KidStat, and AIDStat) that are held in less formal settings (some in a conference room in which a computer and projector are set up, some simply around a conference table). Recreation and Parks has created RecStat, ParkStat, and VendorStat (which tracks the performance of vendors that, for example, mow the grass in the city's parks).

AgencyStat meetings are typically held a day or two before the agency appears at CitiStat. Indeed, these sessions were originally designed to be similar to debate preparation—insuring that the agency head knows what questions might be asked at the coming CitiStat session and has appropriate answers. But as some agency heads become more comfortable with the CitiStat process and as they become more familiar with how it works and what it might accomplish, they have used their own AgencyStat meetings not only to anticipate and prepare themselves for CitiStat questions but also to actually manage their own operations. After all, an agency director's best preparation for a CitiStat sessions is to manage well the tasks on which the mayor and his executive team are focused.

The data, the maps, and the technology

Compstat's original analytical tool was the precinct map, with colored pins to display the data of particular crimes. When he was a police lieutenant in Boston, Bratton was already using data, maps, and pins (Bratton 1998, 99). By the time Bratton became police commissioner in New York City, be could use computer technology to create more sophisticated maps with colored dots. The pins were gone, but the analytical approach—mapping the patterns of crime—remained the same. Then, to use the phrase of Jack Maple, Bratton's deputy commissioner for crime control strategies, the crime-fighting strategy was to "put cops on dots" (Maple 1999, 128).[2]

For policing, maps with dots are a quite effective first-order analytical tool. They display data on crimes in a way that can dramatize some patterns. How many burglaries occurred on a block during any month or any week? How many robberies occurred at an intersection between 2:00 and 5:00 a.m. on the last five Saturdays? Maps with dots display the data in a way that can suggest possible crime-fighting strategies. Maps with dots display data in a way that can help to follow the impact of any specific crime-fighting effort. Moreover, although creating the computer maps with the dots requires individuals with significant technological savvy, people need little analytical training to identify where the dots clustered. In policing, maps with dots are a great first-order pattern-recognition tool.

For some city agencies in Baltimore, maps with dots are also an effective analytical pattern-recognition device. For example, a city map with dots on vacant buildings quickly dramatizes where the problems are though not what to do about them.[3] During most CitiStat sessions, however, the maps are hardly driving the discussion. Indeed, often what is projected on the screen is not connected to the discussion. Instead, the person in the control room is frantically following the discussion—trying to find and put on the screen a map or picture or other graphic that is somehow related to the questions being raised.

Of the various graphics that are displayed on the screen in the CitiStat room, the one that most quickly captures attention is the bar chart. A bar chart that compares the performance of various subunits, or the performance of the managers of various subunits, creates obvious questions: Why is that unit doing better than others? Why is that manager doing worse than others? Why has this unit improved significantly while others haven't? Such questions often have no clear answers; for often the units (even though they are subcomponents of the same agency) do not have identical areas, identical staff, or identical problems. Still, these bar charts are the analytical display of data that most often focuses attention on real questions of performance. The maps are a nice touch, but they do not play the same central role for most CitiStat sessions as they can for Compstat.

The questioning

This is the fundamental format of both Compstat and CitiStat meetings: The mayor and his executive team questioning key agency managers (people with real operational responsibilities) about everything from a particular problem (What are we doing about a water main break at this major intersection?) to a troubling trend (Why has our response to this priority service request continued to deteriorate over the last two months?) to the development of a long-term strategy (Can we learn from our response to this problem how to prevent similar problems in the future?). A CitiStat session may start with a question about a particular problem that occurred yesterday, with an issue that has come up during the last three bi-weekly sessions, or a trend that a CitiStat analyst has just recently discovered.

Regardless, the fundamental format of a CitiStat session is questions from the mayor and his executive team, followed by answers from the agency director and/or others from the agency's top staff, followed by more questions. Often, this give and take will end with the agency director committing to return in two weeks with a more detailed answer, with a new strategy, or with an unequivocal clear statement that the problem has been fixed. And thus the next meeting is apt to begin with the relevant follow-up question.

Still, what is CitiStat exactly? Is it simply the room, the meetings, the data, the maps, the technology, and the questioning? If so, any city ought to be able to replicate CitiStat easily.

The four tenets of CitiStat

It's a well-established urban legend: One night in the winter of 1993–1994, at Elaine's—a restaurant, bar, and in-crowd hangout on Manhattan's Upper East Side—Jack Maple was drinking either double espresso or champagne. (As is befitting of any urban legend, this one comes in multiple versions: Bratton 1998, 223; Maple 1999, 31.) Inspired by his drink, Maple scrawled on a napkin his four principles for Compstat:

(1) Accurate and timely intelligence;

(2) Rapid deployment;

(3) Effective tactics; and

(4) Relentless follow-up and assessment (Bratton 1998, 224; Maple 1999, 32; Silverman 1999, 161–163).

With only slight modifications, these have become the "four tenets" that "constitute the foundation of CitiStat" (http://www.ci.baltimore.md.us/news/citistat/).

In addition to the six, very visible characteristics of CitiStat and the four tenets defined by Maple, there exist other aspects that are not so obvious. They are not hidden. Still, compared with these six conspicuous and easily described features of CitiStat, they can be easily missed, obscured, or ignored. Moreover, although they may become evident to someone who repeatedly participates in CitiStat (or even to someone who watches a series of CitiStat sessions over several weeks or months), these more subtle aspects may not be discernible from just one or two sessions. CitiStat is much more than the meetings and the maps.

The six core drivers of CitiStat: A hypothesis

The six visible features and Maple's four tenets are two different hypotheses about what makes CitiStat a useful performance strategy for a city such as Baltimore. I have a set of different hypotheses:

> The management strategy that Baltimore calls CitiStat contributes to the performance of individual city agencies because it keeps agency managers and employees focused on improving specific outcomes by:
>
> (1) the active engagement of the city's top executives;
>
> (2) the breadth, depth, disaggregation, and "nowness" of the data plus the thoroughness of the analyses of these data;
>
> (3) the perseverance of the questioning, feedback, and follow-up (which is more persistent than relentless);
>
> (4) the consequences for both good, poor, and improved performance;
>
> (5) the focus on problem solving, continuous experimentation, and learning; and
>
> (6) the institutional memory of the city's top executives.

None of the six "core drivers" contained in this hypothesis is sufficient to make a CitiStat strategy effective. None may even be necessary. I suggest, however, that—collectively—

these core drivers contribute more to the effectiveness of this performance strategy than do the six visible features or Maple's four tenets.

In a half-day visit to Baltimore—and many of those who make the pilgrimage to the mother church of CitiStat spend only half a day—a convert is not apt to observe many of these six core drivers. And a briefing from Matt Gallagher, CitiStat's director of operations, or even from Mayor O'Malley himself is apt to focus more on the details of the CitiStat liturgy than on the underlying theology. For example, the technology is celestially radiant and apparently omniscient; thus, visitors can be easily tempted into thinking that, if they want to replicate CitiStat, all they need do is conjure up a similar, computerized sacrament. Certainly, the six core drivers that I suggest do not come with the same apostolic blessing as Maple's four-part canon.

Nevertheless, the six-core-driver hypothesis is more consistent with what we know about organizational behavior and the leadership of public agencies. Any government jurisdiction or agency that seeks to adapt the CitiStat approach to performance management—while replicating the six visible features and venerating Maple's tenets—ought not to ignore the six core drivers that sustain the entire strategy.

Active engagement of top executives

Large organizations require, in the words of Alfred Chandler, "the visible hand of management" (1977, 1). Such organizations exist, he (and others) have argued, because they do a better, less expensive job of coordinating the various activities of their subordinates than would the invisible hand of the market. At the same time, this coordination requires a coordinator—someone or some group at the top of the organizational hierarchy whose very visible hands do the coordinating (Ibid., 7). For a large organization—be it a large corporation or a large city—to accomplish anything significant, the organization's top executives must be actively engaged in coordinating the efforts of multiple subordinates, both individual and organizational subordinates.[4]

Like Compstat, CitiStat requires the visible commitment of the city's top leadership. At the beginning of his first term in 2000, Mayor O'Malley made CitiStat one of his key initiatives. O'Malley is known for CitiStat. O'Malley wants to be known for CitiStat.

By the end of his first term, however, O'Malley was no longer a regular participant in CitiStat sessions. He does drop in occasionally. But O'Malley has delegated the conduct of the meetings—and thus the coordination of his agenda within and across city agencies— to Michael Enright, his first deputy mayor, and CitiStat Director Gallagher. Nevertheless, CitiStat works fine under this arrangement. Why? Because Enright and Gallagher speak for the Mayor. (O'Malley and Enright have been friends since their freshman year at Gonzaga High School in Washington, D.C.) No agency head will seriously consider anything more than a polite appeal to the mayor about an operational failure that was exposed at a CitiStat session, or about an operational improvement for which Enright and Gallagher were pressing. He or she would, of course, want to take a major policy decision to the mayor. But an end-run around Enright and Gallagher would be unthinkable and ruinous.[5]

CitiStat sessions are conducted primarily by Enright, or when a pressing political issue forces him to miss a meeting, by Gallagher. And during these sessions, there is no doubt that Enright or Gallagher speak for the mayor. If O'Malley didn't care about CitiStat, his first deputy mayor would not be spending more than six hours every week conducting these meetings.

After all, for any public official, time is a most valuable resource. It can't be wasted on issues, problems, or tasks that are not high priority. Moreover, how these officials *spend their time* sends signals to the rest of the organization. In any organization, people have a very simple way to gauge what is important: They watch how the top officials spend their time. This is how they learn what top leadership thinks is important. The people in the organization may listen to the speeches; they may read the memos. But they will not pay any attention unless these verbal and written messages correlate with how these officials actually *spend their time.* People who work for the city of Baltimore understand that O'Malley cares about CitiStat not because he talks about it but because his chief deputy spends so much time on it—and because their own agency director (and twenty or thirty managers in their agency) also have to spend so much time on it.

CitiStat *requires* the ceaseless, active engagement of the top officials in the city. If these officials do not spend their most valuable resource—their time—in regular, frequent time-consuming meetings, CitiStat will be nothing more than a hollow charade attended by the assistants to the assistants of the assistants.

"Now," disaggregated data and analysis

A century and a half ago, David McCallum, superintendent of the New York and Erie Railroad, wrote in his annual report that "a system of operations, to be efficient and successful, should be such as to give to the principal and responsible head of the running department a complete daily history of details in all their minutia." To run his railroad, McCallum wanted "the means of knowing whether such responsibilities [of subordinates] are faithfully executed" with "such information to be obtained through a system of daily reports and checks" that "will not only enable the General Superintendent to detect errors immediately, but will also point out the delinquent" (1856, 1987, 47).

Baltimore is a city. The mayor of Baltimore has operational responsibility for a large number of nitty-gritty, service-delivery chores: fixing potholes, plowing snow, clearing downed trees, delivering clean water, putting out fires, organizing basketball leagues. Each of these activities can be counted, each of these activities can be measured, and thus each of these activities generates data. Through its daily operations, Baltimore generates lots of data.

Baltimore has the data provided by standard management systems—the data-producing systems that existed when O'Malley took office. Typically, these data were collected for reasons of financial accounting or personnel record-keeping. Some might be put in an annual report. None, however, were being used to think about how to improve performance. But these data did exist. In addition, O'Malley's administration has since created new forms of data. It now has the data generated by the 311 telephone number that citizens call—3,000 to 4,000 times per day—to request that city government fill a pothole or clean up a fallen tree. It has the data compiled by its CitiTrak computer system that follows the status of the city's response to these "service requests" or "SRs."[6] And it has the data that it explicitly collects as it identifies and probes possible performance shortcomings.

These are not, however, highly aggregated data that were compiled after the fiscal year was over and later bound into a thick report required by the city charter. These are not data for the last quarter that must be submitted to the city council sometime before the end of the next quarter. These are the very latest data about what has happened during the last two weeks; call them "now data." Moreover, these are very disaggregated data about what has happened in different parts of the city—about who did what and when. Business executives don't run their organizations using annual data; to know what is working and what isn't, to learn what changes have had what impact, and to ensure that at the end of the year they will have made a profit, business executives need the latest, disaggregated data. To improve performance, public agencies need the same thing. They cannot work with highly aggregated, end-of-the-year data. If they are to make adjustments that will have a real impact on the performance of their operational responsibilities—if they are to respond to a new February crop of potholes along an arterial corridor, or to the failure to plow the secondary streets on the West Side during a late April snow storm, or to a growing waiting list for basketball court times—they need very disaggregated, very *now* data.

Such data—no matter how recent and no matter how disaggregated—do not, however, speak for themselves. Data never do. They speak only through some lens—through some analytical framework that suggests what is important and what is not. Only such an analytical framework can convert data into information. It is the job of the CitiStat analysts and the CitiStat leaders to provide that framework. CitiStat not only requires disaggregated, now data; it also requires the *analysis* of these data.

The CitiStat analysts do this in a formal way. These young analysts—originally just in the mayor's CitiStat office, but now also individuals hired by city agencies—examine the data with a variety of simple but powerful analytical tools, seeking to identify new patterns and problems, and new perspectives on old patterns and problems. This is not high-theory policy work; it is basic operational analysis: Are pothole SRs being completed within the guaranteed time? Why is it taking longer to complete SRs on the West Side than on the East Side? Why did we have a spike in uncompleted SRs during the last two-week reporting period? What is being done to rectify this lapse in service? What could be done to rectify it more quickly? What operational change might prevent a similar lapse from occurring in the future?

Before every CitiStat session, the CitiStat analyst responsible for that agency prepares a memo of ten to twenty pages, outlining a series of issues to be discussed. The memo is delivered to Enright and Gallagher the day before the session—sometimes before 5:00, sometimes later in the evening. This memo examines the data from the last two-week reporting period suggesting areas of concern or progress, recalls the issues raised and commitments made during the previous session (which the analyst had summarized in a memo to the agency head hours after that previous meeting), and notes a recent, singular failing (or three) that requires immediate attention or that may suggest a more fundamental, underlying operational weakness.

For Compstat, the elemental data are crimes: What crimes were committed? Where? When? What have we done about them? What patterns can we detect? What strategies should we adopt in the future in response to these patterns? For CitiStat, the elemental data are service requests:

What service requests were received? Where? When? What have we done about them? What patterns can we detect? What new strategies should we adopt in response to these patterns? For Compstat, some crimes—particularly violent crimes—are more important than others. Similarly, for CitiStat, some service requests—categorized as "priority service requests"—are more important than others. For example, the Bureau of Water and Wastewater has nine priority SRs (see Table 1).

Thus, data for priority SRs receive more attention. The analysts focus on these data as they seek to identify trends, patterns, and responses. And so do agency managers. For they both know that citizens evaluate their mayor and their agency based on how well they do the nitty-gritty chores, particularly the *important*, nitty-gritty chores.[7]

Persistent questioning, feedback, and follow-up

Compstat emphasized "relentless follow-up," and so does the CitiStat Web site. Nevertheless, at the many CitiStat sessions I have witnessed, the questioning, feedback and follow-up are more "persistent" than "relentless." Enright and Gallagher are no pushovers,

Table 1. Priority service requests for the Bureau of Water and Wastewater, August 28, 2004 to September 10, 2004.

Priority Service Request	Resolution-Time (in days)		Percent of Requests Completed by the Target (%)
	Target	Average	
Sewer Overflow	1	0.2	100.0
Sewer Water in Basement	1	0.3	97.1
Rip Rap*	7	3.0	94.3
Storm Inlet Choke	10	17.5	15.6
Discolored Water	7	2.2	99.2
Exterior Water Leak	4	0.7	98.6
Low Water Pressure	14	3.8	100.0
No Water	1	0.4	89.6
Water in Basement	2	0.9	91.8

* "Rip Rap" is the debris left at the end of a construction project.
Source: Bureau of Water and Wastewater, Memorandum dated September 22, 2004, "DPW: Bureau of Water and Wastewater Executive Briefing," p. 12.

but they are hardly "merciless" or "implacable."[8] They do not beat up on agency directors. Despite the popular characterizations of CitiStat, those who conduct these sessions are not abrasive or abusive in their questioning.[9]

Enright and Gallagher are persistent but practical. They do listen to reason. If an agency director can make a coherent and persuasive case that he or she needs something to improve performance to the next level prescribed by the mayor's agenda (be that resources, cooperation, or time), Enright is quite willing to grant the request. Dr. Peter Beilenson, who served as commissioner of health for the first five years of O'Malley's administration, was known among his colleagues for his ability to use the CitiStat process to obtain additional resources or flexibility. Indeed, he did so quite consciously.

Still, there should be little doubt that Enright and Gallagher are persistent, persistent, persistent—though the level of their perseverance may not be obvious to those visiting CitiStat for a day and watching a session or two. This persistence implements the commitment of O'Malley, Enright, and Gallagher to CitiStat. If they were not persistent—persistent in their questioning, persistent in their feedback, and persistent in their follow-up—CitiStat staff, agency directors, and agency personnel would not take the process seriously.

Moreover, this persistence is what solves the intractable problems and impels the city's agencies to improve performance. CitiStat sessions ignore the easy problems. If a problem were easy to solve, the agency would have solved it by itself. CitiStat sessions ignore performance improvements that can be easily implemented. If an improvement was easy to implement, the agency would have done so itself. Thus, almost by definition, the agenda of any CitiStat session is dominated by problems and performance challenges that require persistence.

Consequences for performance

In *A Comparative Analysis of Complex Organizations,* Amitai Etzioni (1961) argued that organizations with different kinds of goals require different strategies for obtaining compliance. Organizations that seek to maintain order can best obtain compliance through coercion. Organizations whose goals are economic will find a utilitarian strategy based on "remunerative sanctions and rewards" to be more effective. "Organizations that serve culture goals have to rely on normative powers because the realization of their goals requires positive and intense commitments of lower participants to the organization" (Ibid., 80, 82).

What is the appropriate strategy for a government jurisdiction, such as a city? What kind of goals does it have, and thus what kind of compliance strategy should it use to achieve such goals? Obviously, a city has order goals; for example, it is responsible for maintaining the order of its finances. To create this financial order, the city employs a coercion strategy that consists of accounting, auditing, and severe punishments for compliance failures. A coercion strategy may be effective for preventing city employees from doing bad things; but will it work to get them to do good things? And the city's economic and normative goals do require its employees to do more than refrain from bad behavior; to achieve either of these kind of goals, city employees must actually accomplish something positive. And a city does have economic goals; after all, it exists to provide a variety of very material services for its citizens. To achieve such goals, "remunerative sanctions and rewards" would appear to be more effective. Unfortunately, given the politics of governmental budgets and the constraints of civil-service regulations and union contracts, city executives are limited in the use of a utilitarian strategy. Moreover, a city also provides many of its economic services with a very cultural purpose. Consequently, to the extent that the managers of a city or a city agency are limited in their use of utilitarian rewards, they may choose to emphasize their cultural purposes and to rely on normative rewards.

If there are no consequences, either utilitarian or normative, for improved or unimproved performance, CitiStat will accomplish little. And, indeed, some agency managers in Baltimore were relieved of their responsibilities (a very utilitarian consequence) because of the lack of performance improvement in their agencies.

Still, CitiStat won't work if the only consequence is the firing of a few conspicuously and indisputably inadequate agency directors. That isn't enough. CitiStat needs to create consequences for everyone involved—not merely for a few, obviously non-performing managers.

The most obvious consequence—for both the directors and other top managers of city agencies—is the need to answer questions at the next CitiStat meeting. Even if the questioning is merely persistent, not relentless, it is still questioning. And these questions require answers—public answers, sensible answers, defensible answers. These questions require answers about your and your organization's performance, answers about problems with which you were familiar when you walked into the room, and answers about problems that you didn't know existed. For even the most poised and self-assured public official, these questions can be intimidating. For some, just anticipating these questions can be unnerving, inflicting torturous, sleepless nights.

To create such consequences, CitiStat simply needs officials who can ask authoritative questions—questions backed by data and analysis, questions based on the discussion in previous CitiStat sessions, questions driven by the mayor's agenda. By simply asking probing questions about the details of the agency's performance, O'Malley, Enright, and Gallagher are imposing consequences. CitiStat's biweekly requirement that its agency heads face persistent questioning, itself, creates normative consequences.

Moreover, these consequences are not just for the agency director. Every agency official who comes to the CitiStat meeting can be questioned. Most are not. Their director has brought them to these sessions so that they will understand exactly what the mayor wants and exactly why the agency needs to make specific performance improvements. Some, however, know that they too will be asked questions; they know what issues were discussed at the last meeting, know that they have some operational responsibilities and information for one or more of these issues, and know that Enright, Gallagher, or their agency director will call on them to provide a detailed answer. Others recognize that, if some issue for which they share responsibility comes up, they can be immediately called upon to provide a few key facts or a detailed explanation. And although the agency director may not lose too much sleep over tomorrow's CitiStat session (after all, that is one of the personal characteristics that lead to this individual being offered and actually accepting the position), others may be more worried about the persistent questions, even if they have never been called to answer the simplest one.

There can be, of course, some positive consequences as well. The mayor's office has season tickets to both the Baltimore Orioles and the Baltimore Ravens, and it awards these tickets to individuals and teams that have accomplished something significant. And, although the city has a limited number of tickets that it can distribute, it has no constraint on the amount of praise it can offer—either with a simple "thank you" or "well done" during a CitiStat session, or with the Jack Maple Awards that it gives to agencies that have made significant performance improvements.

Problem solving, continuous experimentation, and learning

In *The Bureaucratic Phenomenon,* Michel Crozier defines a bureaucracy as "an organization which cannot correct its behavior by learning from its errors" (1964, 187). If that is the case—or if it is only partially the case; if a bureaucracy can, but has a hard time, correcting its behavior by learning from its errors—one of the challenges of those who lead and manage such bureaucracies is to devise mechanisms by which they can identify errors, learn from these errors, and make corrections in their behavior.

At the most obvious level, CitiStat is a confrontational, accountability-holding process. After all, there is the podium at which the agency director is obliged to stand. There are the questions from the mayor, first deputy mayor, and others in the mayor's office. There is the explicit expectation that the agency director is responsible for answering these questions—for solving the service-delivery and service-request problems that these questions probe. The room and the process are designed to create an accountability hierarchy with the mayor and his immediate staff as the "accountability holders" and the agency director and other top managers as the "accountability holdees" (Behn 2001).

In fact, however, the CitiStat process is less hierarchical, more collegial than the conspicuous layout of the room or the obvious direction of the questioning might suggest. Indeed, to improve the performance of city agencies, CitiStat would have to be so. The mayor's office doesn't have sole responsibility for identifying the problems. The agencies don't have the sole responsibility for fixing the problems. They have a mutual, collective responsibility to do both.[10]

Sometimes the questions from the mayor's executive team are of the form: "Have you thought about X?" "Have you tried Y?" "What do you think would happen if you did Z?" Sometimes the responses from the agency are of the form: "If we got A, we think we could do B." "We are trying C, but it will take a while to see if it will work." "We've figured out that D won't work, so we're about to try E."

If the solution to every service-delivery deficiency were obvious, these problems would be simple—and thus would not warrant discussion at a CitiStat session. The problems that deserve attention at CitiStat are those for which the correct response is not obvious. Consequently, although there is a clear organizational and political hierarchy in the room, the higher levels in this hierarchy do not possess all the wisdom or have all the answers. The mayor's executive team is, in fact, dependent upon their key agency managers not only for energetic implementation of the mayor's priorities but also for their ideas and suggestions about how best to go about that implementation.

To the one-time visitor or casual observer, CitiStat can, indeed, appear to be adversarial and confrontational. But if it is to be successful, a CitiStat strategy has to foster a spirit of problem solving, continuous experimentation, and learning.

Institutional memory

CitiStat can't depend upon numerical data and quantitative analysis alone. It also depends upon human memory. Sure, the quantitative data provide some of the memory—for these data are cumulative and thus can provide not only the most current snapshot of an agency's performance over the last two weeks but also a long-term picture of changes in performance over the last two years or more. But these data don't provide a record of CitiStat discussions over the last two months or last two years. These data don't capture the questions asked let alone the answers, explanations, or excuses that have periodically been offered. If the first deputy mayor, the director of CitiStat, and the CitiStat analyst are not consistent participants in the biweekly meetings, if they don't remember the problems that they probed, the questions that they asked, the justifications that were offered, and the promises that were made weeks, months, or years ago, they won't be able to recognize when an agency is making progress. They won't be able to determine what kind of tactical modifications or strategic transformations might help.

Thus CitiStat's leaders are constantly engaged in an analysis of data but in a less technical but nevertheless powerful way. Their primary analytical tool is their own memory. They remember what was said at the same CitiStat meeting two weeks, or two months, ago. They remember what was said at a different CitiStat meeting yesterday. And they remember what was said at a City Council session, or during a meeting with a stakeholder organization, or by a civic leader. At a CitiStat meeting, the mayor's executive team is not just relying on the briefing papers provided by their staff. They are not automatons being silently manipulated by the analytical wizards behind the screen. Instead, they are combining the analytical data provided by the staff with the anecdotal data that they are continually absorbing to probe for both the underlying nature of particular problems and for possible strategies for attacking these problems.[11]

Talented people

CitiStat isn't a computer. It isn't technology. It isn't a system. A mayor or other public official can't just create something that looks like CitiStat—build a room, buy some technology, hire a few analysts—press the start button, walk away, and expect this new gizmo will automatically produce a steady stream of performance improvements. That won't happen. Yet, if you watch a CitiStat session or two, you may easily come away with the impression: "Hey, anyone can do this."

CitiStat requires talented people. It requires talented people to set it up. It requires talented people to run it—and not just every other week when it is time for the meeting, but every single one of the thirteen days in between. In particular, to make CitiStat work in a city, county, State, or other jurisdiction, the top political executive requires three types of talented people:

Talented leaders

Someone or some team has to run a CitiStat-type performance strategy. In Baltimore's case, this is done by the team of Enright and Gallagher, who actively share the responsibility for leading the discussion at CitiStat sessions.

They also split other responsibilities. Gallagher manages the day-to-day operation of the CitiStat staff, a task in which Enright is hardly engaged. But Enright is closer to the mayor, to his political and policy strategy, and to his current thinking. One individual might be able to take on both responsibilities, but managing the CitiStat staff is itself a significant and time-consuming undertaking. It would be difficult to manage the CitiStat staff and simultaneously keep up on the political activities, stakeholder interactions, and policy thinking of the elected chief executive.

Talented analysts

To prepare for each biweekly CitiStat meeting, someone has to prepare a detailed analysis of immediate concerns about unfulfilled service requests as well as of long-term strategic progress. To do this work, CitiStat has relied on a staff of half-a-dozen young, committed, energetic, hard-working analysts. Occasionally during a CitiStat session, Enright or Gallagher will call on an analyst for clarifying information, and more senior analysts may need no prompting to join in the questioning. Nevertheless, these analysts perform mostly behind the scenes, although everyone involved knows who has responsibility for which agencies.

Talented agency managers

Finally, CitiStat won't work without public managers who grasp the strategic concept and managerial value of CitiStat, who understand how to lead and motivate public employees, and who can learn how to use CitiStat not only to keep City Hall happy but also to ratchet up their own agency's performance. In the New York City Police Department, many precinct commanders were unable to do this; they retired or were replaced. In Baltimore, a few agency directors could not do this either—with similar consequences. Indeed, two of O'Malley's agency directors—Kimberly Flowers, director of the Department of Recreation and Parks, and Jay Sakai, head of the Bureau of Water and Wastewater—were members of the CitiStat staff before the mayor promoted them to these positions. And, as they moved from staff analyst to agency manager, they drew on their understanding of the purpose behind CitiStat, their appreciation of its managerial and motivational philosophy, and their insider knowledge of what made the mayor and city hall tick. If Gallagher, Enright, and O'Malley had not concluded that these individuals were capable of implementing CitiStat within an agency, they would have never offered them the job. And if Flowers and Sakai had viewed CitiStat as merely a biweekly irritant, they would not have taken the job.[12]

You can't just measure things and expect miraculous improvement. Yes, the industrial psychologist Maison Haire said, "What gets measured gets done" (Peters and Waterman 1982, 268). Yes, Mayor O'Malley frequently says, "What gets watched gets done." But no matter bow much something is measured and no matter how much something is watched, if people don't know *how* to get it done, it won't get done. CitiStat requires talented people, with the required talent being the ability to get things done within the complicated environment of a government agency.[13]

The functions of CitiStat

In Baltimore, CitiStat is not some add-on to municipal government. It is not merely a set of performance measures published in an annual report. It is not a performance-budgeting attachment to the city's regular budgetary process. It is not another nice requirement imposed by the city council or state legislature with which every city agency formally yet grudgingly complies in a way that completely satisfies all of the prescribed guidelines and yet is completely irrelevant to the agency's operations. It is not a fad that could disappear tomorrow without anyone in city government noting or caring. In Baltimore, CitiStat is the vehicle that Mayor O'Malley and his top people use to run the city.

In his classic, *The Functions of the Executive*, Barnard (1938) conceives of organizations as "associations of cooperative efforts" where this cooperation is "conscious, deliberate, purposeful." Thus, he writes, "An organization comes into being when (1) there are persons able to communicate with each other (2) who are willing to contribute action (3) to accomplish a common purpose." From this three-part definition of the "elements" of an organization, Barnard concluded that any such organization (public or private) required three "essential executive functions":

(1) "to provide the system of communication";

(2) "to promote the security of essential efforts"; and

(3) "to formulate and define purpose" (Ibid., 4, 82, 217).

That is, to Barnard, the job of the executive is to establish the organization's purpose and to communicate it, using both incentives and persuasion, so as to convince individuals to make an effort to achieve that purpose.[14]

A comparison of the six core drivers of CitiStat with Barnard's three functions reveals that each core driver performs one or more of Barnard's three tasks. Indeed, most of the six core drivers contribute in some way to all three of Barnard's functions. Thus, each of CitiStat's core drivers helps to produce the cooperative efforts required to achieve the purposes of Baltimore's city government.

Is CitiStat a dominantly better way to carry out Barnard's three executive functions? Not necessarily. It is, however, one very good way.

Creating a performance culture

CitiStat, argues O'Malley, "moves us from spoils-based patronage politics to results-based performance politics." But is this change in the external politics (assuming that this change is, indeed, occurring) accompanied by a change in the internal behavior of city agencies and city employees? Are Baltimore's city agencies moving from rules-based, bureaucratically-constrained passivity to results-based, performance-driven action? That is, has CitiStat changed the implicit organizational culture of the various agencies of city government?

Schein defines organizational "culture" as "a pattern of shared basic assumptions that the group learned as it solved its problems of external adaptation and internal integration, that has worked well enough to be considered valid and, therefore, to be taught to new members as the correct way to perceive, think, and feel in relation to those problems" (1992, 12). Certainly within many governments, people solve the individual and collective problem of staying out of trouble by learning to follow to the letter all of the bureaucratic rules. And since, within most governments, there is little opportunity to earn meaningful rewards for positive contributions, but multiple opportunities to incur serious penalties for some major (or even minor) error, the problem that many individuals and groups believe to be one of their most significant is how to stay out of trouble. (As a public manager in an entirely different jurisdiction once allowed: "I guess if I keep my name out of the newspaper, I'm doing a good job" [Behn 1994, 3]). Thus, a challenge that the leaders of any governmental jurisdiction or public agency face as they seek to improve performance is how do they "unfreeze" the old rule-based culture, "change" it to a new performance-based culture, and then "freeze" this new culture in place (Lewin 1947, 1951).

Siehl and Martin (1984) suggest that an organization's culture contains three components: (1) the "content" or "core values of the organization," including its "basic philosophy or mission"; (2) the "forms" consisting of the "oftentimes indirect, implicit, and subtle means of value transmission," including particularly "organizational stories and scripts" and its "rituals and ceremonies"; and (3) the "strategies that managers can use as a means of reinforcing the content or underlying values of the culture" (Ibid., 228). From this perspective, a strategy for unfreezing a rule-based culture would destroy (somehow) the old core value that focuses people and organizations on staying out of trouble by, perhaps, undermining the validity and utility of the old stories (examples of how people got into trouble only when they didn't follow the rules and how they stayed out of trouble when they did) and the rituals that reenforced them. Then, the freezing step needs new stories and new rituals that reenforce the new performance culture.

Those who seek to implement a performance strategy in any government jurisdiction or public agency certainly need to disrupt the belief that the only consequences that individuals or groups can provoke are the penalties for not following the rules. They also need to create positive consequences for excellent performance and negative ones for failing to perform (perhaps consequences that are more negative than those imposed for failing to follow the rules). They need to tell and repeat the stories about their use of these consequences. Finally, they need to create the rituals that reenforce these consequences.

The obvious ritual of CitiStat is the biweekly meeting. It is here that the mayor and his executive team seek to establish that performance is one of their top values—that performance should be a top value of every agency head, every deputy, and every frontline worker. It is here that they seek to unfreeze the old, rule-based culture by creating new, positive consequences for improving performance that are at least (if not more) significant than the traditional, negative consequences for failing to obey one of the rules and by creating new, negative consequences for failing to achieve performance objectives. It is here that they seek to convey their new performance-based culture and to freeze it into the shared assumptions under which every city agency operates. It is here that they create and tell their stories about people and organizations who improved performance—as well as the stories about those who failed to live up to expectations. Certainly, the CitiStat strategy employed in Baltimore would appear to contain the three components suggested by Siehl and Martin.

Schein offers a similar perspective on the challenge of unfreezing an organization's culture—or what he calls "creating a motivation to change"—that requires three different catalysts:

> (1) enough *discomforting data* to cause serious discomfort and disequilibrium; (2) the connection of the discomforting data to important goals and ideas causing *anxiety and/or guilt;* (3) enough *psychological safety,* in the sense of seeing a possibility of solving the problem without loss of identity or integrity, thereby allowing members of the organization to admit the discomforting data rather than defensively denying it (1992, 298–299).

Further, for leaders of "mature organizations," Schein offers three specific strategies for promoting this change: (1) the "systematic promotion" of an existing organizational subculture; (2) "organizational development" ("defined as a planned change process") or the "creation of parallel learning systems"; and (3) "technological seduction" (Ibid., 313–321).

In many ways, Baltimore's CitiStat would also appear to employ, if only implicitly, Schein's insights. Certainly, the bi-weekly CitiStat meetings repeatedly confront city agencies with "discomforting data" about the inadequacy of their performance and connect that inadequacy to the mayor's goals in a way that is consciously designed to cause both anxiety and guilt. At the same time, these meetings create the sense that these performance problems can be solved and that the mayor's office is prepared to help. Moreover, once an agency has created a subculture that focuses on performance rather than rules, the mayor's executive team is quick to promote its success. And although Jack Maple would hardly be accepted by the organization-development profession as a qualified OD consultant, he certainly did help the mayor's office design a change process with the CitiStat meeting as an alternative way for agency managers to experiment with and learn new performance strategies. Finally, 311, CitiTrak, and the computerized presentations in the CitiStat room are all seductive, new technologies that both permit an analytical focus on performance and create the discomforting data that demand change.

Will CitiStat last?

Still, even if CitiStat has unfrozen the traditional, rules-based organizational culture of Baltimore's agencies, has the mayor's office managed to replace it with a new, refrozen performance-focused culture? Schein suggests that the creation of a new culture (at least through organizational development and new learning systems) requires "anywhere from five to fifteen or more years if basic assumptions are really to be changed without destroying and rebuilding the organization" (Ibid., 317). Yet no big-city mayor has the opportunity to destroy and rebuild his city agencies; they provide essential services and have to keep continuously functioning. Nor does a mayor, who seeks to change the culture of city government, have the luxury of undertaking a process that will take five or fifteen years to produce results.

Thus although O'Malley and his executive team may be able within just a few years to foster a new performance culture among the top managers of every city agency, it is not obvious what will happen when the mayor, his staff, and his key managers all leave office. For unless the new performance culture has been adopted by the city's permanent civil service or unless the next mayor decides to continue CitiStat—complete with biweekly meetings and constant pressure to improve performance—the old rule-based bureaucratically constrained culture can easily reemerge.

Nevertheless, there are two pressures that may prevent the next mayor from dismissing CitiStat as just O'Malley's fad. These two pressures—one political, one technological— may force a real (not just nominal) continuation of some kind of aggressive performance strategy even if it is no longer formally called "CitiStat."

First, O'Malley has built political support within the city's business community for many of his programmatic and management initiatives, including CitiStat. After he was elected mayor in 1999, but even before he was inaugurated, O'Malley asked the Greater Baltimore Committee (the biggest business organization in the city) and the Presidents' Roundtable (a group of African-American business leaders) to create a combined task force to make suggestions on how to improve the work of city agencies. The report recommended that the city "establish accountability as a priority by setting quantifiable goals and regularly measuring performance" and that it "create an Office of Management Initiatives" (Greater Baltimore Committee and the Presidents' Roundtable 2000). By July 2000, when the two business organizations issued their report, *Managing for Success,* the Mayor had already moved to create CitiStat. O'Malley's willingness to solicit and act on the business community's recommendations established a working relationship.[15]

"The business community gets it," says O'Malley. If the leaders of the business community do, indeed, "get it"—if they continue the active interest in the management of city government that they demonstrated in *Managing for Success*—they are unlikely to want the next mayor to abandon CitiStat.

Second, the technology that creates the Service Requests that provide much of CitiStat's data—311 plus CitiTrak—will not go away. And given CitiStat's public emphasis on the timely response to citizen Service Requests, the next mayor will be hard pressed to ignore them. O'Malley has established a "48-hour pothole guarantee." (Within 48 hours of when it receives a citizen's SR about a pothole, the city will fill it.) What will the next mayor do? Create a 72-hour pothole guarantee? Simply forget about filling potholes?

What if an enterprising reporter bounces over a pothole three days in a row? What if this reporter calls in an SR for the pothole? What if this reporter then drives around looking for other potholes and calls in an SR for each? And what if these potholes aren't filled for 48 or even 72 hours? The subsequent story will get the attention of lots of citizens, the business community, and the mayor too.

CitiStat isn't the only management mechanism that a mayor can use to ensure that a city responds to citizen requests to fill potholes in a timely fashion. But it is one such mechanism. Thus, regardless of whatever official name the next mayor gives his or her management strategy, it is likely to employ the core drivers of CitiStat.

Acknowledgments

My thanks to all those in Baltimore who have permitted me to observe their meetings and who have "spent time" explaining to me what they are doing and why. My thanks also to colleagues Alan Altshuler, Randy Aussenberg, Eugene Bardach, Phineas Baxandall, John D. Donahue, Leif Dormsjo, Steven Kelman, David Luberoff, John Pierce, Michael Powell, Jeffrey Tryens, and Julie Boatright Wilson, plus (of course) the two anonymous referees, each of whom read earlier versions of this paper and "spent time" providing comments to help keep me from making yet another foolish mistake.

Endnotes

1. This article is based on information collected from attending five presentations on CitiStat by Baltimore officials at the Kennedy School and from five visits to Baltimore during which I observed ten CitiStat sessions as well as eight "AgencyStat" sessions and interviewed a dozen city officials (some several times). The details of the data-collection process can be found at http://www.ksg.harvard.edu/TheBehnReport/CitiStatDataCollection.

2. Bratton, Maple, and the New York Police Department did not invent the analytical approach of putting dots on a map. Over 200 years ago, Dr. Valentine Seaman used this approach during the yellow fever epidemic in 1798. He even did this in New York City (Stevenson 1965).

3. For more CitiStat maps of Baltimore, go to: http://www.ci.baltimore.md.us/news/ citistat/reports.html.

4. Chandler was writing exclusively about the private sector. "Modern business enterprise is easily defined," he wrote; "it has two specific characteristics: it contains many distinct operating units and it is managed by a hierarchy of salaried executives" (1977, 1). Still, Chandler's definition, does not distinguish in any way among large organizations in the for-profit, nonprofit, and governmental sectors.

5. In the administrations of many elected chief executives, it is much easier for agency heads to fool the elected official than to fool the chief of staff, first deputy, or whomever is the top assistant who is closest to the elected official. A mayor, elected county executive, governor, or president has a variety of political and ceremonial responsibilities that limit the time that he or she can devote to operations. Thus, elected chief executives usually delegate most day-to-day operational duties to a chief of staff or other top deputy. If such a deputy understands the elected chief executive's priorities, has earned the elected executive's full confidence, and speaks with him or her frequently, this deputy speaks *for* him or her as well. In Baltimore, Enright is such a deputy.

6. Whenever a citizen calls 311 to complain about a pothole or a downed tree, that service request (SR) is entered into the CitiTrak database and assigned an SR number. Baltimore has a different template in its CitiTrak system for each of its over 300 different categories of service requests, and each such SR category is assigned to a particular agency. (An SR to fill a pothole goes to the city's Transportation Department; an SR to clear a downed tree goes to the Department of Recreation and Parks.) And when the department has completed the SR (when it has filled the pothole or cleared the downed tree), it enters that accomplishment into the CitiTrak database.

   Thus, this database provides a plethora of data. CitiStat analysts can use such data to answer simple questions, such as how well is the city doing in fulfilling its priority service requests on time. Or they can use these data to explore trends in both service requests and in the city's response to them. And, because each SR has a number, and because the citizen is given that number when he or she first makes the request, citizens can use the CitiTrak system to check on the status of their individual requests.

7. Yes, if you run for the city council in Cambridge, Massachusetts; Berkeley, California; or Tacoma Park, Maryland, the voters want to know your foreign policy. But in Baltimore, they want to know if you can get the potholes fixed.

8. The *Dictionary of Synonyms* lists four synonyms for "relentless"—"unrelenting, merciless, implacable, grim"—and reports that relentless and unrelenting "both imply an absence of pity or of any feeling that would cause one to relent and to restrain through compassion the fury or violence of one's rage, hatred, hostility, or vengeance." That hardly describes what happens at a CitiStat session; there is no rage, hatred, hostility, or vengeance. In contrast, this dictionary's one synonym for the verb to "persist" (the adjective "persistent" is not listed) is to "persevere." "Persevere nearly always implies an admirable quality," while persist "may imply a virtue . . . but it more often suggests a disagreeable or annoying quality, for it stresses stubbornness or obstinacy more than courage or patience and frequently implies opposition to advice, remonstrance, disapproval or one's own conscience" (Gove 1968, 676, 383, 606). Indeed, to some (or many) agency directors, the questioning, feedback, and follow-up during a CitiStat session can be annoying or even disagreeable. And often Enright and Gallagher may appear stubborn or obstinate in their repeated efforts to improve the city's performance on just one particular category of service requests. Nevertheless, both have repeatedly demonstrated their openness to advice—to new strategies or new resources or new thinking that might be required to reach the next level of performance.

    If the phrase "persevering questioning, feedback, and follow-up" was not so awkward, I would use it.

9. In the early days of Compstat, the questioning could, indeed, be abrasive or abusive. Bratton and Maple were looking to change not just the culture of the New York City Police Department; they also wanted to get rid of the people—particularly the precinct commanders—who embodied and sustained that culture. But they concluded that, given all of the other changes they were making, they could not also directly fire dozens of precinct commanders. But they could help them decide to quit. Some precinct commanders experienced their first Compstat grilling and put in for retirement. Some precinct commanders watched their colleagues experience their Compstat grillings and put in for retirement. In the early days of Compstat, the questioning, feedback, and follow-up was, indeed,

relentless—relentless with a purpose. A decade later, after having filled the precinct commander positions with individuals who understood and could use the Compstat process to manage their own units, the questioning at a Compstat meeting has become (some report) more persistent than relentless.

    I did not observe any of the first three years of CitiStat sessions. So I cannot say whether the original questioning was relentless or persistent. There has been some significant turnover in agency directors in Baltimore, much of it driven by the inability of these managers to accept and employ the CitiStat concept to improve their organizations' performance. Still, O'Malley, Enright, and Gallagher could, through merely "persistent" questioning, easily identify which agency directors they needed to replace.

    A government or a public agency does not need relentless people to make a CitiStat-like process work. But it does need people who are persistent.

10. Indeed, the relationship between the mayor's office and the line agencies is much more of a "compact of mutual, collective responsibility" (Behn 2001, chapter 7) than the hierarchical nature of the room and the questioning would suggest.

11. For explanations of how executives absorb (and use) anecdotal data, see Kotter (1982), Mintzberg (1975), and Peters (1979).

12. One of the secondary benefits of CitiStat is that it helps the mayor and his executive team identify their weak agency managers. If you are meeting with each agency director every other week, and if you are questioning and re-questioning them about very specific aspects of their organization's performance, you are getting much better feedback on who are your good managers and who are your weak ones. You still have to be willing to do something about these weak managers. But you have much better data on who is weak and who isn't.

13. The new public management has come in two forms: (1) the make-the-managers-manage form and (2) the let-the-managers-manage form (Kettl 1997, 447–448). Both forms require, however, that the managers know how to manage. Regardless of whether the managers are (1) required to manage or (2) permitted to manage, they still have to know *how* to manage. That's why I have argued that—in addition to making or letting the managers manage—it is essential to "help" the managers manage. Maybe a mayor, county executive, governor, or president can hire all of the managerial expertise he or she needs. In fact, however, most elected chief executives will find that they cannot simply

hire the army of managerial talent required to run their government. If that is the case, they will have to "help" smart, energetic people also become talented public managers (Behn 2004, 5–6).

14. Barnard argues that "organization, simple or complex, is always *an impersonal system of coordinated human efforts*" (1938, 94, italics in the original). Impersonal? Why impersonal? Because if the system has to be personal, it may be impossible to create or sustain. **Still,** the personal coordination of human efforts is (in most circumstances) more effective than the impersonal coordination. And CitiStat is an effort to make the coordination personal by bringing into contact with the mayor's executive team not just the agency heads and their immediate deputies but two dozen or more members of their own organization.

Thus, for the task of reformulating and defining the purpose of the agency (within, of course, the boundaries of the mayor's macro thinking about his purpose for the city), CitiStat permits the engagement and contribution of many more individuals who are making an effort to achieve that purpose. Further, CitiStat communicates, directly to many more individuals, both the mayor's macro purposes and the operational purposes that he and his leadership team have defined for the agency. Finally, CitiStat provides a direct, personal mechanism for the city's leadership team to use incentives and persuasion to obtain the cooperative efforts of many more city employees.

15. It didn't hurt that in August 2000, O'Malley hired Matthew Gallagher, who had been working at the Greater Baltimore Committee as director of this Managing for Success project, to be CitiStat's director of operations.

References

Allis, Sam. 2002. "Baltimore tutorials," *Boston Sunday Globe,* September 29, A2.

Barnard, Chester I. 1938. *The Functions of the Executive.* Cambridge, MA: Harvard University Press.

Behn, Robert D. 1994. *Bottom-Line Government.* Durham, N.C.: The Governors Center at Duke University.

Behn, Robert D. 2001. *Rethinking Democratic Accountability.* Washington, D.C.: Brookings Institution Press.

Behn, Robert D. 2004. *Performance Leadership: 11 Better Practices That Can Ratchet Up Performance.* Washington, D.C.: The IBM Center for the Business of Government.

Branch-Brioso, Karen. 2001. "Slay Hopes Baltimore Model Will Boost City Efficiency." *St. Louis Post Dispatch.* July 1.

Bratton, William and Knobler. 1998. *Turnaround: How America's Top Cop Reversed the Crime Epidemic.* New York: Random House.

Chandler, Alfred D., Jr. 1977. *The Visible Hand: The Managerial Revolution in American Business.* Cambridge, MA: The Belknap Press of Harvard University Press.

Clines, Francis X. 2001. "Baltimore Uses a Databank to Wake Up City Workers. *The New York Times,* June 6.

Cross, Michael. 2004. "Public Domain." *The Guardian* (London), March 4, 17.

Crozier, Michel. 1964. *The Bureaucratic Phenomenon.* Chicago: University of Chicago Press.

DiCarlo, Rachel. 2004. "Irish Times: Baltimore Mayor Martin O'Malley is Speaking at the Convention Tonight. Is he a rising star in Democratic politics?" *The Daily Standard,* July 28, at: http://www.weeklystandard.com/Content/Public/Articles/000/000/004/395vcyct.asp.

Etzioni, Amitai. 1961. *A Comparative Analysis of Complex Organizations.* New York: Free Press.

Giuliani, Rudolph W., and Ken Kurson. 2002. *Leadership.* New York: Hyperion.

Gove, Philip B., ed. 1968. *Webster's New Dictionary of Synonyms.* Springfield, MA: G. & C. Merriam Company.

Greater Baltimore Committee and the Presidents' Roundtable. 2000. *Managing for Success: Report to the Mayor.* Baltimore: Greater Baltimore Committee (July). http://www.gbc.org/Mgmt%20Studies-1/Mgmt%20Studies.htm.

Henderson, Lenneal. 2003. *The Baltimore CitiStat Program: Performance and Accountability.* Washington, DC: IBM Endowment for the Business of Government.

"How To Torture Your Contractors." 2004. *The Times* (March 9): Features; Public Agenda 4.

Kettl, Donald F. 1997 "The Global Revolution in Public Management: Driving Themes, Missing Links." *Journal of Policy Analysis and Management* 16 (Summer): 446–462.

Kotter, John P. 1982. "What Effective Managers Really Do." *Harvard Business Review* 60(6): 156–167.

Lewin, Kurt. 1947. "Group Decision and Social Change." In Theodore M. Newcomb and Eugene L. Hartley, eds., *Readings in Social Psychology.* New York: H. Holt.

Lewin, Kurt (Dorwin Cartwright, ed.), 1951. *Field Theory in Social Science: Selected Theoretical Papers.* New York: Harper.

Maple, Jack, and Chris Mitchell. 1999. *The Crime Fighter.* New York: Doubleday.

McCallum, Daniel C. 1856, 1987. "Superintendent's Report." *Annual Report of the New York and Erie Railroad Company.* New York. Reprinted on pp. 46–47 in Jay M. Shafritz and J. Steven Ott, ads., *Classics of Organization Theory.* Chicago: The Dorsey Press.

Mintzberg, Henry. 1975. "The Manager's Job: Folklore and Fact." *Harvard Business Review* 53(4): 49–61.

Peirce, Neal. 2004. E-mail to "Colleagues" including the author, January 17.

Peters, Thomas J. 1979. "Leadership: Sad Facts and Silver Linings." *Harvard Business Review* 57(6): 164–172.

Peters, Thomas J. and Robert H. Waterman, Jr. 1982. *In Search of Excellence.* New York: Harper & Row.

Scales, Joan. 2004. "Mayor Playing With Fire." *The Irish Times* (Dublin), July 12, 13.

Schein, Edgar H. 1992. *Organizational Culture and Leadership,* 2nd ed. San Francisco: Jossey-Bass.

Shields, Gerard. 2000. "City Figures To Improve Efficiency," *The Baltimore Sun,* November 19, lB.

Siegel, Fred, and Van Smith. 2001. "Can Mayor O'Malley Save Ailing Baltimore?" *City Journal* 11 (1 Winter): 64–75.

Siehl, Caren and Joanne Martin. 1984. "The Role of Symbolic Management: How Can Managers Effectively Transmit Organizational Culture?" Pp. 227–239 in James G. Hunt, D. M. Hosking, C. A. Schriesheim and R. Stewart, eds., *Leaders and Managers: International Perspectives on Managerial Behavior and Leadership.* Elmsford, New York: Pergamon Press.

Silverman, Eli B. 1999. *NYPD Battles Crime: Innovative Strategies in Policing.* Boston: Northeastern University Press.

Stevenson, Lloyd G. 1965. "Putting Disease on the Map: The Early Use of Spot Maps in the Study of Yellow Fever." *Journal of the History of Medicine* 20: 226–261.

Swope, Christopher. 2001. "Restless for Results." *Governing* (April): 20–23.

The Varieties of CitiStat

Robert D. Behn

Baltimore's performance strategy, CitiStat, has been adapted by a number of cities in the United States. None of these adaptations is identical to the original or to any of the others. In fact, this analysis identifies five important features of CitiStat along with 20 sub-traits of these features that can be used to specify the important differences among these various CitiStats.

—Introduction by Robert D. Behn

In 2000, Mayor Martin O'Malley of Baltimore, Maryland, established CitiStat, a management strategy modeled after the Compstat program of the New York City Police Department (NYPD) and designed to improve the performance of city agencies.[1] Since then, numerous cities in the United States have created their own versions of CitiStat. For example, Atlanta, Georgia, has ATLStat; Chattanooga, Tennessee, has Chattanooga Results; Providence, Rhode Island, has ProvStat; St. Louis, Missouri, has CitiView; San Francisco, California, has SFStat; Somerville, Massachusetts, has SomerStat; and Syracuse, New York, has SyraStat. King County, Washington, is creating KingStat, and Palm Bay, Florida, is creating PalmStat.[2]

Each of these replications of CitiStat is an adaptation of Baltimore's innovation.[3] None is a perfect copy; none was designed to be a perfect copy. In each city that has created its own CitiStat, the mayor's leadership team took what they perceived to be the key features of the Baltimore version and modified them to mesh with their own specific purposes and their own particular circumstances. Although these versions of CitiStat have many features in common, no two are identical. Each has its own distinct characteristics. This raises an important question: What are the significant differences among the varieties of CitiStat?

Robert D. Behn, "The Varieties of CitiStat," *Public Administration Review* 66, no. 3 (May/June 2006): 332-340. Copyright © Blackwell Publishing. Used with permission.

Moreover, if none of the cities' versions of CitiStat is identical, what performance strategies can be included in the class of programs called "CitiStat"? What features must an individual city's performance strategy possess for it to be categorized as a CitiStat? In my investigation of cities that have implemented some version of the CitiStat strategy, I employ the following classification: A city is conducting CitiStat if it holds a series of *regular, periodic meetings* during which the mayor and/or the mayor's top aides *use data* to discuss, examine, and analyze, with the individual director (and the top staff) of different city agencies, past *performance,* future *performance* objectives, and overall *performance* strategies.

This is not a very exclusionary classification.[4] It certainly fits almost every management strategy that an American city has designated as its own version of CitiStat. The three important components of my classification are (1) the regular periodicity of the meetings, (2) the use of data, and (3) the examination of past performance combined with the development of strategies for future improvement, if a city is doing these three things, I classify it as engaging in a variety of CitiStat.

Nevertheless, the varieties of CitiStat can be quite different. In particular, from my conversations with city officials who have launched their own CitiStat programs, from my visits to CitiStat meetings in different cities, and from what I have learned from others who have observed or analyzed different versions, at least five distinct features of CitiStat can be used to distinguish the different varieties. These five features concern:

1. The *room* in which the CitiStat meetings are held
2. The *staff* who manage the CitiStat process and analyze the data
3. The *data* that form the basis of the discussion at the meetings
4. The *meetings* themselves
5. The *follow-up* to the decisions and commitments made during these meetings

Most of these five features have subfeatures, so the number of traits that characterize any city's CitiStat process totals 20.[5]

1. The room

Every city that has adopted a version of CitiStat (at least every CitiStat that I have observed[6]) has also constructed a specially equipped room for holding its CitiStat meetings. This is, in fact, the most visible feature of Baltimore's CitiStat.[7] Visitors who seek to understand how CitiStat works so that they can replicate it in their own city spend most of their time in Baltimore's specially designed CitiStat room. This raises the following question.

Question 1: What are the key features of the room?
Although the CitiStat room in each city has a slightly different layout, all have five common features:

- A *table* at which the mayor and his or her key staff sit in permanently assigned seats
- A *podium* at which the director of the agency whose performance is being examined stands
- A *projector* for projecting maps, data, and pictures from a *computer* onto a *screen*

The CitiStat room may be used for other purposes. Thus, the table, podium, projector, computer, and screen may be moved around among CitiStat meetings. For the next CitiStat meeting, however, the room will be arranged in exactly the same way.

The design of the CitiStat room is the least important of the five dimensions of CitiStat. Yet it is also the characteristic that is most faithfully replicated, if only because it is the easiest to observe and reproduce. Every CitiStat room I have visited has not only a *table* at which the mayor and his staff sit but also permanent seat assignments. The mayor sits here, the budget director sits there, and the director of the agency always stands—behind a *podium*. And then the *projector, computer,* and *screen* display maps, data, and pictures for everyone in the room to see.[8] (Indeed, many CitiStat rooms—following the example of Baltimore, which followed the example of the NYPD's Compstat—have two screens so that different data can be projected simultaneously.)

Of course, all of this technology is not essential. Indeed, in some cities, the data are not only projected on the screen but given to everyone in the room at the beginning of the meeting in the form of a handout that contains everything that will be projected onto the screen. Thus, in these cities, the CitiStat staff project onto the screen nothing that is not already in everyone's lap.

The formality of the room is not unimportant. Creating a specific CitiStat room establishes, if only symbolically, that the mayor believes CitiStat is important. Nevertheless, the mayor has a variety of other ways—using the other four features (and the other 19 traits)—to signal that CitiStat is important. Moreover, if these other signals suggest that CitiStat is not all that important, the symbolism of the formal room will have little impact.

2. The staff

To make CitiStat work, a city needs staff. But who are these people and what are their responsibilities? There are at least four different traits of the staff of CitiStat that might differ from city to city.

Question 2A: Is there a full-time director of CitiStat?

This would appear to have an obvious answer. One of the first things that Mayor O'Malley did when he created CitiStat was hire Matthew Gallagher as its full-time director. Yet not all cities have done this. In some, the person with the lead responsibility for making the CitiStat process work is borrowed from an existing agency. This person may have several other responsibilities; indeed, CitiStat may not even be his or her primary job.

Question 2B: How many full-time staff work for CitiStat?

In addition to the director of CitiStat, Baltimore has a half-dozen staffers, mostly analysts but also an investigator. Of course, many of the cities that have started their own CitiStat programs are smaller than Baltimore; thus, their CitiStat staff would be appropriately smaller. Nevertheless, if the CitiStat process is designed (as my definition suggests) to "use data to discuss, examine, and analyze [a city] agency's recent performance," the city needs at least one person to work with these data.[9]

Again, however, in some cities, the CitiStat staff are borrowed from an existing agency. And the people responsible for working with the data may have other responsibilities—perhaps multiple and higher-priority responsibilities.

Question 2C: What is the analytical capacity of this staff?

To improve performance, CitiStat requires not only data but also the analysis of these data. Thus, CitiStat requires some staff with the analytical talent to examine the data—to sift through the reams of available information, to determine what is relevant (why and how), to figure out whether performance is improving or not, to suggest how an improvement in performance might be reflected in changes in the data, and even (if the staff possess managerial as well as analytical skill) offer some strategies for obtaining that improvement.

Some cities have followed Baltimore's practice of hiring staff precisely because they possess these skills. In other circumstances, particularly when staff are borrowed from other agencies, these individuals may have some technical but not necessarily analytical skills. Because CitiStat appears to be a high-tech operation[10]—if only because a computer is used to generate the information projected onto the screen—it also appears natural to assign responsibility for the data to the city's information technology department. Although these individuals may be very good at keeping the city's technology infrastructure humming, they may not have the analytical dexterity to figure out what the data reveal about an agency's performance let alone to determine what these data suggest about strategies to improve future performance.

Question 2D: What do these staff do?

They certainly collect and organize data. They may also analyze the data, though this depends on their analytical skills, how many other assignments they have, and the nature of the CitiStat responsibilities they are given. For example the more explicit the mayor's purposes for establishing CitiStat, the more likely the staff will be to focus their analytical efforts on those purposes. In contrast, if they have other (perhaps higher priority) tasks, they may be able to do little more than collect and organize the data just in time for tomorrow's CitiStat session.

Indeed, the frequency of a city's CitiStat meetings correlates well (theoretically as well as empirically) with the amount of staff time dedicated to CitiStat. If a city has several full-time CitiStat analysts, it also has the ability to conduct CitiStat meetings on a frequent schedule. If, to work on CitiStat, a city is borrowing portions of time from existing staff members with other assignments, it simply lacks the capacity to conduct such sessions for many city agencies or to do so frequently.

In any organization public, nonprofit, or for-profit—people quickly gauge the importance of an activity by noting the number and capabilities of the staff who have responsibility for that activity.[11] The mayor signals the importance of CitiStat not only with the room but with the staff.

3. The data

A performance strategy requires performance data. To improve its performances a city, a state or province, a nation, a public agency a nonprofit organization or a business firm needs some data that describe or illuminate that performance. But what data? There are at least three important traits of the data that are used by different cities.

Question 3A: What kinds of data are used?

Almost every city that has launched a version of CitiStat began with available data. When Baltimore started, it simply told city agencies "Bring us whatever data you have." Thus Baltimore, and other cities, began by using personnel and financial data—data that were already being collected for other administrative purposes. Little wonder that in Baltimore, CitiStat first focused on reducing the cost of personnel overtime.

As a city develops some experience with its CitiStat process—as it develops an understanding of the important performance deficits of specific agencies—it begins to think about what data it would like to collect: What data do we need to determine whether we are improving or not? Because each city has its own unique problems and because each mayor has his or her own unique performance priorities the data a city seeks to collect for its CitiStat performance strategy are also unique.

Today, six years after Baltimore began CitiStat, it relies notably on data obtained from its 311 phone system. In Baltimore (as in Chicago, New York, and other U.S. cities), when a resident has a problem that city government is supposed to solve, the citizen can call a single phone number, 311. For true emergencies, of course, citizens call 911. But for any and all nonemergency services (the classic example is a pothole that needs fixing), a citizen simply calls 311.[12]

At Baltimore's call center, a 311 staffer enters the citizen's problem into one of the templates on the CitiTrak system—gives the citizen a "Service Request" (or "SR") number, and tells the citizen how long it should take to get the problem resolved. Moreover, the data in the CitiTrak computer provide the basis for determining how well an agency is doing. For each service request category, a city department has a "target resolution time," measured in days. And CitiTrak permits the CitiStat staff to determine for each service request category the percentage of requests that were resolved within the target time. All this is because Mayor O'Malley decided that improving the timely response of city agencies to 311 service requests was one of the most important performance improvements that his administration could make.

Other U.S. cities have 311 phone systems. Other cities have versions of CitiStat. Baltimore, however, is the only city (of which I am aware) that uses the 311 data (as organized by CitiTrak) to drive much of its CitiStat process.[13]

Question 3B: What is the source of these data?

Initially, in every city, the CitiStat staff are dependent on city agencies for data. As it makes progress, however, the staff can learn what data they really need. In some circumstances, the staff still need to obtain these data directly from the agencies. But CitiStat staffers may also develop the capacity to collect data on their own. In such circumstances, the CitiStat staff—and thus the mayor—have an independent source of information on the performance of these agencies.

In Baltimore, the service request data from CitiStat provide this independent source of performance information. Is a city agency meeting its resolution-time targets for different service-request categories—particularly for its *priority service* requests? The CitiStat staff and the mayor don't have to worry about whether an agency is somehow using a definition of the start time or of the resolution time that makes their performance look better than it is. The percentage of service requests completed within the target resolution time is calculated from the data within the CitiTrak system.[14]

Question 3C: Who has done what kind of preliminary analysis of these data?

The simplest presentations of any data are bar charts and tables. But what kind of bar chart? What do the bars measure? For what or for whom? And what kind of table? What are the columns? What are the rows? What counts as data to be included? What data can be (or should be) excluded? The creation of a simple bar chart or table involves numerous choices, each of which have a major impact on the message that it conveys—or, at least, on the message that it permits (or encourages) people to infer.

Thus, the analytical skill of the CitiStat staff is reflected in the sophistication of the presentation of data during a CitiStat session. In these circumstances, analytical sophistication does not mean regression analysis—not even simple, two variable, linear regression, let alone a more complex model. The analysis of data consists primarily of bar charts and tables. Nevertheless, to present data in formats that permit city officials to make legitimate comparisons—comparisons across units, comparisons across time, comparisons with established targets—the CitiStat staff need an appreciation of both the legitimate value and the limitations of the data, as well as an understanding of how different presentation formats will affect people's understanding and conclusions.

The NYPD's Compstat and Baltimore's CitiStat were originally conceived as data driven. Both rely on analysis of data—whether it is the geographic analysis of crime data presented on a map or the analysis of the percentage of service requests resolved by the target time presented in a table. The data never speak for themselves. They only speak through some kind of systematic methodological, intellectual, or ideological framework. Any bar chart or table of data establishes a framework, if only through the selection of the data and its form of presentation. The mere creation of a bar chart or table is also the creation of a framework through which the data will speak.

A CitiStat analyst can also create a framework—an analytical framework that reflects the mayor's performance priorities. Thus, the skill of a CitiStat analyst is reflected in the data that are used, the methods for obtaining the data, and the analysis and presentation of those data.

4. The CitiStat meeting

If it is nothing else, CitiStat is a series of regular, periodic meetings. Although the various CitiStat rooms are quite similar and although the meetings may (at first glance) appear to be quite similar, there exist at least seven traits of these meetings that can differ significantly.

Question 4A: How frequent are the meetings?

For its key city agencies Baltimore holds a CitiStat meeting every other week. (For a few others, the meeting is every fourth week.) This is certainly on the very frequent end of the spectrum. In some cities, an agency might only appear at a CitiStat meeting semiannually.

Question 4B: How firm is the schedule of meetings?

Most cities that have created their own CitiStat program have also created a schedule of CitiStat meetings for different departments that extends months into the future. In some of these cities, this schedule is followed religiously; in other cities, scheduled CitiStat meetings are occasionally cancelled or postponed. In Baltimore, the key city agencies are scheduled to show up at CitiStat at *precisely the same time* every other week (e.g., Thursday at 1:00 or Friday at 8:30), and this schedule is *never* modified. Months into the future, everyone knows which agency will be at CitiStat at 1:00 on any Thursday.

Question 4C: Who attends from the mayor's office?

In most situations, the mayor's key staffers attend. In different cities, these people have different titles. Nevertheless, they almost always include the mayor's chief of staff or deputy mayor, the budget director, the personnel director, or the director of a department of administration—the people who run the mayor's key support units.

Question 4D: Who attends from the agency?

In some cities, the agency is represented by only two or three people: the director, the deputy director, and perhaps the agency's internal analyst. In Baltimore, however, most agency directors bring their top two-dozen managers; often, several of these managers are called on to answer specific questions for which they have direct operational responsibility.[15]

In part, the number of people from the agency who attend is a function of the size of the city, and thus the size of the agency. In part, this number is a function of the size of the room. Even with these constraints, the number of attendees does vary. The director of one agency in Baltimore explained that she brought more than two dozen of her agency's top managers to every CitiStat session so that they could learn (from listening to the discussion, even if they were never called on to answer any questions) the issues and problems on which the mayor was focused.[16] And the presence of agency managers who have detailed operational knowledge of different components of the agency's tasks ensures that logical follow-up questions can be answered immediately and accurately (or not, and embarrassingly!).

Question 4E: Who runs the meeting?

In most cities, the mayor does not personally run the meeting. The mayor may attend. The mayor may stop by. The mayor may be there at the beginning of the meeting (indeed, the meeting may not start until the mayor arrives) but then leave for another appointment. Or the mayor may attend sporadically. So who really runs the meeting?

In some cases, it is a top mayoral staffer or the director of CitiStat. This is a person who attends all (or at least most) of the meetings, has an established, ongoing responsibility for the program, and is prepared and able to keep the meeting focused on the agency's performance—particularly on its key performance indicators and its most consequential performance deficit(s). This person understands the mayor's priorities and conducts the

Linking Budget Dollars to Results

Jonathan Walters

In the late 1990s, as an alderman in Somerville, Massachusetts, Joseph Curtatone was perpetually frustrated by the budgets his local legislature was supposed to be helping shape and approve. "Budget time really used to get me," he recalls. 'It was a straight line-item budget. There might be a small paragraph for each department briefly describing what they do, but there was nothing that told you how much we spent on what–no inputs, outputs or outcomes."

It was classic best-guess budgeting, coupled with a typical tactic: Any department that had any money left in its account at year's end was guaranteed to get a budget cut. "If you're the DPW director and you have $15,000 left in your account, then that's how much we cut your budget for the next year," Curtatone recounts. "So the message to all our departments was, 'Spend down your budget.'"

While this was one of the most significant points of aggravation, Curtatone also was nettled by how the city managed its decisions in general. "Here we were, a multimillion-dollar operation with absolutely no real-time information on even the most basic services. We weren't measuring anything. How many potholes were we filling? How were we filling them?"

The simple fact that Curtatone harbored such frustration, though, made him an unusual breed of elected legislator. Nationally, those who follow budgeting and managing for results in the public sector note that his impatience with a lack of information about what the city was trying to accomplish, and whether it was getting important jobs done efficiently set him apart from most legislators. Even in cities where mayors are preaching performance, the last public officials who seem to tune in are city council members.

Those in the trenches agree. When asked to comment on the average city council member's familiarity with the concepts surrounding performance measurement, Jackie Nytes, an eight-year veteran of the Indianapolis City Council, lets out a long sigh. "Theoretically, if I ask city council members if they're in favor of using data to make decisions, they'll say, 'Of course.' But a lot of that is just lip service. A lot of council people are part timers, and the fact is that making budget decisions based on information about results is just harder."

But if her counterparts around the country are going to deal effectively with delivering services in times of tight resources, she thinks the way to do that is elevate the conversation. "If we're really going to get a handle on budgeting, then the question shouldn't be, do we have enough money for this many jail beds? The question should be, do we have the programs in place so that we don't need so many jail beds? If legislatures are acting responsibly, then they should be focusing on those kinds of outcomes."

The ranks of governments that are turning to more results-based programming and budgeting seems to be slowly adding up, frequently because one or two people, such as Curtatone or Nytes or Martin O'Malley,

(Continued on page 187)

meeting to ensure that the agency, its director, and the other members of the agency's staff are focused on these priorities.

In other cities, the agency director runs the meeting, which is organized around a series of Microsoft PowerPoint slides that report on key performance indicators. The agency director leads the mayor's staff through this presentation, which describes the implica-

---

(Continued from page 186)

former mayor of Baltimore and now governor of Maryland, become frustrated enough to try moving government in a new direction.

For Curtatone's part, he took the most direct route possible to that position of influence: running for Somerville mayor. Upon taking office in January 2004, Curtatone promptly organized a series of field trips to Baltimore with top staff. The result was "SomerStat," which he says is now standard practice in his city. "For the first year, our aldermen were saying, 'Oh yeah, SomerStat. Explain that to me again.'" His early budgets had both line items and performance-related costing to ease them into the program. Now, using data to discuss budgeting has become standard operating procedure within his local legislature.

What hasn't happened in Somerville yet, Curtatone says, is taking the information being collected on government performance and results and pushing it out to citizens so that they can be more tuned in to what's being accomplished with their tax dollars. That's the city's next big step.

Some elected legislators think that is the best reason of all for making a clear connection between dollars and results. "Revenues are getting tighter and tighter, and we're not going to micromanage our way through this," Nytes says. "We have to reframe the discussion with the taxpayer. This isn't about looking for fluff in budgets, for waste. We're already efficient. The question is, are we efficient at the right things? So this is about what we want to budget for: What are our priorities and what do those cost, and then explaining to citizens the tough choices. If you want all these services, then you may need to increase taxes to pay for them."

Meanwhile, there is evidence that pushing performance–and transparency in government–can actually have significant political payoffs. Kansas City auditor Mark Funkhouser parlayed his reputation as a tough protector of taxpayers' interests into a successful mayoral run, winning a close election against a popular incumbent city councilman. Funkhouser's high-profile and tough performance audits were frequently so nettling to the mayors he worked for that he was directly threatened with being fired if he didn't back off. He ran on a campaign of government transparency and accountability.

And in Somerville, Curtatone says he ran for mayor on a straight platform of "performance-based budgeting and costing out and measuring activities and results." In Somerville, citizens were certainly ready to support a mayor who knows his ABCs.

Source: Excerpted from Jonathan Walters, "Data-Driven Decisions," *Governing* 20, no. 9 (June 2007), pp. 76-78. Reprinted with permission of the author.

tions of the data, explains why the data may not look as good as they might, and perhaps summarizes the agency's plans to improve performance.

Sometimes, it appears, no one is running the meeting.

Who runs the meeting is not inconsequential. A meeting conducted primarily by the agency director is fundamentally different from a meeting conducted by a member of the mayor's staff. And the informal status of such a mayoral staffer is also consequential. Is this staffer close to the mayor? Does he or she know the mayor's political and performance agenda? Does he or she speak for the mayor? If a mayoral aide runs the meeting, his or her standing can affect how focused the meeting is on strategies for improving the agency's performance.

Question 4F: Who sets the agenda?

Usually, the agenda is set by the CitiStat staff. In Baltimore, the CitiStat staffer who is responsible for the agency sets the preliminary agenda by preparing a memo (running a dozen or more pages) that lists key issues to be discussed during the meeting (usually more issues than can possibly be covered in an hour and a half). The evening before the meeting, this memo is delivered to the mayor, the first deputy mayor, and the director of CitiStat. Then, about 10 minutes before the CitiStat meeting is to begin, the first deputy mayor, the director of CitiStat, and this staffer meet in the CitiStat director's office (50 feet from the CitiStat room) to go over the issues.

In other cities, the CitiStat staff prepare (perhaps in collaboration with the agency) the PowerPoint slides that will be the de facto agenda of the meeting. Moreover, the CitiStat staff often give these slides to the agency director before the meeting. And the agency director may use these slides to conduct the meeting. Thus, by creating the slides, the CitiStat staff explicitly set the agenda. Nevertheless, in choosing how to use these slides, the agency director has the opportunity to influence—if only at the margins—how that agenda unfolds.

In other cities, the agency director and the agency staff prepare their own slides. In this case, the agencies set the agenda by themselves.

Question 4G: Who knows the agenda before the meeting begins?

In Baltimore, the agency directors do not see the CitiStat memo that is delivered to the mayor, deputy mayor, and CitiStat director. Nevertheless, given that they were at a CitiStat meeting only 14 days before, and given that they are (or ought to be) on top of their agency's operations, they should be able to predict the items on the agenda.

Of course, if the CitiStat staff prepare PowerPoint slides and give them to the agency, its director knows exactly what the agenda will be and how it will unfold, and he or she is able to influence that unfolding.

Show-and-Tell or Gotcha: These seven traits of any CitiStat meeting directly affect the tenor and spirit of the discussion. Are the mayor and his or her staff harassing and abusing agency managers? Or is the session yet another in a series of multiple meetings—no more productive or significant than all the others that take place in city hall?

Baltimore's CitiStat has been described as "a highly confrontational" system complete with "a 'star chamber' room for frequent grilling of chief officers on their performance"

(6, Perri 2004). The *New York Times* offered a similar portrait, "Some department supervisors seemed to writhe like medical interns fumbling for the city's pulse" (Clines 2001), and columnist Neal Peirce (2004) described "the probing" as "excruciatingly specific and penetrating." The *Baltimore Sun* reported one city manager at a CitiStat meeting "looking as if he needs a cigarette and blindfold" (Shields 2000). "The managers who are forced to go through these inquisitions are less than thrilled," reported *Governing;* they "often emerge from the sessions red-faced and embarrassed before their peers" (Swope 2001).[17]

Such popular depictions of Baltimore's CitiStat have worried some mayors and their staff. They are concerned that their own CitiStat will become a "gotcha game," intimidating agency managers but not improving performance. If, however, a city is worried that its meetings will become excessively adversarial, their sessions may morph into agency "show-and-tell."

Neither extreme is apt to foster the kind of agency behavior that will significantly ratchet up performance. If CitiStat meetings become a gotcha game, the agencies will focus their energies on avoiding mistakes—or at least, on avoiding big mistakes that are apt to produce highly embarrassing gotchas. If CitiStat meetings become show-and-tell sessions, the agencies will not take them seriously—or may even strive to manipulate their presentation to distract attention from their biggest performance failures.

5. Follow-up

One of Jack Maple's four tenets of Compstat and CitiStat is "relentless follow-up and assessment."[18] I have argued that relentlessness is not essential; those who run CitiStat need not be unrelenting, merciless, implacable, or grim. Follow-up, however, is essential. And for this follow-up to be effective, the mayor and his or her staff do need to be persistent (Behn 2004, 2005). If they do not follow up, either relentlessly or persistently the CitiStat exercise—room, staff, data, and meetings—will have little impact.

If the CitiStat process is to have an impact on performance, something significant has to happen *during* the CitiStat meetings; something significant has to *come out* of these meetings; and something significant has to happen *after* the CitiStat meetings. To foster an improvement in performance the meetings have to produce some decisions and some commitments. But unless there is some follow-up, these decisions and commitments will not significantly improve agency operations. This follow-up has five critical traits.

Question 5A: What kinds of assignments are made during the meeting?

If the objective of CitiStat meetings is to review past performance so as to improve future performance then this review must (at least occasionally) lead to some kind of policy or operational changes that will, indeed, improve future performance. These changes might be initiated by the mayor's staff: They analyze the agency's recent performance data, uncover some important deficiencies that they want fixed, and prepare a set of changes that they want the agency to make. These changes might be initiated by the agency: The director comes to the meeting having already analyzed the agency's recent performance data and reports on a plan that the agency already has implemented (or will implement).

Alternatively, these changes might result from a discussion and negotiation during the CitiStat meeting: The mayor's staff may emphasize an important deficiency that they want fixed, and the agency director proposes some corrective actions.

Regardless of the process that generates a suggestion for change, this suggestion can become an *assignment* for future action. Of course, this suggestion for change may be little more than a mere suggestion—something that everyone recognizes would be nice to do but also something that no one cares enough about to make sure that it is really done. A CitiStat session can generate lots of generalized suggestions for improvements—suggestions that come without enough specificity to determine whether they have been done, let alone a deadline for getting them done. But a CitiStat session can also generate *assignments:* specific tasks to be completed by a certain date.

Assignments need not, however, come in the form of vague suggestions or specific tasks. Rather than hint at what the agency might do or tell the agency precisely what to do, the mayor's staff may make *assignments* in the form of expectations for an improvement in the performance data (again by a specific deadline). The mayor's staff may express assignments in the form of performance targets for the agency to achieve while leaving it up to the agency to decide how to achieve them.

Question 5B: Who makes these assignments?

If a real assignment is made, it will be made by the key mayoral aide who runs the meeting. Even if the assignment results from some kind of plan proposed by the agency director, it is promoted from suggestion to assignment by this mayoral aide when he or she requests an explicit progress report by a specific date, whether it is two weeks or two months. Mayoral aides make assignments not necessarily by issuing directives but by establishing deadlines, either for specific sub-tasks that are part of the overall plan or for reports on progress toward achieving specific performance targets.

Question 5C: How are these assignments communicated?

These assignments are, presumably, communicated during the CitiStat meeting. Indeed, it is the specificity with which the key mayoral aide describes an assignment that transforms it from a suggestion to a specific task or performance target. To an outside observer who is unfamiliar with the personalities engaged in the meeting or the informal connotations that words and phrases have acquired within the city's administration, it may be unclear whether the assignment is a suggestion, a task, or a target. Nevertheless, those who have obtained the status within the city's administration that permits or requires them to be in the room will not miss the subtle signals.

In Baltimore, the CitiStat staff communicate assignments in one additional way. By the end of every CitiStat meeting, the CitiStat staffer with responsibility for that agency prepares a memo listing everything to which the mayor's staff and the agency director agreed during the meeting. This memo eliminates all possibility of ambiguity. It prevents the agency director from saying at the next meeting, "I didn't know you wanted that" or "I didn't promise to do that."

Question 5D: Do city agencies prepare for their CitiStat meetings by conducting their own mini, internal "AgencyStat" sessions?

If, after every CitiStat meeting, the mayor's office engages in detailed follow-up, the agency directors will pay attention to their assignments. And one way to judge whether these directors are truly engaged in the CitiStat process is to observe how they prepare for their next CitiStat meeting.

In Baltimore, many agency directors do so by conducting their own internal "AgencyStat" sessions several days before. After all, they know (or should know) what the data are and how the mayor's office will interpret those data. They know (or should know) what their agency's performance deficits are—particularly the ones about which the mayor really cares. They know (or should know) what they will be asked at their next CitiStat meeting. They know (or should know) on what tasks or targets they will be asked to report. Consequently, to develop answers to these anticipated questions—answers that the mayor's staff will accept or even welcome—agency directors may find their own AgencyStat sessions quite productive. Moreover, in Baltimore, several agency directors have learned that their own AgencyStat sessions are not only an effective means of preparing for CitiStat meetings but also an effective strategy for managing their own agency.

Of course, if the mayor's office does not undertake effective, persistent follow-up to its own CitiStat meetings, agency directors are unlikely to conduct their own AgencyStat sessions.

Question 5E: When and with whom are the results of these assignments examined?

Mayoral follow-up comes full circle at the next CitiStat meeting. Does the meeting begin with the mayor's staff asking about the critical assignments that were made during the previous meeting? Does the meeting begin with the mayor's staff introducing an entirely new set of miscellaneous concerns? Or does the meeting begin with a brand-new version of show-and-tell?

Does the mayor's staff focus CitiStat sessions, meeting after meeting, on the key performance concerns of the mayor? Does the mayor's staff bring continuity to their expectations for agency performance by making clear, specific assignments and expecting frequent and detailed reports on progress? Or does the mayor's staff bounce from issue to issue, driven by the latest blip in the data or the latest story on the front page of the newspaper?

Conclusion: Designing CitiStat

There is not just one CitiStat. There are many. They come in numerous varieties, with multiple combinations of these five features and 20 traits. After all, each city creates its version in response to the mayor's specific objectives and priorities.

Moreover, it is not immediately obvious that one specific combination works optimally in all circumstance for all mayoral objectives and priorities, while others are mere imposters. Nevertheless, in designing their own CitiStat, mayors and staff ought to think analytically and consciously about each of these five features and 20 traits.

Endnotes

1. Because Baltimore's CitiStat was the first one that I observed (and the one for which I have observed the most CitiStat Sessions), it is the standard against which I implicitly compare the others. This need not be the case: I could have taken another city's version as the benchmark, or I could have established my own, hypothetical benchmark (with specific characteristics that I invented or pieced together from different Cities). Still, Baltimore is also the original benchmark from which every city that has created a CitiStat began; no city (at least that I know of) created its own CitiStat without first having visited Baltimore. In fact, every time I have visited a CitiStat session in Baltimore, a visitor (or a dozen visitors) from one or more jurisdictions has also been in the room. Thus, for every city in the United States that has created its own CitiStat, Baltimore is the natural and obvious benchmark.

2. I have not visited all of these versions of CitiStat.

3. In 2004, Baltimore's CitiStat won one of the Kennedy School of Government's Innovations in American Government Awards.

4. Indeed, given the nature of this classification, some cities in the United States or elsewhere may have been doing something that fits within the CitiStat class even before Baltimore launched its version in 2000.

5. These 20 subfeatures are not the only traits of CitiStat. Others include the following: (I) Who has access to the data? (Baltimore gives it to the Baltimore Neighborhood Indicators Alliance; Schachtel 2001); (2) How visible is CitiStat? Can citizens learn about it on the Web, or is it completely invisible? (3) Is this one of the mayor's few signature initiatives, or is it simply one of many policy and managerial programs that the mayor has launched? I don't discuss these traits because, at this stage of my research, I believe they are apt to have less of an impact on the effectiveness of any CitiStat performance strategy than the 20 traits discussed here.

6. These and the other features and traits examined in this article reflect only those CitiStats that I have observed. Other versions may have additional characteristics.

7. For a description of this room and other features of Baltimore's CitiStat, see Behn (2004, 2005) and Henderson (2003).

8. This is why I consider the room to be one trait, not five. Every CitiStat room that I have seen has the table, the podium, the projector, the computer, and the screen (or a blank white wall that serves as the screen).

9. As with a lot of other operational needs, smaller cities face the irreducibility problem. What if the city needs only half a city attorney or half a snowplow? The obvious solution is to contract for this service. Still, some responsibilities are best carried out internally.

10. Many of the journalistic descriptions of Baltimore's CitiStat program explicitly call it a "high-tech" operation (Behn 2004).

11. People can also gauge the importance of an activity by how close its key staffers are to the organization's leader.

12. To those who focus on large-scale public policy problems, potholes may appear a trivial concern—a minor annoyance to a few habitual complainers. But to city residents—and thus to city mayors—potholes can be a significant problem. In June 2005, Citizens for NYC, a nonprofit organization in New York City, released a citywide survey of residents and neighborhood leaders that revealed the biggest problem in the city was—you guessed it—potholes. Potholes ranked above litter and garbage (2), street noise (3), and dangerous intersections (4). (Citizens for NYC 2005). For the data, see http://ccnyc.neighborhoodlinkcom/ccnycfiles/CNY C%20Spring05%20Charts%204%20emailing.pdf.

13. Syracuse has CitiLine. Service requests for the Department of Public Works are recorded by the CitiLine staff, and thus the city can track these data. For all other departments however, service requests are forwarded to the department.

14. Of course, there are other ways to cheat. For example, a city agency could report to the CitiTrak system that it completed a Service Request that it has yet to finish. To prevent this behavior, Baltimore audits 100 completed Service Requests each week.

15. This raises, perhaps, Question 4Da: Who speaks for the agency? In Baltimore, any member of an agency's staff who attends a CitiStat meeting may be called on to answer a question or address an issue in his or her realm of responsibility. In other cities, only the agency director (or perhaps the deputy) ever speaks—often because these are the only people from the agency who are in the room.

16. In terms of the attendance at the meetings, there is one important difference between CitiStat and Compstat. A Compstat meeting may focus on the performance of one or two precincts; neverthe-

less, the commanders or representatives of the other precincts are in the room. This gives these other precinct commanders the opportunity to learn about the effectiveness of the crime-fighting strategies employed by other precincts—strategies that they may be able to adapt to their own work. Thus, Compstat meetings provide an effective means of disseminating successful innovations. CitiStat meetings could also be designed to provide an opportunity for such learning. But this would require (at least in Baltimore) agency directors to attend a large number of meetings per week; the relevance of one agency's effective strategy to another agency might not be as obvious, direct, or immediate.

17. In my visits to Baltimore's CitiStat, I have not, however, observed any city manager writhing under excruciating probing, let alone asking for a cigarette and blindfold.

18. For references to Maple's four principles as applied to Compstat and CitiStat, see Bratton (1998, 224), Maple (1999, 32), Silverman (1999, 161–63), and http://www.ci.baltimore.md.us/news/citistat/.

References

6, Perri. 2004. *Rewiring Local Decision Making for Political Judgment.* London: New Local Government Network.

Behn, Robert D. 2004. The Core Principles of CitiStat: It's Not Just about the Meetings and the Maps. Paper presented at the 26th Annual Research Conference of the Association for Public Policy Analysis and Management, Atlanta, GA, October 28.

———. 2005. The Core Principles of CitiStat: It's Nor Just about the Meetings and the Maps. *International Public Management Journal* 8(3): 1–25.

Bratton, William, with Peter Knobler. 1998. *Turnaround: How America's Top Cop Reversed the Crime Epidemic.* New York: Random House.

Citizens for NYC. 2005. Potholes, Noise and Litter are Top Concerns in NYC Neighborhoods. News release, June 22.

Clines, Francis X. 2001. Baltimore Uses a Databank to Wake Up City Workers. *New York Times,* June 6.

Henderson, Lenneal. 2003. *The Baltimore CitiStat Program: Performance and Accountability.* Washington. DC: IBM Endowment for the Business of Government.

Maple, Jack, with Chris Mitchell. 1999. *The Crime Fighter.* New York: Doubleday.

Peirce, Neal. 2004. A More Efficient Approach to Governing our Cities. *Seattle Times,* January 19.

Schachtel, Marsha R. B. 2001. CitiStat and the Baltimore Neighborhood Indicators Alliance: Using Information to Improve Communication and Community. *National Civic Review* 90(3): 253–65.

Shields, Gerard. 2000. City Figures to Improve Efficiency. *Baltimore Sun,* November 19, 1B.

Silverman, Eli B. 1999. *NYPD Battles Crime: Innovative Strategies in Policing.* Boston: Northeastern University Press.

Swope, Christopher. 2001. Restless for Results. *Governing,* April, 20–23.

Appendix: For Further Reading

Books and Articles

Ammons, David N. *Municipal Benchmarks: Assessing Local Performance and Establishing Community Standards.* 2nd ed. Thousand Oaks, CA: Sage Publications, 2001.

Ammons, David N. Performance Measurement and Managerial Thinking. *Public Performance & Management Review* 25, June 2002: 344–347.

Behn, Robert D. The Psychological Barriers to Performance Management. *Public Performance & Management Review* 26, 1, 2002: 5–25.

Behn, Robert D. Why Measure Performance? Different Purposes Require Different Measures. *Public Administration Review* 63, 5, 2003: 586–606.

Berman, Barbara J. Cohn. *Listening to the Public: Adding the Voices of the People to Government Performance Measurement and Reporting.* New York: Fund for the City of New York, 2005.

Broom, Cheryle, Marilyn Jackson, Vera Vogelsang Coombs, and Jody Harris. *Performance Measurement: Concepts and Techniques.* Washington, DC: American Society for Public Administration, 1998.

Coe, Charles K., and James R. Brunet. Organizational Report Cards: Significant Impact or Much Ado about Nothing? *Public Administration Review* 66, 1, 2006: 90–100.

Coplin, William D., and Carol Dwyer, *Does Your Government Measure Up? Basic Tools for Local Officials and Citizens.* Syracuse: Maxwell School, Syracuse University, 2000.

de Lancer Julnes, Patria, Frances S. Berry, Maria Aristigueta, and Kaifeng Yang, eds. *International Handbook of Practice-Based Performance Management.* Los Angeles: Sage Publications, 2008.

Epstein, Paul D., Paul M. Coates, and Lyle D. Wray, with David Swain. *Results That Matter: Improving Communities by Engaging Citizens, Measuring Performance, and Getting Things Done.* San Francisco: Jossey-Bass, 2006.

Epstein, Paul D., Lyle Wray, and Cortney Harding. Citizens as Partners in Performance Management. *Public Management,* November 2006: 18–22.

Folz, David H. Service Quality and Benchmarking the Performance of Municipal Services. *Public Administration Review* 64, 2, 2004: 175–186.

Forsythe, Dall W., ed. *Quicker Better Cheaper? Managing Performance in American Government.* Albany, NY: Rockefeller Institute Press, 2001.

Fountain, James, Wilson Campbell, Terry Patton, Paul Epstein, and Mandi Cohn. *Reporting Performance Information: Suggested Criteria for Effective Communication.* Norwalk, CT: Governmental Accounting Standards Board, 2003.

Hatry, Harry. *Performance Measurement: Getting Results.* 2nd ed. Washington, DC: Urban Institute, 2006.

Hatry, Harry, Donald M. Fisk, John R. Hall Jr., Philip S. Schaenman, and Louise Snyder. *How Effective Are Your Community Services? Procedures for Performance Measurement.* Washington, DC: International City/County Management Association and the Urban Institute, 2006.

Heikkila, Tanya, and Kimberley Roussin Isett. Citizen Involvement and Performance Management in Special-Purpose Governments. *Public Administration Review* 67, 2, 2007: 238–248.

Ho, Alfred, and Paul Coates, Citizen-Initiated Performance Assessment: The Initial Iowa Experience. *Public Performance & Management Review* 27, 3, 2004: 29–50.

Holzer, Marc, and Kathryn Kloby. Helping Government Measure Up: Models of Citizen-Driven Government Performance Measurement Initiatives. In *International Handbook of Practice-Based Performance Management,* ed. Patria de Lancer Julnes et al. Los Angeles: Sage Publications, 2008: 257–281.

Holzer, Marc, and Seok-Hwan Lee, eds. *Public Productivity Handbook.* 2nd ed. New York: Marcel Dekker, 2004.

Holzer, Marc, and Kaifeng Yang. Performance Measurement and Improvement: An Assessment of the State of the Art. *International Review of Administrative Sciences* 70, 1, 2004: 15–31.

Kelly, Janet M., and David Swindell. A Multiple-Indicator Approach to Municipal Service Evaluation: Correlating Performance Measurement and Citizen Satisfaction across Jurisdictions. *Public Administration Review* 62, 5, 2002: 610–621.

Lee, Mordecai. Credibility and Trust Are Enhanced When Public Reporting Precedes Citizen Participation. *PA Times,* 26, 7, 2003: 4.

Lee, Mordecai. Empirical Experiments in Public Reporting: Reconstructing the Results of Survey Research, 1941–42. *Public Administration Review* 66, 2, 2006: 252–262.

Lindblad, Mark Richard. Performance Measurement in Local Economic Development. *Urban Affairs Review* 41, 5, 2006: 646–672.

Melkers, Julia, and Katherine Willoughby. Models of Performance-Measurement Use in Local Governments: Understanding Budgeting, Communication, and Lasting Effects. *Public Administration Review* 65, 2, 2005: 180–190.

Metzenbaum, Shelley H. *Performance Accountability: The Five Building Blocks and Six Essential Practices.* Washington, DC: IBM Center for the Business of Government, 2006.

Moynihan, Donald, What Can Baseball Teach Us about Performance Management? *Public Administration Review* 66, 4, 2006: 647–648.

Newcomer, Kathryn, Edward T. Jennings, Jr., Cheryle Broom, and Allen Lomax, eds. *Meeting the Challenges of Performance-Oriented Government.* Washington, DC: American Society for Public Administration/Center for Accountability and Performance, 2002.

Nicholson-Crotty, Sean, Nick A. Theobald, and Jill Nicholson-Crotty. Disparate Measures: Public Managers and Performance-Measurement Strategies. *Public Administration Review* 66, 1, 2006: 101–113.

Pizzarella, Carla. Achieving Useful Performance and Cost Information in a Comparative Performance Measurement Consortium. *International Journal of Public Administration* 27, 8 and 9, 2004: 631–650.

Plant, Thomas. The Performance Measurement Paradox in Local Government Management. *Public Management* 88, 4, 2006: 16–20.

Poister, Theodore H. *Measuring Performance in Public and Nonprofit Organizations.* San Francisco: Jossey-Bass, 2003.

Poister, Theodore H., and Gregory Streib. Elements of Strategic Planning and Management in Municipal Governments: Status after Two Decades. *Public Administration Review* 65, 1, 2005: 45–56.

Poister, Theodore H., and Gregory Streib. Performance Measurement in Municipal Government: Assessing the State of the Practice. *Public Administration Review* 59, 4, 1999: 325–335.

Popovich, Mark G.. ed. *Creating High-Performance Government Organizations: A Practical Guide for Public Managers.* San Francisco: Jossey-Bass, 1998.

Rivenbark, William C., ed. *A Guide to the North Carolina Local Government Performance Measurement Project.* Chapel Hill: University of North Carolina, Institute of Government, 2001.

Smith, Dennis C., and William J. Grinker. *The Transformation of Social Services Management in New York City: Compstating Welfare.* New York: Structured Employment Economic Development Corporation [Seedco], 2005.

Streib, Gregory D., and Theodore H. Poister. Assessing the Validity, Legitimacy, and Functionality of Performance Measurement Systems in Municipal Governments. *American Review of Public Administration* 29, 2, 1999: 107–123.

Swiss, James E. A Framework for Assessing Incentives in Results-Based Management. *Public Administration Review* 65, 5, 2005: 592–602.

Van Ryzin, Gregg G., Stephen Immerwahr, and Stan Altman. Measuring Street Cleanliness: A Comparison of New York City's Scorecard and Results from a Citizen Survey. *Public Administration Review* 68, 2, 2008: 295–303.

Walters, Jonathan. *Measuring Up 2.0: Governing's New, Improved Guide to Performance Measurement for Geniuses and Other Public Managers.* Washington, DC: Governing Books, 2007.

Wang, XiaoHu. Assessing Performance Measurement Impact: A Study of U.S. Local Governments. *Public Performance & Management Review* 26, 1, 2002: 26–43.

Wang, XiaoHu, and Montgomery Van Wart. When Public Participation in Administration Leads to Trust: An Empirical Assessment of Managers' Perceptions. *Public Administration Review* 67, 2, 2007: 265–278.

Yang, Kaifeng, and Kathe Callahan. Citizen Involvement Efforts and Bureaucratic Responsiveness: Participatory Values, Stakeholder Pressures, and Administrative Practicality. *Public Administration Review* 67, 2, 2007: 249–264.

Yang, Kaifeng, and Marc Holzer. The Performance-Trust Link: Implications for Performance Measurement. *Public Administration Review* 66, 1, 2006: 114–126.

Useful Web Sites

Alfred P. Sloan Foundation, Performance Assessment of Municipal Governments Program
www.sloan.org/programs/govt_projects.shtml

Association of Government Accountants
www.agacgfm.org/performance/sea/

Governmental Accounting Standards Board
www.seagov.org/

Government Finance Officers Association, Performance Measurement page
www.gfoa.org/index.php?option = com_content&task = view&id = 479&Itemid = 250

International City/County Management Association, Center for Performance Measurement
www1.icma.org/main/bc.asp?bcid = 107&hsid = 1&ssid1 = 50&ssid2 = 220&ssid3 = 297

National Academy of Public Administration, Performance Management Consortium
www.napawash.org/pc_government_performance/index.html

National Center for Public Productivity
www.ncpp.us/

Public Performance Measurement Reporting Network
http://ppmrn.rutgers.edu/

University of North Carolina, North Carolina Benchmarking Project
www.iog.unc.edu/programs/perfmeas/